SEWING FOR EVERYONE

MARY BROOKS PICKEN

Sewing for Everyone

Detail drawings by C. FLORENCE VALENTINE

Fashion drawings by PATRICIA LINGANE ROWE

THE WORLD PUBLISHING COMPANY

CLEVELAND AND NEW YORK

PUBLISHED BY *The World Publishing Company*
2231 West 110th Street · Cleveland · Ohio

First Published October 1944

A Message For You

YOU ARE READING this book because you want to learn to sew, or because, in sewing, you have met problems on which you needed help. Whether you are a beginner or one with sewing experience, this material should help you and insure quick and easy sewing throughout your future.

For a Beginner or an Experienced Worker. For the beginner, an easy, natural starting point for sewing that should give immediate satisfaction is suggested. For those with some experience, there are quick and easy methods that should save time and make all future sewing easier.

Your Modern Guide. The more we learn about any subject, the more interesting it becomes. Let this book bring you, for the first time, or as a stimulating review, the essentials of sewing, show you the creative possibilities, and lead you ultimately, through the range of sewing information it covers, to the pleasure and recreation that comes with skill in this craft.

There Are Wider Fields. This recreation may lead to an important future for you—a future full of the joy of creating beautiful things for yourself, your family, for your home, or for others, and the satisfaction of saving and conserving, of being self-sufficient and of having a new, deep and absorbing interest worthy of your efforts.

Know the Requirements of Types of Garments. We have given in this book the basic instructions for certain types of garments. Turn to these when making any one of them, and find there the information necessary for success with that type. This should save time for you and make for greater satisfaction in the finished garment.

Acknowledgments

The author wishes to express her appreciation for the help of the following: C. Florence Valentine, Patricia Rowe, Theresa Brakeley, Vera Tuman, Elsie Gullick, Marie Fasolo, Margaret Wollenhaupt, Thelma Manne, Paula Bolli and Eleanor Wrightnour.

Appreciation is also due to Alma Kitchell, who has made it possible for the author to give voice to her conservation ideas, especially of fabric, over the Blue Network and Station WJZ. Many of these thoughts and ideas have taken form in this book.

Again, appreciation is due to the Singer Sewing Machine Company for the inspiration their machines have been throughout the years, and credit is due to the Mary Brooks Picken School for some text material reworked in this book.

Contents

[x]

SEWING FOR EVERYONE

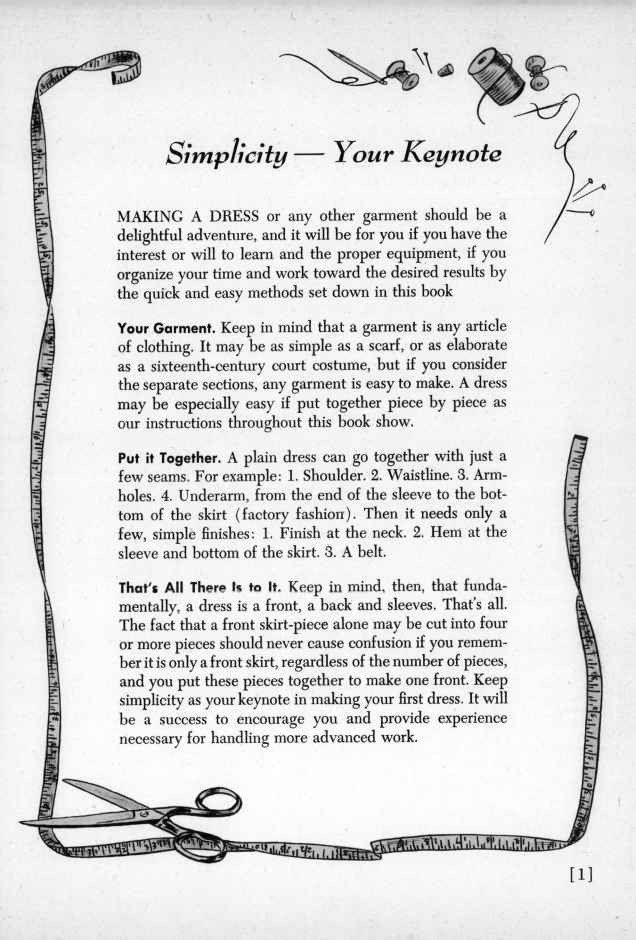

Simplicity — Your Keynote

MAKING A DRESS or any other garment should be a delightful adventure, and it will be for you if you have the interest or will to learn and the proper equipment, if you organize your time and work toward the desired results by the quick and easy methods set down in this book

Your Garment. Keep in mind that a garment is any article of clothing. It may be as simple as a scarf, or as elaborate as a sixteenth-century court costume, but if you consider the separate sections, any garment is easy to make. A dress may be especially easy if put together piece by piece as our instructions throughout this book show.

Put it Together. A plain dress can go together with just a few seams. For example: 1. Shoulder. 2. Waistline. 3. Armholes. 4. Underarm, from the end of the sleeve to the bottom of the skirt (factory fashion). Then it needs only a few, simple finishes: 1. Finish at the neck. 2. Hem at the sleeve and bottom of the skirt. 3. A belt.

That's All There Is to It. Keep in mind, then, that fundamentally, a dress is a front, a back and sleeves. That's all. The fact that a front skirt-piece alone may be cut into four or more pieces should never cause confusion if you remember it is only a front skirt, regardless of the number of pieces, and you put these pieces together to make one front. Keep simplicity as your keynote in making your first dress. It will be a success to encourage you and provide experience necessary for handling more advanced work.

Tools — For Quick Easy Sewing

PROVIDE GOOD TOOLS. Good tools help you to sew quickly and easily and only good tools, like good friends, are worthy of you.

For Your Sewing Basket. Essential tools are the foundation of your sewing. They are the small and inexpensive things that centuries of constant use have perfected to the point of smooth excellence for quick and easy work.

Needles, Thread and Pins. Your needles and thread should be right for your work— fine ones for fine fabrics and strong, sturdy ones for coarse materials. Take only one needle at a time from the packet and keep the packet closed to prevent rust. If needles become rusty, run them through an emery bag or a well-packed steel wool pincushion. Remember, if a needle needs to be pushed through the fabric, it is too large, and your fabric requires a smaller one. Use thin, sharp dressmakers' pins, sold in ¼ or ½ pound boxes. Good pins do not mar fine fabrics. Wash pins every month or so—scald and scatter on a paper to dry.

YOUR QUICK and EASY CHART for NEEDLES—THREADS—STITCHES					
Fabrics—Type of Sewing	Size of Thread		Size of Needle		Machine Stitches to the Inch
	Cotton	Silk	Hand	Machine	
For basting.	50–80	A (for velvet)	Milliners' No. 8	Same as for stitching	6
Dainty hand-work. Delicate finishing on gossamer fabrics.	150 200	00 000	10		
Light-weight or sheer fabrics, fine dimity, batiste and light-weight rayon.	100 120 150	A 0		Fine	15 to 20
For summertime fabrics, inconspicuous stitching, dainty aprons, dresses, children's clothes and glass curtains.	80 90 100	A	8	Medium-Fine	14 to 18
Firm dress silks and cottons, finely woven woolens. For general household sewing, draperies, men's dress shirts.	50 60 70	B	6 or 7	Medium	12 to 15
Heavy cretonne, madras, muslin, brocade. For quilting, sturdy aprons, men's work shirts. For buttonholes and buttons.	30 36 40	B	5 or 6	Medium-Coarse	10 to 12
Light-weight canvas, duck and ticking. For awnings, upholstery, mattresses. For buttons on children's underclothing and men's wash clothing and for heavy mending.	16 20 24		4 or 5	Coarse	9
Heavy weaves of canvas, duck, ticking, drilling, and sacking.	8 10 12 (or 40 linen)		3 or 4	Coarsest	8

Scissors, Shears, Razor Blade and Thimble. It is important to have a set of two pairs of scissors, one 3″ and one 5″ long, and a pair of shears or bent trimmers 7″ or 8″ long. These should be used only for fabrics. If they need to be sharpened, choose a reliable shop. Do learn to cut long, even lines with your shears and to use the points of your scissors for snipping and for corners. Keep a razor blade handy for ripping. Use a thimble for protection and for speed in hand-sewing. Be sure your thimble fits your finger. It should fit as comfortably as a shoe or glove and should be smooth, and not too heavy. Aluminum and plastic thimbles are very satisfactory, yet inexpensive.

Tape Measure, Ruler, Yardstick. For quick and easy sewing there must be no guess-work. Have good measuring equipment: a 60-inch tape which may be read from either end; a 6-inch ruler for measuring seams, hems, and button-holes; and a yardstick to mark long seam lines and skirt lengths. Many women find a 5-foot rule a real convenience, and some like a triangle such as artists use, for marking bias, for chalking lines, etc.

Tracing Wheel, Awl, Pencil and Pad, Tailor's Chalk. A sharp-pointed, good steel tracing wheel is an aid in marking seam lines and notches in firm cotton fabrics. A thin, sharp awl can be used for punch marks for pocket and plait position and for eyelets. A lead pencil and a pad are handy for taking measurements and notes. Use tailor's chalk for pattern perforations and for marking joining lines and corrections made in fitting. A stick of school chalk is always convenient in a sewing box.

Sewing Equipment. Keep a drawer, box or chest just for your sewing things, so that you can keep your tools together and have them easy to get at when you want to sew or mend. Keep it near the radio, if you enjoy sewing while listening.

Cutting Table. A cutting surface is important. A cutting board or collapsible table 36″ to 40″ wide, and 5′ to 6′ long, is satisfactory. If a dining table must serve, clear it of everything except your sewing before you start and cover it with newspaper or felt to avoid scratching. Some find a spick-and-span linoleum-covered floor satisfactory for cutting. Others use a piece of composition board on the bed, or place the work on two chairs. The space you have and the frequency of your sewing periods should determine your equipment. Many cut several garments at one time and find it worth while to prepare a cutting surface for such occasions.

Mirror. Seeing is believing, so a full-length mirror and a hand mirror are necessary equipment. If you lack a long mirror, a length of mirror may be purchased and put on the inside of a closet door with molding or metal rosettes.

Ironing Board, Sleeve Board, Tailor's Cushion, Iron, Press Cloth and Basin. For quick and easy sewing, press as you sew; that is, press every seam before it joins another. Keep the necessary materials always ready for use. Have the pressboard surface clean and smooth. Use a sleeve board for pressing sleeves and seams, and a tailor's cushion, which is a firm ham-shaped pad, for shrinking out sleeve fulness, for pressing darts or any shaped sections of a garment. You need an electric iron, of course. The steam iron has many points to recommend it, because it steams as it presses and, when used with care, does not scorch or leave press marks on the fabric. A press cloth and basin are "must" items if you lack a steam iron. For shrinking fabrics, provide yourself with a 3-yard length of unbleached muslin, well washed to remove sizing. Wet this, smooth your fabric out over it and roll the material. Such a length of fabric can serve for years, especially if given a tubbing occasionally. A tiny sponge is ideal for dampening seams.

Dress Form. This is an aid in fitting yourself, because it can be adjusted to your height and garments may be hung properly. Buy a form a size smaller than your own bust measurement. Make a fitted lining for yourself, slip it on the form and pad it with batting to conform to your measurements. Mark waist, neck and hem lines on this for convenience in fitting. Cover the form with a bag-like slip-cover to keep it clean when not in use.

Sewing Machine. This is to today's sewing what the airplane is to travel. It provides speed, efficiency and a completely modern result. A separate section is devoted to sewing machine sewing.

Findings Find Their Places. Notions or findings are fairly standard but each season usually introduces some new and handy sewing aid for quick and easy sewing. Keep in touch with the notion department of a good store and provide yourself with new time-savers. Notions include such standard items as threads, mending threads, sewing threads, needles, pins, snap fasteners, hooks and eyes, zippers, dress shields, tape and bias bindings, edge finishes, weights, beltings, etc., etc. These do not change often, and a supply should be purchased ahead of sewing time. Make a note of other items, as new trimming tapes, edges, cordings, fasteners, and similar articles, and keep the list pinned up or in a reminder file, and have the essentials at hand for any garment you undertake. Sewing to be successful must be enjoyable. Planning ahead to have the necessaries is one way to get good results and enjoy the whole experience of garment creation.

Sewing Supplies. Keep your sewing supplies labeled. Don't lose time hunting for them. Your space may be only a dresser drawer, or it may be an entire cabinet or closet, but it is the way you keep it that is important. A limited space may prove more useful than more room for it demands a tidy, ship-shape arrangement to fit things in. Use strong boxes for your sewing materials. Make labels, as "Cotton Scraps," "Silk Scraps," "Cotton Threads," "Tape, Binding, and Elastic," and any other items you may have. Keep buttons, buckles, hooks and eyes, snaps and similar items in small glass jars, so you can see at a glance the needed notions. If you have no available space in which to keep sewing supplies, purchase a roll-away chest which can be kept under the bed, or make a cabinet from orange crates

[4]

or do as theatrical people do—keep a suit case just for your sewing and bring it out when the sewing urge is on.

Extra Tools. There are helpful tools that may be added as time-savers if you do considerable sewing. For example, pinking shears, gauge (for marking skirt lengths), bodkins, belt turner (a long wire gadget for turning belts and bias bands), spool rack and a pressboard for velvets. There is also a small plastic tracing wheel that holds loose chalk. It is in the form of a small flat case, with a tiny toothed wheel that revolves through a narrow slot at the bottom to carry the chalk to the fabric. Similar time-savers appear in the shops. Examine them if they appeal to you, try them out.

Fashion Magazines, Sewing Instruction Books, Clippings, Pin-Up Board and File. Fashion magazines and pattern books are especially necessary for the woman who sews. There is no point in sewing unless what you make is smarter than what you can afford to buy. Sewing instruction books are valuable for reference. Keep your sewing instruction books with your sewing, not in a book case. Subscribe to a good fashion magazine and a pattern book and have these always at hand for reference— for ideas. Clip ideas that appeal to you—and never be at a loss as to how to finish a neckline or what to do with a waistline or sleeve. Copy smart ideas from expensive clothes. Remember the rule of three. The style of your frock is one-third of its worth, the fabric, one-third and your workmanship, one-third. An 8 x 24 piece of soft wood or composition board, fastened on the wall or inside a closet door, is helpful for pinning up fashion notes and fashion clippings. If space does not permit this, a letter file may be used.

The Sewing Machine — Your Power Plant

OF COURSE, you have a sewing machine or can rent or use one belonging to a relative or friend. A machine is essential for quick sewing. Make sure that the machine you use is kept in the best possible condition. If it is a new one, give it the care and attention that will keep it in perfect order. If it is old, have it oiled and adjusted as needed.

The first step in the successful use of a machine is to know the instruction book. A book is provided for each machine. If yours is mislaid, get another from the manufacturer. Once you know what the sewing machine will do for you and how to use it to get the best results, it will be both servant and friend.

Local machine shops have special instructors who will help you to get the most service from their make of machine, show you how to use the attachments and how to keep a machine in good running order.

Instructions on using your machine are not given here, but practice machine stitching until you can handle it well. Learn to stitch straight. Practice on lines on tablet paper with an unthreaded needle. The following suggestions will help you to locate and correct minor difficulties that may develop in your machine sewing.

Needle Thread Breaks. This may be caused by:
1. Improper threading. (Always pull both bobbin and top thread back out of the way when you start to sew.)
2. Tight tensions.
3. Thread too fine or too coarse for needle.°
4. Needle blunt, bent, or set incorrectly.
5. Presser foot not properly adjusted. (In beginning to sew, always have material correctly placed under presser foot.)
6. Glazed or poor quality thread.

Machine Skips Stitches. This may be caused by:
1. Needle improperly set into needle bar.
2. Needle too long or too short.
3. Needle blunt or bent.
4. Needle too fine for thread.°

Stitching Puckers the Material. The cause may be:
1. Tight tensions.
2. Blunt needle.
3. Stitch too long, especially on fine material.
4. Fabric too light in weight to carry over feed. For this, use newspaper or tissue under the fabric.

Bobbin or Shuttle Thread Breaks. This may be caused by:
1. Incorrect threading of bobbin case.
2. Tight lower tension.
3. Bobbin wound too tightly or irregularly.
4. Bobbin wound too full.

° See Thread and Needle Chart on page 2.

[6]

Machine Works Heavily. This may be caused by:
1. Dust, lint, or threads clogging the working parts.
2. Lack of oil.
3. Thread ends caught in the shuttle or bobbin case.

Breaking Needles. This may be caused by:
1. Use needle of correct size.°
2. Use a good quality needle that is right for the machine.
3. See that the presser foot or attachment is securely fastened.
4. Use a heavy needle when sewing with heavy thread on thick seams or heavy material.°
5. Let the feed carry the work along without your pushing it.

Other Points to Remember:
1. To avoid injuring the machine, don't run the machine with the presser foot down when there is no cloth under the presser foot.
2. Be certain that the same kind and size of thread is used in both bobbin and needle. Test your threads by pulling the tension and bobbin threads together. If their tensions are in harmony, the pull on each thread will be the same. A little testing by pulling will reveal which one is tight or loose and which to adjust.
3. Be sure that the needle is the right size for the thread.°
4. Make certain that the needle, the thread, and length of stitch are suited to the material and purpose.°
5. See that the machine is perfectly clean.
6. Work to have the tension, the stitch, the thread, all in accord so that the seam may flow out from the machine without restraint, straight and perfect in every stitch.
7. In learning to stitch straight with the machine, mark pieces of paper with straight lines, squares, and triangles for practice work. Take the thread out of the needle and the bobbin out of the machine, and practice stitching on the marked lines, turning corners accurately, and keeping even spaces. This will soon train the eye and accurate work will result.

Machine Attachments. These serve two important steps in your sewing; they speed your work, and they give it a professional appearance. Let us introduce you to some of the machine attachments that will insure quick and easy sewing for you. To use each attachment, follow instructions given for them with your make of machine.

Cloth Guide. This is simply designed and easy to attach. It insures accuracy and speed for edge stitching where the width is greater than the presser foot.

Foot Hemmer. Attaches to machine in place of presser foot. Do learn to use it.

Binder. Takes width #5 ready-made binding; convenient for children's clothes, curtains, etc.

Gathering Foot. Have one by all means; easier to use than ruffler; efficient for many types of fabrics.

Ruffler. Ideal for lawn, organdie, any fabric that will hold tiny plaits.

Edge Stitcher. Use to sew on lace or insertion. For overlapping ribbons, braids, etc.

Under Braider. Stamp your design to wrong side of fabric; work from this side. Beautiful work and intricate designs possible with this aid.

Zigzagger. Expensive to buy, but saves hours of work; ideal for children's clothes and lace-trimmed lingerie.

Cording Foot. As essential as scissors, a necessity for every machine, especially for home furnishings.

Quilter. Essential for machine quilting, as it guides stitching line, helping to keep rows even.

Machine Craft Guide. A marvel of efficiency for craft work, especially rug making.

Pinker. Grand for chintz, taffeta and all firmly-woven fabrics; saves time in finishing edges.

Fabric Facts

A NEVER-ENDING RIBBON of fabrics is designed for garments and house furnishings. Each season brings the old favorites and fabric designers are ever giving us new offerings in timely colors and designs.

Fibers and Yarns. All fabrics are developed from fibers. Cotton and linen are vegetable fibers; silk and wool, animal. Rayons are synthetic and, therefore, man-made, as are also fabrics of glass. All these fibers are spun into yarns of many kinds. Tight yarns, loose, hard, soft, thick, fuzzy, bulky, heavy, thin or light, depending on the kind of material to be made from them.

Weaves and Finishes. Hundreds of different types of looms weave yarns into textiles of all kinds, and the surface effect may be varied from a satin smoothness to a knobby roughness. The fabric finish may change the effect again. Finishes vary. Some fabrics have a sizing or glazing added. Such a finish may give the fabric firmness, stiffness, smoothness, gloss, deep dull tones and many other effects. Special finishes also render fabrics showerproof, spot or germ repellent, crush resistant, and give it other properties suitable to the use to which it is to be put. Certain fabrics are felted in finishing to make them seem heavier than they really are.

Tags and Labels. Watch tags and labels on materials and garments to know how to handle and wash them. This is important since new fibers, blends and combinations of yarns make it increasingly difficult to know the material through the simple home tests we usually make. Have a special place to keep textile and garment tags. Mark each with the date of purchase and treatment recommended.

Nap, Pile and Sheen. Some fabrics have a standing surface known as nap, or pile. To determine whether a fabric is napped, brush the hand over the surface. It will usually feel smooth, running with the nap, and rougher, against it. Pile is the term used in reference to velvet and velveteen; and nap, to the relatively smoother fabrics such as wool broadcloth. In making a garment, the fabric is generally cut so that the nap runs downward to insure smoothness, but some velvets will give a desirable deep or rich effect if the pile runs upward. This is especially true of rayon velvets. Fabrics with nap reflect light one way when the nap runs upward, and another way with the nap downward. This effect of light is known as sheen, and changing the direction of the nap may give the material the appearance of different color. It is important, therefore, to have all pieces in such fabrics cut "heads up," that is, with the tops of each pattern piece facing the same way. Cotton chambray, for example, has no nap, but because of the way it is woven, it "shades off," and it is best to cut all garment pieces running in the same direction.

Test a piece of fabric as you begin to handle it. See whether it mars or crushes easily, whether it slips or puckers in stitching. Use more pins if it slips—paper underneath if it puckers. Take care in pressing—be sure water does not spot, or the iron mark or mar the surface of your fabric. An ounce of prevention is worth a pound of cure, you know.

Color Fastness. Most good cottons and rayons are vat dyed, which means that they are, to all intents and purposes, fast in color. Reasonable care in washing and drying will keep their color intact for the life of the garment.

Shrinking, Sponging, Pressing. All fabrics shrink slightly—wool, cotton and linen most of all. Fabrics of wool should be preshrunk. Sometimes this is done by the manufacturer. Even so, it is a safeguard to shrink the fabric before cutting. For doing this, keep on hand a 3-yard length of unbleached muslin. Wet this, wring it out, lay the wool fabric folded over the muslin, roll both fabrics together smoothly. Lay this roll aside for 12 hours. Then remove the wool and hang it over a door to dry. Be sure to put a cloth over the top of the door to protect your fabric. Rayon and silk do not require shrinking before cutting. A rayon dress, if washed, should be measured first and then stretched to the original size during the ironing.

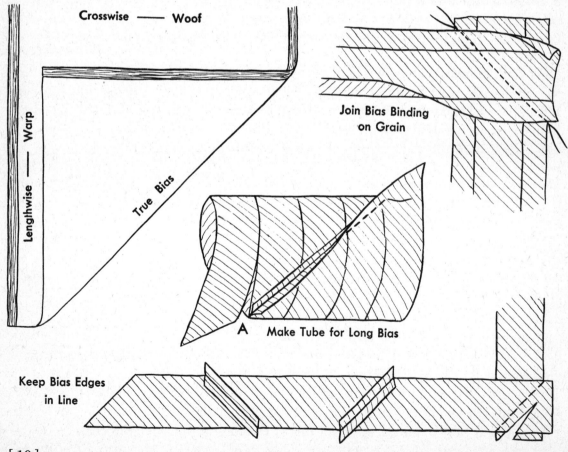

Cottons that are not sanforized, i.e., preshrunk, should be shrunk before cutting as described for wool above if they are color fast; otherwise, garments must be made slightly larger to allow for shrinkage. Firm cottons shrink approximately ½″ per yard in length, while loosely woven fabrics shrink twice that. Cotton garments should never fit snugly, as they shrink slightly each time they are laundered.

Note the information on the tag or label accompanying fabric or garment before treating it.

Prints, Stripes, Plaids, Motifs. Care in cutting is necessary to have all such fabric designs correctly placed in a garment. Novices should choose small prints, narrow stripes and even checks and plaids until they feel expert enough to match designs properly. Usually there is some waste when designs must be matched. Flower motifs should run with tops of flowers up in a garment. Consider the best location on the figure for large motifs and so place them when you lay your pattern on. Printed material often causes difficulty, because the printing is not "straight with the goods," that is, in line with the woof of the fabric. In buying printed fabrics, it is always well to notice whether the print is straight and avoid those that are printed off grain. A dress that is not cut with the grain of the fabric will never "set" well and will not be attractive when worn. A dress that is printed and is not cut with the design will be equally unattractive. Therefore, be cautious in buying the fabric at the outset.

Fabric Grains. Warp threads are lengthwise in all fabrics; woof or filling threads, crosswise. When a corner of the fabric is folded so that the lengthwise threads are parallel with the crosswise threads, the diagonal fold forms a true-bias line. Play with a piece of fabric; stretch, fold and refold until these points are clear. We illustrate here lengthwise, crosswise and true bias. Study the illustrations and know these essentials of fabric. Notice also how bias is pieced on the lengthwise and crosswise grains to obtain one long strip of bias fabric for binding or facing. From a small piece of true bias, mark the piece with pencil lines and make it into a tube with these lines joined as shown; then cut off a strip beginning at **A** and cutting around and around on the lines.

Estimating Material Requirements. Often, when shopping, you see just the material you would like to have for a dress. The question of how much to buy is always a problem, and if the material is expensive, it is particularly important to estimate correctly. A rule that may be safely followed in the case of material 35″ or 40″ wide is to measure twice the length of your dress plus 5″ for hem and ¾ of a yard for sleeves. If a plaited skirt is desired, an additional skirt length should be added. For fabric 54″ wide, 2 yards will usually cut a plain tailored frock; 1¼ yards, a plain skirt. In 39″ chiffons and crepes, if bias skirts or long skirts are the fashion, then 5 to 8 yards will be needed.

Your Mending Routine

IF YOU HAVEN'T a wholly satisfactory mending routine, plan one now. Every woman has her share of mending to do, and it depends upon you whether you enjoy doing your mending or have it forever hanging over you, depriving you of the use of articles and apparel that need only a few stitches to make them really satisfactory. Sooner or later, almost everyone meets mending problems, such as resewing seams, taking tacking stitches, sewing on buttons, or sewing down parts of a garment that have become frayed. Do you keep your mending up to date?

The Mending Basket. Tuck into your mending basket all the necessary time-saving articles: a darning egg, small sharp-pointed scissors, a safety-razor blade, darning needles, sewing needles, darning thread, pins, tape, buttons, snaps and hooks and eyes. Your mending basket or box should also be large enough to hold the garments to be repaired.

Darning-Stitch. The stitches most used in mending are darning-stitches. These look like weaving. Just use the running-stitch, alternating over-and-under-stitches in each successive row, and then pick up with stitches made in the opposite direction, so that the weave is replaced. Darning-stitches are a substitute for the original material, so the thread should be as nearly as possible the same color and texture as the material. In mending wool or linen, it is an excellent plan to unravel a thread of the material itself and darn it into the worn place. Weave the stitches into the material, so that they blend into it without bulk or seam.

Darning-stitches are used for mending holes in stockings, tears in table linen, and worn places in garments of wool and linen. When an otherwise good garment becomes thin at the knee or at the elbow, its life may be prolonged by reinforcing these points by a net of darning-stitches on the wrong side. If the hole to be darned is very large, it is sometimes advisable, as in the case of knitted underwear, to baste a piece of fine net over the hole and darn through. This will keep the hole from stretching, and give the darned portion a flat and permanent appearance.

Mending Dainty Garments. Dainty lingerie and baby clothes should be carefully mended by hand with fine thread and small stitches. Lace should always be mended with tiny overhand stitches.

Machine Mending. The machine is best for mending firmly woven cotton material such as muslin, drilling and firm shirtings. A silk stocking with a long run may also be mended by machine. To mend, crease the stocking lengthwise of the run on the wrong side and stitch the length of the run. Be sure your stitching line comes just outside the run portion, stretch the stocking slightly as you stitch to give sufficient length in the stitching line to prevent its drawing or breaking. Then overcast the seam with loose stitches to give it the appearance of a line rather than a seam. This same method may be used for runs in most knitted garments.

Mending Shirts or Blouses. To mend a shirt that is worn across the shoulder or at the front, place a piece of sturdy light-weight material, such as net, underneath the worn surface, and stitch back and forth with very fine thread on the machine, or mend by hand with running-stitches. Men's shirt cuffs and collars that are worn should be ripped off, reversed, and stitched on again.

Patches, Make-Overs. Mending and altering are akin, because both are usually made on garments that have been worn. There is economy in making over clothes for children, but the design, the fabric and the color must be suitable. Do not merely shorten mother's skirt for daughter; rip it, and make it fit as it should. Dye the material if the color is not suitable.

Altering Garments for Children. Garments of growing children often need alteration. The skirt and sleeves may be lengthened by inserting a band of contrasting material to give the necessary length. The hem may be let down to the proper length. If the bottom of the hem is worn, let it make the top of the new facing line and put a narrow tuck at the top to conceal the worn edge.

Lengthen a short-waisted dress by inserting a strip of material at the shoulder line or around the blouse three or four inches above the waistline, or use a new yoke. The strip may be of contrasting color or of the same material, washed and left in the sun if necessary, to take off the new look.

To make an armhole larger, insert a 1½" to 2" square gusset at the underarm. If more fullness is needed through the body, insert a piece the full length of the underarm seam.

Salvage Materials. Good materials may be redyed, recut, and remade. Keep the scraps of new fabrics; they may be used for trimming, facing, lengthening, making new collars and cuffs, pockets—in fact for many things that will save your time and money. See information on storing such items, page 4.

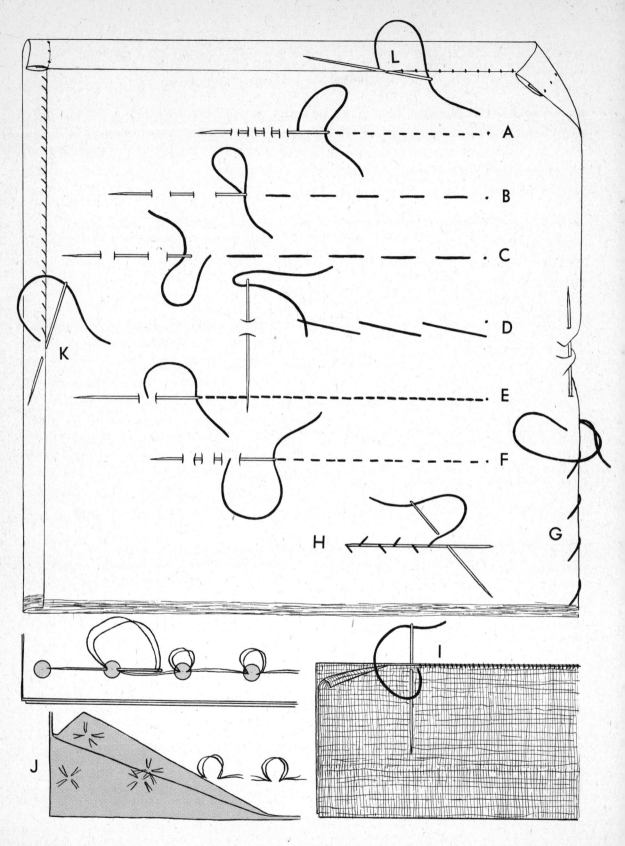

KNOT THE THREAD by lapping it over the end on the first finger of the left hand. Twist the lap with the thumb upward. Make a tiny knot to begin. Make a new knot each time you begin with a new needleful of thread. Run your needle along the seam of the fabric. If running-stitches are being made, take a tiny back-stitch for security as you begin each needleful.

Always Use a Thimble That Fits You, that is light in weight, and entirely comfortable. Work to develop an easy position of your hands for sewing. Your fingers must aid you in many ways in doing fine sewing, smoothing, creasing, and turning the material. So keep your hands in good condition and immaculately clean so that they may serve you well in all your sewing.

If your hands perspire easily, dust them with French chalk as you start to sew. This will allow the work to move more quickly in your hands, and it will also protect it. You can buy French chalk at your drug store.

A. Running-Stitches are the most used of all stitches—for sewing plain seams, for dainty hand sewing, and for gathering and basting. Fine running-stitches require a fine needle. For instance, a #10 needle should be used with size 100 thread. For running-stitches, choose a long slender needle; then take up several stitches on the needle, as shown, and pull them through; experts put seven to ten stitches on the needle. This makes the work progress quickly and insures even stitches and a straight line, as the needle itself aids in keeping the sewing line straight.

B. Even-Basting-Stitches are made in the same way as running-stitches, except that they are longer, their length measuring from ¼″ to ½″. Use a knot in beginning your basting, as the basting thread must be removed when replaced with permanent stitching. Basting is seldom used on hand-sewed seams as one can keep the seam together accurately with pins without basting when handling it for a running-stitch. Basting is a great safeguard in particular machine work and very necessary with wool garments or any materials that stretch or that are inclined to pull under the presser foot, such as velvet, crepe, satin or chiffon. Clip basting threads at intervals to remove them.

C. Uneven-Basting. This stitch is used merely to hold two pieces of material together for stitching or handling. The stitches are practically twice as long as for even basting. Because of the speed possible with uneven-basting, it proves a real convenience to one experienced in handling materials.

D. Diagonal-Basting. This easy to do basting stitch, serves much the same purpose as uneven basting, but it is used to keep materials from slipping, to hold the facing in a coat or lining in a sleeve until it is felled in, that is, until it is permanently secured. Large diagonal bastings are used in making draperies.

Pin-Basting. (No illustration.) After one is experienced in handling fabric, one will know when pinning of the seams is safe. Cottons of even weave are good for pin-basting and if enough pins and a little caution are used safety is assured.

E. Back-Stitching. For secure seams, a back-stitch is sometimes used. To do this you take a short stitch on the top and a stitch twice as long on the underside. This will make the seam appear as a machine-stitched seam on the right side and will be practically as secure, but it will require, of course, a great deal more time to make. Single back-stitches finish off sewing lines and are useful in a running-stitch seam to give added strength.

F. Combination-Stitches. These are the same as running-stitches except that every three or four stitches a back-stitch is taken. This stays the seam, prevents the thread from catching and pulling out, and is in many ways satisfactory.

G. Overcasting. Used as a finish for seams. On heavy materials, such as wool, take one stitch at a time. On light-weight materials, take a number of stitches on the needle as shown. In this way the work progresses rapidly and provides a nice finish. Always overcast seams in bulky materials or in material that ravels easily. The more the material is inclined to ravel, the closer the stitches must be. Never allow your overcasting thread to draw tight; rather, let it be very easy.

H. Fishbone-Stitch. This is a variation of the blanket-stitch and is ordinarily used in embroidery, but it may be used to hold two edges together, as shown. Bring the needle through. Then, holding the thread along the line to be sewn, take a diagonal stitch from one side toward yourself, as shown, crossing the thread with the needle as you pull it through. Repeat to the other side of the line and continue alternating from side to side.

I. Overhanding is used to hold two selvages together, or two edges where a very secure seam is desired. The stitch is taken over and over, directly in the extreme outside edge of the selvage. It is never used where overcasting will do because the latter works up much more quickly. The basting thread is removed after the seam is overcast and then when the seam is pressed, it should appear perfectly flat.

J. Tailor's Tacks. Where material overlaps, or where two edges are to be brought together in a dart or for a plait, use tailor's tacks to mark where perforations come in the pattern. Then, when the pattern is removed, there will be no confusion as to the correct assembling of the garment. To make tailor's tacks, simply combine an uneven-basting and a back-stitch, using a colored thread, preferably, as it is more easily seen. Make a loose back-stitch and carry it out in a long basting-stitch. Repeat until all perforations are marked. Clip the long stitches on top, as shown, then gently separate the two pieces of material, and cut each back-stitch. The thread ends left are your tailor's tacks. Remove these when the seam stitching is done.

K. Hemming-Stitch or Whipping-Stitch. To make this stitch, slip the knot of the thread under the folded-in edge, bringing the needle through in position for taking the first stitch; insert the needle just underneath the hem, catching one or two threads of the material, and in this same stitch catch the very edge of the hem. Continue working from the wrong side, taking very small, almost invisible stitches through to the right side and slanting stitches of even length on the wrong side. Be careful not to draw the thread tight.

L. Running-Hem. This stitch is sometimes used in place of regular whipping-stitches when an especially dainty and inconspicuous finish is desired. This kind of hemming takes its name from the direction of the stitches that show on the wrong side, and is also known as vertical hemming. To do vertical hemming, conceal the knot in the fold of the hem, bringing the needle out in the crease, and make each stitch by inserting the needle just outside the hem directly opposite the point where it comes out of the hem, taking up one or two threads of the material, and then bringing the needle out a short distance beyond in the hem, as close to the turned edge as possible, so as to take the next stitch.

Embroidery Stitches

A. Blanket-Stitch. Put needle in; bring it out over the thread as shown. Use as an edge finish for collars, front closings. Make of embroidery thread, floss or yarn. Three variations of the stitch are shown in the border at the left. Variation made simply by spacing or grouping.

B. Chain-Stitch. Make a loop by putting needle through, then back from the wrong side across the thread. Insert it as shown and make another loop and thus continue the chain. Used as a decorative stitch on peasant-type clothes, lingerie and linens.

C. Feather or Brier-Stitch. Made by following a line and making a stitch on first one side, then the other, and looping the thread under the needle. To master such stitches, it is good to practice with different sizes of threads and yarns and in drawing the stitch up tight enough to lie straight, and loose enough to curve slightly.

D. Seed-Stitch. A short back-stitch, taken at intervals to fill a space, as in a petal or border.

E. Cross-Stitch. One of the oldest of the decorative stitches. Use for conventional embroideries, for borders, for fill-in, for motif, and especially for sampler work. One row of slanting stitches is often made over a transfer-marked design. Then a row slanting in opposite direction is made across the first row, as shown. Draw the stitch up but never tight. Even stitches enhance the beauty of the work.

F. Satin-Stitch. A long over-and-over stitch, which is the same on top and underneath. For stems, for leaves, for borders and fill-ins. Lay the threads parallel to each other, placing them in the direction the design requires.

G. Long-and-Short-Stitch. Over-and-over whipping type of stitch. Used for applique, for edging designs, especially fruit and leaves. Use fairly heavy thread or yarn and make stitches as deep and as far apart as is appropriate to the size of the motif.

H. Lazy Daisy. Worked around a center point to form a group of stitches resembling the petal of a daisy. Make a loop as deep as you want the petal. Bring the needle out over the thread that is to form the loop. Draw it through. Put needle in directly ahead of the center of the loop, holding the loop in place, and bring it out at the center point, at the side of the beginning stitch. Repeat until as many petals are made as the motif requires. Occasionally three or more petals are made and attached to a stem. If large loops are made, thus making a large center, this may be filled in with French knots or seed-stitch to give a field-daisy effect.

I. Outline-Stitch. Used to outline edges, to make thin stems. A slanting back-stitch worked away from you. The degree of slant and size and kind of thread determine the weight of the line.

J. French Knot. Bring needle through from wrong side. Twist needle around thread several times as shown. Put point of needle down into fabric near where it came up. Pull through to wrong side and then draw thread through, thus bringing knot snugly against fabric. Repeat until you have as many knots as desired.

K. Arrowhead-Stitch. Good for borders and edges, especially for children's clothes. Bring needle up from wrong side to left of a line (1), where stitches are to go. Put needle in near the line (2), taking an upward diagonal stitch on the opposite side (3). Bring it through and insert at (4) and out at (5). Continue from side to side until you have filled the space desired. A little practice insures even spacings and speed in making.

L. Hemstitching. Draw threads, 4, 6, 8, etc., according to the depth you want the hemstitching to be. If necessary, baste a hem as shown. Start at the left of the fabric. Put needle in at the right and bring it around the number of threads necessary to get the effect you desire. In linen, sometimes only three threads are surrounded; in lighter-weight fabrics, six is not too many. Put the needle into the hem edge, as shown, directly over the center of the group of threads. Continue until the row is finished. When a corner is reached and hem is double, then stitches need to be closer together to accommodate same number of threads.

M. Bar Fagoting. Baste to paper the edges that are to be fagoted together, placing them the desired distance apart. Begin at the left side. Put needle in at right and twist the needle around the thread three, four or more times. Pull needle through at a point just above the first left-side stitch. Put it in again and carry it underneath the vertical edge for the next stitch. Repeat until the row is finished.

N. Cross-Stitch Fagoting. Baste edges the desired distance apart and make a cross-stitch back and forth one side to the other, as shown, until row is complete.

Smocking. There are various ways of smocking. The type shown is known as honeycomb and is the simplest and a great favorite. Unless you are working on a fabric having even squares of dots or checks, use a transfer pattern to mark your fabric. Use a knot to begin and work from left to right. After bringing needle up through first dot of second row, take a small back-stitch over the dot. Next insert the needle under the second dot as at 1, and also under the first dot as at 2. Draw dots

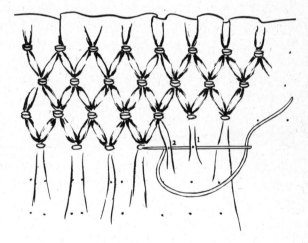

together. Carrying the thread up to the first row, take a back-stitch through the second dot. Taking a stitch through the third dot, first row, draw them together as before. Continue alternating between first and second rows until end of row. After turning work around so you can still work from left to right, repeat your stitches, alternating between second and third rows. Continue doing this until you have as many rows as desired. See page 138 for machine smocking.

Essential Seams

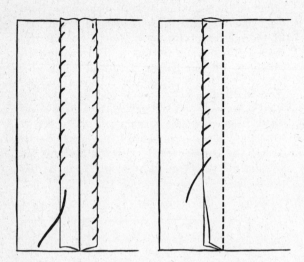

Plain. Seam used in every type of garment. Lay the two edges together in as straight a line as possible, so that both edges come together smoothly, neither drawn or eased. Pin or baste. Stitch plain seams with moderately short stitches. Press the seam open, perfectly flat. There are four ways to finish such seams on the wrong side —Overcast, Pinked, Clean-stitched, Bound.

Overcast. This seam has no unnecessary thicknesses. Used for nearly all fabrics. Make a plain seam. Open it by pressing between the raw edges, laying the seam edges flat against the fabric. Clip the seam at intervals if it is curved so that it will lie flat. Overcast each edge to prevent raveling; take several stitches on the needle at a time for speed and avoid tight stitches.

Pinked. Seam suitable for firm woolens, broadcloth, flannel, chintz, etc. Not too practical for wash garments as the edge has a tendency to roll. A pinked seam saves finishing time. Make a plain seam first. Press this open. Notch the raw edges with scissors or pinking shears.

Clean-Stitched. Seam used by dress manufacturers. Particularly practical for finely woven, nontransparent fabrics. Stitch as for a plain seam; then turn each raw edge to the underside and stitch, holding it free from fabric. When using this on shaped seams, as at under-arm or sleeve, snip edges and stretch slightly before stitching to insure flatness.

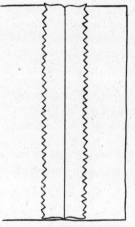 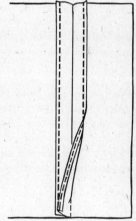

Bound-Seam. Practical for material that frays easily; also for unlined jackets and coats. Stitch as for a plain seam, and press open. Press one raw edge of the binding over ¼"; place the free edge under the seam edge, and stitch directly on the turned edge, taking care to catch the under piece and the fabric the full length of the seam.

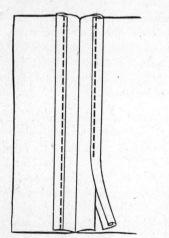 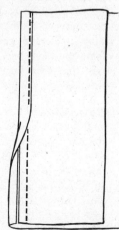

Self-Bound. Suitable for light-weight fabrics. Often used for straight seams of children's clothes, underwear, house dresses and aprons. Place one edge over other, stitch, and trim upper edge to within ⅛" of seam line. Turn raw edge under, fold over the trimmed edge, and stitch. This seam can be made without the first stitching.

[21]

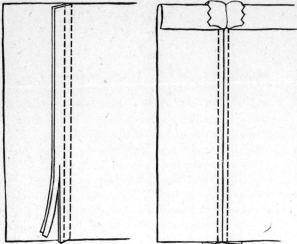

Double-Stitched. For soft materials or those with an embroidered design, such as eyelet embroidery on which it would be difficult to make a French seam, the double-stitched seam is practical. First stitch on the seam line as for a plain seam. Then, ¼" outside the first stitching, make a second row. If the material frays easily, trim away only the frayed edges; then overcast it. The two rows of stitching will give a firm, flat seam.

Top-Stitched. Desirable for medium or light-weight woolens and suitings. Make a plain seam; then, from right side of garment, add a row of stitching along each side of the pressed-open seam. On curved seams, clip the seam before adding the stitching, to make the seam lie perfectly flat.

French. Favored for sheer, firm materials, such as batiste, lawn and organdie. Make a ⅛" seam on the right side. Trim it close to the stitching line, press the seam from the wrong side, and make a second row of stitching from the wrong side, deep enough to cover the raw edges. For a hand-finished effect, make first stitching by machine and run the second in by hand.

Imitation French. Some feel that this is an easier seam to make than a French seam, and it does give much the same effect. Especially suitable for crispy fabrics such as lawn or rayon crepes. Stitch on the seam line on the wrong side of the garment; then turn the raw edges in and stitch them together to give a firm, sturdy seam.

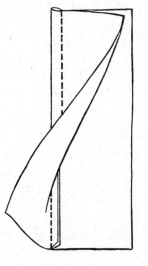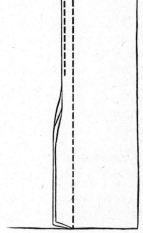

Decorative-Lapped. Used to accent a seam line. Suitable for silks, woolens and heavy cottons. For curved joinings, make the seam line with tailor's tacks for accuracy. Turn the over-lap edge along marking, and baste the turning. Clip edge over the seam line, tailor's tack lines matching. Stitch on very edge of over-lap.

Plain-Lapped. Used principally for piecing interlinings of coats, etc., or where flat concealed joining is necessary, as in felt or flannel. Lap one edge over the other ⅜" to ½" and stitch down center of overlap. This seam may also be used on heavy net and lace with a close all-over pattern. On such fabrics, stitch over paper to prevent puckering. Trim off extra width on each side of the seam.

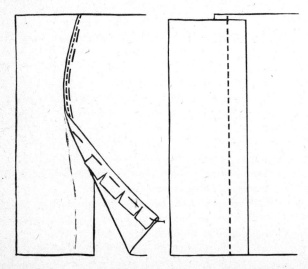

Flat Fell. Used in tailored blouses, men's and boys' shirts and pajamas, all sturdy clothes that are changed frequently and washed after each wearing. Stitch first on seam line from right side. Trim one edge away to within ⅛″ of the stitching. Turn other edge flat over this, turn in raw edge, and stitch the seam from the right side.

Welt. Practical for all tailored-type fabrics. Stitch on seam line. Trim one seam edge up close to stitching; press from right side, pressing crosswise of the seam to prevent overlapping of the seam line. The narrow edge is concealed inside the wide one; a second row of stitching from right side holds wide edge in place. Raw edge may be overcast before final stitching.

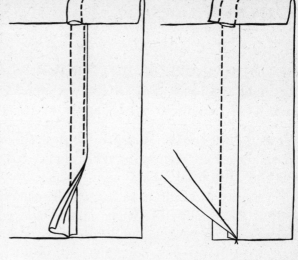

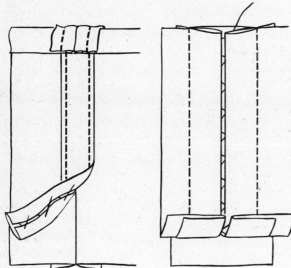

Strap. Used on tailored garments chiefly to add line or design or to extend width, as in a too-tight skirt. For the strap, make a true bias, and overcast the raw edges together. Baste the strap on the right side of the garment over the plain, pressed-open or whipped-together seam. Stitch the strap on each edge to hold it securely in position.

Slot. Used in tailored-type fabrics. Cut a lengthwise strip of material twice the width of the seams plus 1″. Mark the center of the strip with a basting line or a crease. Place a basted, pressed-open garment seam line right side up, directly over center line of strip. Add a row of stitching on each side of seam. Press seam; remove basting.

Baseball-Stitched. Used to join two edges that do not overlap as on a baseball. Put needle in under edge on one side of the opening. Bring out needle; then insert under other side. Continue from side to side all along seam. Close stitches appear straight; widely spaced, slanted. Used for stocking patches, gloves, and where seams are lacking, as under a strap in a skirt which has been let out.

Corded. Used for slip-covers, draperies, and cushions, also a decorative seam for garments. Make as many yards of true bias as you need cording. Cut this 6 times as wide as diameter of cord. Place this bias over cable cord, raw edges together; make a seam. Use cording foot to hug the material up close to the cord. Insert covered cord in seam and stitch from wrong side.

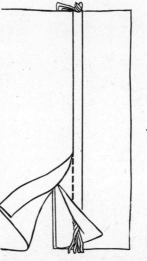

Buttonholes

DETERMINE WHERE BUTTONHOLES and buttons will go on a garment. Lap the right side over the left for women; left over the right for men. Pin the lap exactly so that there is no danger of its slipping.

Worked Buttonholes. Measure the desired distance between buttonholes and mark these distances accurately with chalk, basting or pins. Mark directly underneath for the button location.

Measure the button and cut a slit usually ¼ longer than the diameter of the button. Use points of sharp scissors and cut cautiously on a thread. Horizontal buttonholes are usually made for medium and small buttons; vertical, for large or decorative buttons such as those in a front plait, where there is no strain.

In materials that fray readily, stitch by hand or machine ⅟16" on each side of the lines on which the buttonholes are to be cut. The stitching will hold the edge firm and give support to the buttonhole stitches.

To make a buttonhole, use a medium-coarse single-thread about ¾ yard long.

Stranding Buttonholes. To prevent the edges from stretching and also to make the buttonhole firm, especially in wool or in fabrics that fray, supply what is known as a stranding thread by bringing the needle out just below the inner end of the buttonhole, taking a small back-stitch to make the thread secure, and then taking

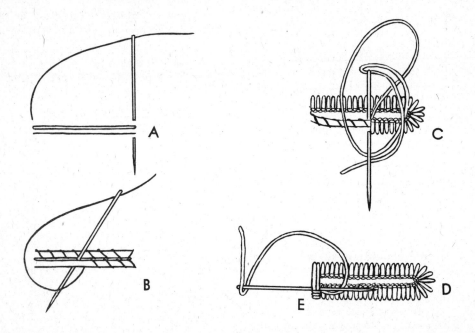

a short stitch under the opposite or outside end, bringing the needle back and taking a small stitch under the inner end, or at the point from which you started, as in **A.** By doing this, you will form two stitches that lie close to the buttonhole opening and are equal in length to this opening. Draw these stranding stitches close, but not so tight as to cause the buttonhole to pucker. This stranding thread should be overcast to the fabric, as shown in **B.**

Working Buttonholes. After completing the overcasting, bring this same thread out about ⅟₁₆″ below the inner end of the opening in preparation for making the buttonhole-stitch. Place the needle under one edge of the slit and in the edge of the buttonhole, to make a short stitch, usually about ⅟₁₆″ deep; bring the threads that come from the eye of the needle around under the point of the needle to the left forming a loop, as in **C,** draw up the thread firm and close, but not tight enough to draw the edges apart. A stitch made in this manner forms a double or buttonhole purl at the edge; this makes a firm and durable finish.

Continue working the buttonhole-stitches across the lower edge of the buttonhole, making them close together and all of the same length, as the illustration shows. When you reach the outer end, take several buttonhole-stitches around it, spacing them evenly, and making these stitches somewhat deeper than those along the edge, thus forming what is known as a round end or fan finish as in **D.**

Next, turn the work and continue making buttonhole-stitches of equal depth.

Making Buttonhole Bar. When you reach the inner end of the buttonhole, finish this with a bar, as in **E.** Take several stranding stitches across this end and then work over them with single-purl stitches by bringing the needle out over the thread just as in making the blanket-stitch. Place these stitches close together, so that they will entirely conceal the stitches underneath, and catch several of them through the material so as to make the bar firm. Finish the buttonhole by taking a couple of tiny back-stitches on the wrong side.

Vertical Buttonholes. Finish both ends of the buttonhole with bars, thus giving a uniform appearance.

Bound Buttonholes. In a bound buttonhole, a welt is formed by covering the slashed edges with ribbon, tape or braid. Although a scant ¼″ welt is the average width, the buttonhole size and weight of fabric may make it advisable to make a wider welt for a more pleasing appearance. (Illustrations on next page.)

A. Mark the position of all buttonholes with chalk or pencil on the wrong side. Be sure they are spaced evenly. If you are using self fabric, then cut oblongs of fabric 1″ longer than length of finished buttonhole and 8 times the width of welt—2″ wide if welt is to be ¼″ wide. These oblongs of fabric can be cut crosswise, lengthwise or bias depending on effect desired.

Center one of the oblongs of fabric directly over each position marked for the buttonhole, right sides together. Baste it in position so that the bastings will be outside your stitching line. Now draw a line to indicate the exact center of the finished buttonhole and a line on each end to indicate the finished length. Starting in the center of one side, machine-stitch the outline as shown. To finish off the stitch, overlap four to five stitches, thus sewing the thread ends.

B. After removing the basting, start cutting the buttonhole in the center, cutting first toward one end, then toward the other. When clipping diagonally at the corners, do not cut through the line of stitching. Bring the edges of the applied piece through the slash to the wrong side.

C. Press the triangular ends out. Fold the fabric piece over the seam edges so that the welts will appear on the right as shown. After the edges are diagonally basted together, the wrong side will appear as in **D.** Tack together the edges of the plaits which are formed on both ends of the buttonhole.

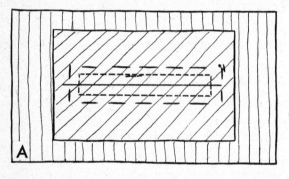

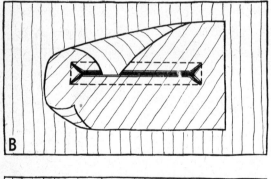

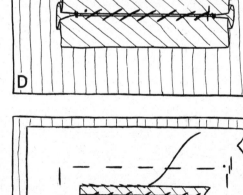

E. Apply your facing to the wrong side. Baste around each buttonhole, then, exactly above the buttonhole, slash the facing in the same manner as you did the buttonhole. Whip down all turned-in edges.

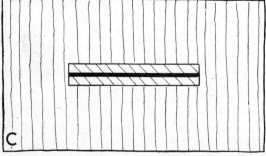

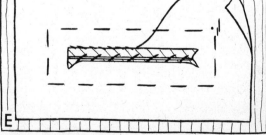

Sewing On Buttons

THE SEWING ON OF BUTTONS is a matter every girl, woman, boy and man should learn—all should be skillful in such sewing. The way in which buttons are placed and secured has much to do with their appearance and function.

For a two-hole button, mark the position for each button by lapping the garment as it is to be worn. Bring a pin up from underneath to the button side directly through the center of each button-hole. Both sides of the garment should be smoothed out so the space between the buttons will correspond to that between the buttonholes.

Use a strong thread, begin with a back-stitch at the point marked by the pin, bring thread up through one hole of the button and down through the other hole and through the fabric; but before drawing the thread down, put one or two pins across the button, as in **A,** so as to provide buttonhole space between the fabric and the button.

Sew back and forth until the button is securely in position. Remove the pin, draw the button away from the material as far as possible, and wind the thread tightly several times around the threads between the button and the material as in **B.** This treatment forms a thread shank for the button, holding the button away from the material and allowing room for the buttonhole. Finish off thread with a tiny back-stitch as in **C.**

Sew a four-hole button on in the same way as a two-hole one, but place pins over the button, as in **D,** and sew diagonally across or parallel so that stitches are a decoration to the button. For four-hole-buttons on coats, the threads should not cross, but should be parallel so as to give a neater finish. **E** shows a decorative way to sew on buttons. Colored thread is often used in this way for bone and pearl buttons on children's undergarments.

F. For shank buttons, locate the positions as explained. Sew on so that the stitches run parallel to the edge of the garment, as the strain will then fall on the shank rather than on the thread.

G. Hooks and Eyes. Place these precisely by marking each side with chalk, pin or pencil, so that the eye is precisely in line with the hook. Use a strong thread or a double thread. Sew over and over the wire to hold flat to the garment. Sew under the hump of the hook so as to hold it in place and prevent gapping. When edges meet rather than overlap, a round eye is used on one edge, as shown in **H.**

I. Worked Eyes. On a placket or narrow edge, worked eyes are better than wire ones, as they show less, especially when made with thread to match the fabric. To make: Provide two or more thread bars in the form of a loop, doing this by taking stitches over each other. Buttonhole over this loop as shown so that it gives a strong bar over which you hook the hook.

J. Snap Fasteners. These need to be placed with precise care. Many types have a hole through the center so that you can locate them easily enough. Over-and-over stitches should be made in the holes of the fastener, both top and bottom, to insure their holding securely in position.

Tailored Pockets

Bound Pocket. Determine the placing of pockets by holding the pattern in place on yourself. The best location may not be exactly the same as in the pattern. Use pins to mark the exact placing and then baste or mark the line with chalk. Cut fabric for the pocket 1″ wider than the finished pocket will be and double the length of the pouch plus 1½″ allowance for welts and seams.

Lay the piece on right side of garment, as in **A,** so that the crosswise center line falls 1″ above the pocket line. Baste this in place. Mark the position of the ends of the pocket line, making this box twice the desired width of the finished welts (usually ¼″ or ⁵⁄₁₆″). Start in the center for this stiching and pivot on the needle at each corner to make it true. Pull out bastings, cut the center line of the rectangle and clip toward the corners at each end, as in **B.** Draw the pouch pieces through the slit to the wrong side. Lay the edges of the welt together and catch them with diagonal basting stitches, as in **C.** Press these edges. Turn to the right side and stitch

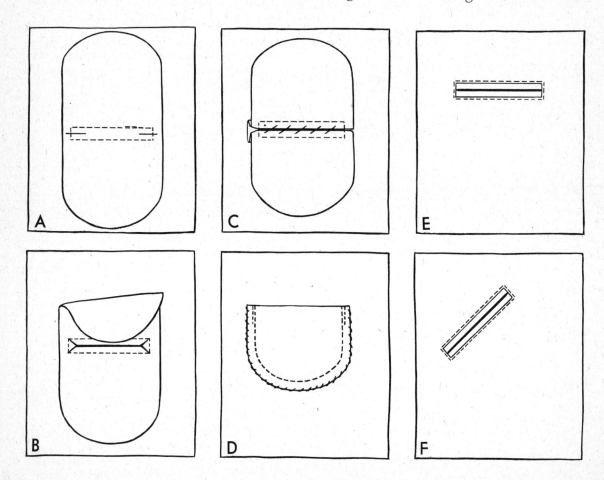

around the edges of the welts, as in **E.** Lay the edges of the pouch together, trim off evenly, and stitch all around, as in **D,** holding the pouch away from the garment. Two stitchings through seams and welts at each end of the seam give added strength. Overcast the seam edges together. **F** shows a pocket on the diagonal.

Welt Pocket. The type of pocket in **G** is often used on women's lounging robes and sports coats and jackets. To make the pouch cut a lengthwise piece of fabric 1″ wider than the desired width of the finished pocket and double the length plus 1½″. Lay this right side down on the right side of the garment, as in **H.** Fold along the crosswise center line of the piece. Lay the crease on the lower edge of the pocket. Stitch a rectangle around this, slit the center and clip toward the ends, as in **I.** Draw the pouch flaps through the slit to the wrong side. Press seams open. Smooth the lower pouch piece up over the opening and stitch, as in **J,** to hold the welt in place. Turn the upper pouch part down to make the back of the pouch and stitch the two halves of the pouch together, holding them away from the garment as you stitch. Stitch twice over the seam at each end, as in **K,** and overcast the raw edges.

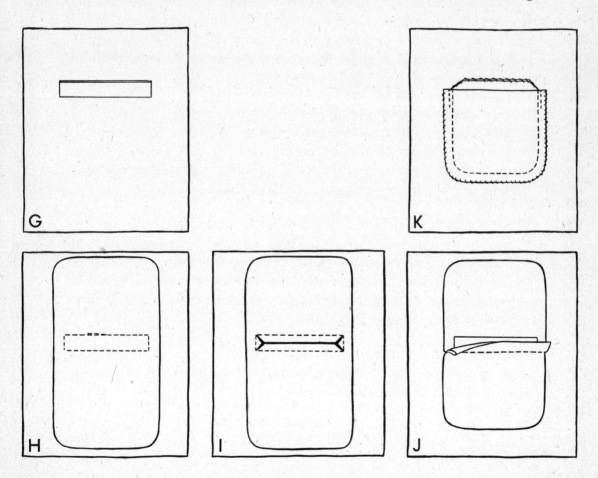

G

K

H

I

J

Fashion

FASHION IS AN ACTIVE, moving force. Fashion—like yourself—wants to be understood and appreciated. And to have Fashion as a friend and companion, you must be sympathetic, alert, and ready to accept that of the new that is appropriate for you.

There are many sources of Fashion, and Fashion gives us an infinite variety each season so that there are lines, designs, and colors appropriate to all. We must, however, know which is becoming to us and how to hold Fashion as a friend. This requires a fidelity to study and an eagerness in shopping—to find what is good in the new and to use it with a regard for details, the little things that make for perfection.

Buy the pattern fashion books. Study the silhouettes, the construction features, types of fabrics recommended, finishing details, etc. When you make yourself a new dress, decide the type of dress you require, find a pattern that is right for your purpose, with lines that are flattering for your type of figure.

Beware of tricky clothes—clothes that are too "cut up" in line. First, because they require time to make; and second, they too often date your dress. A dress of simple, becoming lines that are structurally correct will be good for the life of the garment, and neither you, your friends, or your family will grow tired of them.

When you have learned to appreciate textures in fabric, color quality, beauty in design . . . when you know the season's requirements in silhouette . . . how to choose fabric of a texture or design to express the new silhouette . . . how to use color becomingly and fashionably, you will delight in Fashion's changes, welcome them and find them something to be truly excited about.

We hope that throughout this study you will become increasingly alert to Fashion, and that your intelligent loyalty to her will cause her to be your friend forevermore.

Aprons Three

Materials. Percale in fast color 80 square quality is ideal for aprons for these reasons: Percale of fine, even weave is an easy fabric to handle; it tears, creases, hems, gathers, stitches, and presses easily.

"80 square" is the "thread count," and means that there are 80 warp and 80 woof threads to the inch. You can not see this with the naked eye; but, if you hold the fabric to the light, you can see the evenness of the threads, their closeness, etc. 80 square percale means that the warp and woof threads are of the same size or weight and therefore make a durable fabric that is easy to handle in sewing and pressing. Less expensive percales, 54–68 square or 68–72 square, are good; but they do not sew so easily or wear or iron so well as an 80 square. In the 80 square, hems are as easy one way as another; also, the threads all wear out at the same time, because they are all of the same strength.

Dimity, another favorite fabric for aprons, is sheer and slightly wiry. It should be cut and not torn, because the lengthwise cords in the warp are stronger than the woof. All this makes the dimity definitely different from the percale. An important part of sewing is to learn how to handle all types of fabric. Then you yourself will know when it is necessary to baste before stitching. You will see and understand why narrow hems and tiny tucks are desirable in sheer fabric; also, why fine thread is used. In addition to the construction points, we want you to learn all about fabrics and how to treat them in sewing, so that your sewing will look professional.

Work Apron. Concentrate on making this apron, and others will be easy. All Seams and Hems are allowed for in these patterns.

The A B C's of Sewing. If you have never made a garment, or even if you have made many, start in and make the Work Apron *our way*—which is, we believe, the simplest possible way. We want you to find this so easy that you will want to make many others. Our plan organizes the work just as piece work is organized for a factory worker—to save lost motion and, best of all, to save the delay of wondering what to do next. Our plan also brings the garment to completion quickly and insures your doing each part equally well. We want you really to enjoy—yes, get fun out of—your sewing work. Now, let's begin with A B C:

A. Straighten Fabric Before Cutting. Choose percale. Fabric should be torn, except when either the warp of the woof is heavier. (In dimity, the warp is heavier.) Stretch and pull fabric diagonally to straighten it. Fold and pin according to layout, wrong side of fabric out, in preparation for cutting.

B. Check Your Pattern With Your Measurements. Take from the pattern envelope the pattern pieces—A, B, C, and D are representative of the essential ones. Put other pieces and the instruction sheet back in envelope, because you should follow these simple step-by-step directions, to learn garment-making *our way.*

C. Place the Pattern, and Cut Out Your Apron. With the fold of the fabric next to you, place the pattern pieces on, as illustrated in the layout. Pin each pattern section carefully to the fabric. Each piece is placed for the correct grain, as you see, yet with a minimum of fabric waste. In cutting, allow as much length as practical for neck strap. (Especially necessary for tall person.) Lengthwise apron strings are preferable to those cut crosswise. Cut out the apron. Use sharp shears and cut along the pattern line all the way around each piece. Snip tiny notches where required. Leave pattern pieces pinned to the fabric until darts are indicated.

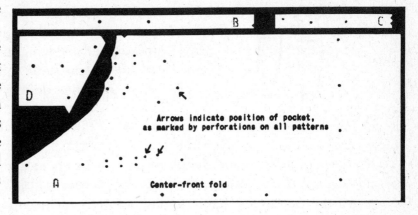

Arrows indicate position of pocket, as marked by perforations on all patterns

Center-front fold

Put in Darts. Darts are used for fitting the garment to the figure. In this apron four hip darts are used, two at each side in the back, to fit your apron to the hips; and two body darts are used to panel the front and to take out excess fulness there. If you are flat in front, you may omit the front darts or make them less deep.

Mark the darts while the pattern is on the fabric. To do this, make a pencil mark in each perforation; then place a pin in each, as shown, so that you can mark the opposite side also with pencil. When all dart marks are made, remove the pattern. Pin each dart, putting the pin through one dot mark and picking up the corresponding mark underneath. Practice marking and pinning darts.

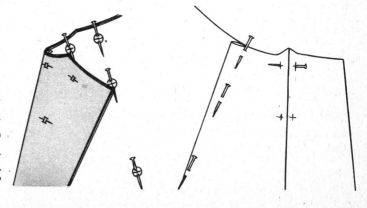

Begin at top of each hip dart, and stitch down to point. Pivot needle; turn and stitch back, stitching on folded edge this time so that dart will be flat. When you have learned how to make hip darts, you will know how to make neck, shoulder, elbow, and waistline darts, because the principle is the same.

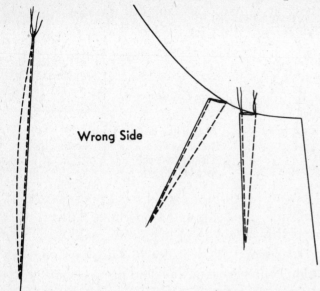

Wrong Side

Stitch body darts, stitching on curved line first, and back on folded edge. Tie the thread ends together on each of these darts. Press hip darts toward center of apron; press body darts away from center of apron, toward the sides. Body darts are used in both the back and front of dresses and jackets. Learn to form, stitch, and press all darts nicely in your aprons; and you will be sure of perfection when you use them later.

Put in Narrow Hems. With your narrow sewing-machine hemmer, hem the lengthwise edges of each tie string; also, the back edges of the apron. If you haven't a hemmer, turn the edges back a scant ⅛″; then make another ⅛″ turn, creasing each turn firmly with your fingers. Baste, if necessary.

In using your hemmer, give your full attention to the hem and go slowly so as to catch the turned edge under the stitching line. If sewing is new to you, practice making a narrow hem on a scrap of the fabric before you begin on the apron.

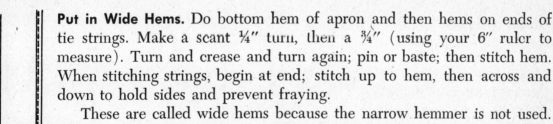

Put in Wide Hems. Do bottom hem of apron and then hems on ends of tie strings. Make a scant ¼″ turn, then a ¾″ (using your 6″ ruler to measure). Turn and crease and turn again; pin or baste; then stitch hem. When stitching strings, begin at end; stitch up to hem, then across and down to hold sides and prevent fraying.

These are called wide hems because the narrow hemmer is not used. The same method is used in making this hem that is used in making a hem several inches wide. Learn now to turn, crease, and measure hems evenly so that you can do them perfectly no matter what their width.

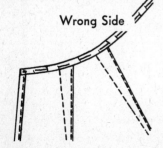

Wrong Side

Make Curved (Underarm) Hems. When the six darts are in, snip the top ends of hip darts off diagonally a scant ¼″, so that darts will not be bulky inside the hem. Turn and crease ⅛″, then ¼″. Baste, drawing the basting slightly tight so as to avoid stretching these curved lines. Stitch the hems.

Apply the Strings. Lay two folds in the top end of each string; stitch across each, as shown. Lay the strings on the wrong side of the apron, with the edge ¼″ in from the hemmed apron edge, as shown, and right side of string up. Stitch. Turn the strings into position. From the right side of the apron, stitch the strings on, stitching in the form of an oblong box, as shown. This conceals the raw edge and at the same time makes the strings secure.

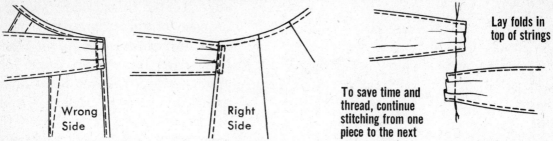

Wrong Side

Right Side

Lay folds in top of strings

To save time and thread, continue stitching from one piece to the next

Prepare Work Pockets. For the pocket hems, turn bias end of each pocket over ⅛″ to wrong side, then back ¾″ to right side, creasing and smoothing flatly so that hems can not twist. Stitch ends at each side for width of hems only, as shown. Clip front corners, turn hem to position, crease, and stitch it down. Turn raw edges of pockets in on the two sides and bottom. Snip corners away, and press or baste turn.

Apply Pockets. The body darts, pressed out from the center of the apron, make it slightly easier to position the pockets. Place each lengthwise front of pocket in line with the body darts, to panel the center front. Pin the pockets in place, having the grain of the fabric in the pocket the same as that in the apron. Baste both pockets carefully. Begin at the stitching line of the hem, and stitch up to the top of the hem; then pivot on the needle, and turn and stitch back. (Go slowly. Hold the wheel with your hand if necessary to take one stitch at a time. This is an essential when finishing a line or when doing intricate stitching.) Stitch all around the

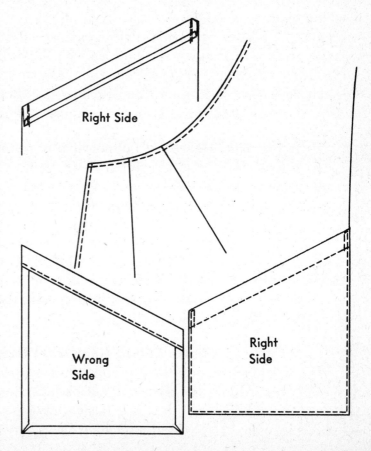

Right Side

Wrong Side

Right Side

three turned edges, pivoting at each corner. At the top of the pocket, turn and stitch back on the hem to the stitching line, as you did on the opposite side. This double stitching at the hem strengthens the pockets at the top and prevents them from tearing if they catch—a precaution to take with all pockets. Pull thread ends through to wrong side, and tie.

Make Neck Strap. When you make belts or bands or double ties in the future, you will want to make them in the same way that you make this neck strap: First, piece the strap if necessary to make it long enough. Fold right side in. Bring the two raw edges together on the long side of the strap and stitch, making a scant ¼" seam; then stitch twice across one narrow end—to hold end later while strap is being turned. Clip raw edges every 3 or 4 inches. Press seam open its full length. This is a very little thing, but it insures an even edge when strap is turned. Place end of orange stick against stitched end, the opposite end next to you; and with your fingers crowd strap down on stick to turn it right side out, as shown. Clip stitched end off, and press strap with seam to one edge.

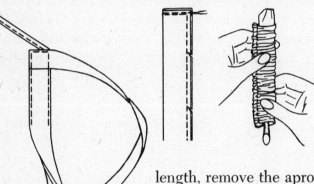

Wrong Side

Apply Neck Strap. Crease and pin bib hem in position. Put apron on, and tie the strings. Adjust strap to a comfortable length for you—not so short as to draw apron from its becoming position at the waistline, or so long as to be uncomfortable. When straps are pinned for correct length, remove the apron. Cut strap to the measured length. Open out the bib hem, place edges of strap ⅜" beyond extreme edge of the bib on each side, and stitch strap ends to raw edge of the bib. Then make hem at top of bib; and stitch it, as shown. Applying straps in this way not only conceals the ends, but serves to make them secure. Tie the thread ends.

Press Your Apron. Fold it lengthwise through the center, right side out. Wring your cheesecloth press cloth out of water. Open it out, and place one thickness over your apron. Press, working from the center out. Press one side; then turn and press the other. You will see from this how very easy this apron is to iron. It is sturdy and practical, protecting your dress at all points—in front, under the arms, and over hips.

Apron With Ruffle. (Illustrated on next page.) Cut and make exactly the same as the Work Apron, with two exceptions: The ruffle and the pocket. For cutting, use the essential pattern pieces and follow this layout for placing them on.

[35]

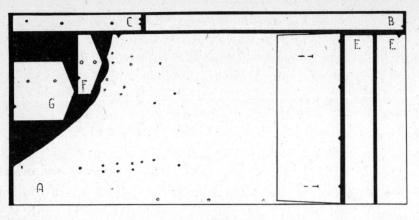

Join the Two Pieces of the Ruffle. Place the edges of the ruffle together with the lengthwise grain, usually two selvages; and stitch in a ⅜″ seam. Hem the ruffle, using the narrow hemmer.

Gather and Adjust Fulness. Gather the ruffle, gathering it very full. Fold the apron lengthwise in the center. Place a pin at the bottom of the apron to mark the center line. Place wrong side of ruffle to wrong side of apron, as shown, with the seam of the gathered ruffle on the center line. Pin ruffle in position, beginning at the center and pinning out to the edge. Baste and stitch it, making a scant ¼″ seam. Trim this seam slightly, just to even it.

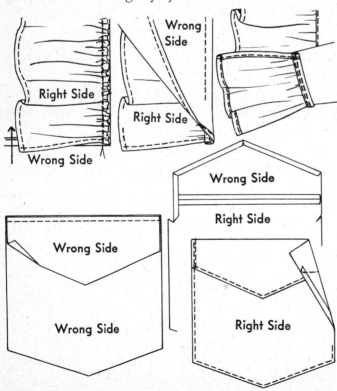

Make a French Seam Turn. Conceal the gathered edge of the ruffle inside a fold of the apron, by turning and making a French seam turn, as shown. Turn and top-stitch on the folded edge, as shown, to secure the seam.

Apply Flap Pieces to Tops of the Pockets. Place right side of flap to wrong side of pocket. Stitch in place across the top, using a ¼″ seam. Press seam open. Turn flap to the right side, turn raw edges under, and stitch. Apply flap pockets, doing this exactly as you applied the work pockets. Press apron when it is finished.

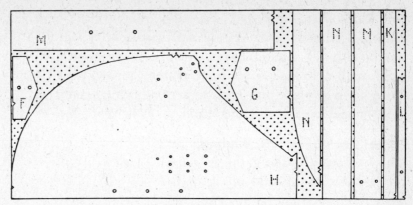

Dress-up Apron. Shape pattern at the bottom to conform to the layout. Place the pattern pieces on, as shown. Cut the apron, strings, and pockets on lengthwise of fabric. Use many pins in pinning pattern pieces on, and cut all edges as true as possible.

To prevent stretching the curved underarm lines, run a row of stitching around the lines ⅛" in from the edge, easing the fabric slightly under the presser foot.

Join apron ruffle sections together. Hem ruffle, neck ruffle, and sides of tie strings, using narrow machine-hemmer. Make ½" hem in bottom ends of tie strings. Gather the ruffles, using the machine gathering foot or ruffler. Adjust stitch on machine to about 7 stitches to the inch.

Because this apron is narrow, only one hip dart is used on each side. Put in, and stitch as in percale aprons.

Make Cluster Tucks. Place cluster tucks on the right side of the apron, on each side of the center front, according to the marks indicated by the perforations in your pattern. These tucks serve to take up the fulness and fit the apron around the waist, the same as the body darts on the other aprons. Make all the tucks the same width and length. To do this: Make three lengthwise tucks on each side of apron, the first tuck on an even line with the outside edge of the top portion. Use thread in the fabric to guide you in stitching straight. Make tucks slightly narrower than narrow side of presser foot, and stitch all to an even depth of 4". Pull thread ends through to wrong side, and tie.

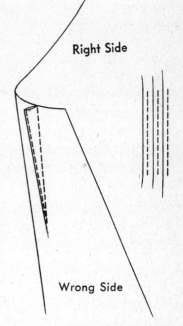

Right Side

Wrong Side

Turn, crease, and press the hem in the top of the bib; but do not stitch it. Turn, crease, baste, and stitch the curved underarm edges, stitching up to the bib hem but not across it.

Full Ruffle Around Curve. Pin ruffle along sides and around bottom of apron. Pin around curve, so that ruffle will be amply full and will not draw on lower edge. Join ruffle with a French seam turn. Gather top ends of tie strings. Pin in place, having side hem of string even with waistline edge of apron; and stitch on, as in Work Apron.

Make Center-Stitched Binding. To join neck band to the gathered neck ruffle, place right side of strap to wrong side of ruffle. With ruffle on top, stitch; then turn raw edge of neck band over ⅜", and crease again so that the raw edge of the ruffle is concealed under the fold. Stitch through the center of fold, to complete the binding. Check length of strap. When the length of the neck ruffle is correct, slip ends

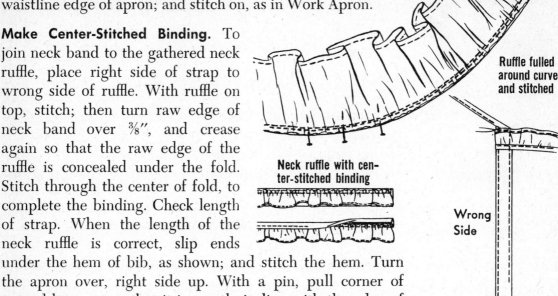

Ruffle fulled around curve and stitched

Neck ruffle with cen-ter-stitched binding

Wrong Side

under the hem of bib, as shown; and stitch the hem. Turn the apron over, right side up. With a pin, pull corner of curved hem out so that it is exactly in line with the edge of neck strap ruffle. Stitch up to the top of hem, across the top of bib hem, and down on the opposite side. This stitching secures ends of bib hem, catches strap at top of hem, and gives a neat finish. Make and apply flap pockets. Press.

Variations. The style of the aprons given you in these instructions is one that has proved satisfactory from many essential points—economy in fabric, ease in making and laundering, and all-round protection for one's dress. Many aprons were made, worn, and experimented with before this style was accepted as ideal.

A set of these aprons nicely wrapped would make a most welcome gift for birthday or Christmas, or for a shower. If you need to contribute something to a bazaar, try these aprons. They always meet with ready sale.

This same type of pattern may be used, without darts, for making denim or ticking work aprons for men and manual training aprons for boys. If the man in your house likes to help with the steak or Sunday suppers, make him an apron of plain percale in any dark colors, such as navy blue or forest green or burgundy. If you want a boy to help with the dishes and housework, make him an apron that looks mannish enough, and he won't mind doing the dishes half so much as he will if he has to wear your apron.

For aprons of heavy fabric use sturdy twilled tape—from a ⅜" to a ¾" width— for the neck strap and tie strings; and stitch them on firmly, of course.

Straight Ruffles. Tear limp fabrics like voil, ninon and marquisette on the straight, crosswise of the fabric. They hang better when handled in this manner. Very narrow French seams are used to join strips together. The end of the seam that is to go through the machine hemmer should be snipped off.

Bias Ruffles. Cut crisp fabrics like organdie and taffeta on the bias. When cut so, they show to better advantage, because they are more perky. Make a true-bias seam to join the strips together, and overcast the raw edges. A French seam can be used on lawn or organdy. Suggestions for the use of ruffles on page 145.

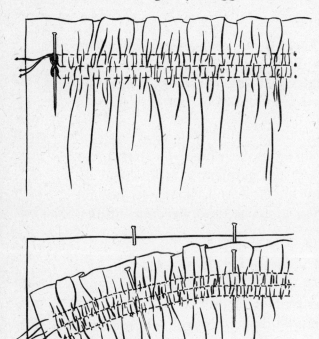

Hand Shirring. Drawing fabric together to make fulness is called gathering. Shirring comprises three or more rows of gathers. Gathering and shirring should not be used on all fabrics—wiry fabrics will not set well. Use small running-stitches and have all rows evenly spaced. Put in stitches for all the rows of gathers and draw up all the threads at once so that all fulness is even. Thread a needle with each surplus thread and, on the wrong side, fasten off each row with back-stitches. Never draw shirring too tight. If there is much to be done, machine shirring is quicker and it is always stronger, evener than that done by hand. See page 143 for suggestions on the use of machine shirring.

Dressmaking

DECIDE AT THE OUTSET that you are going to learn to sew beautifully so that you will enjoy it and through it express the creative urge that is your heritage. Never sew in haste or resentfully. Creative work is not done that way. Relearn any essentials that you consider tedious, if necessary, so that from knowing you may come to find them really fascinating to do.

All good effort shows in sewing. There is no other art or craft where practice pays such big dividends. With each article you make, you have opportunity to work for greater perfection. Your skill increases through practice, and year in and year out your better work will reward you.

Remember when you sew, and realize this each time you start to cut a garment: one-third of the value of the garment is represented by the cost of the fabric; one-third by the style you choose—its fashion rightness and becomingness to you; and one-third by your cutting, fitting and workmanship.

Make your sewing profitable and enjoyable. Take the time now to learn the simple principles given in these pages. Then your sewing will never be disappointing, never tedious or dull. If you know the essentials and strive to improve your workmanship, you will not only enjoy making beautiful garments, but will get excited about the new fabrics and textures, the new and becoming colors, and the new and flattering silhouettes that fashion brings you each season.

Panel-Front Dresses

A. Straighten Your Fabric. (See pages 10 and 11.) Stretch and straighten until lengthwise and crosswise grains line up perfectly. Never pull so hard as to tear or damage fabric. When the fabric is straight, fold lengthwise on your cutting board. (If necessary, press the fabric to have it smooth for cutting.) When placing fabric on your board, place it wrong side up so that you can freely pencil and chalk-mark perforations and notches. If notches are cut too deep, cutting them takes time and presents a problem. If you acquire the habit of marking location of notches with chalk, you will find it satisfactory in many ways. You must chalk both sides exactly alike.

B. Check Your Pattern with Your Measurements. Open out your pattern; and take out the pieces required to cut your dress. Before you start to cut, make adjustments to conform with your measurements so that when you fit your dress there will be no major alterations.

Look on the back of pattern envelope. Locate your size, check each of your measurements with those of your pattern. Pencil your measurements opposite those given on envelope for your size, so that you can compare them. If measurements correspond, proceed to lay out pattern. If there is a difference, note what it is— perhaps it is so slight you can pin in the pattern or separate it to provide the necessary allowance. If your shoulders are size 14 and bust size 16, for example, plan to extend the cutting line in the bust ⅛" in the center back and ¼" on the underarm seam in the waist part. This grading chart will help you to adjust your pattern to your measurements. With tailors' chalk, block out the new line.

Your aim should be to enlarge or decrease the pattern where needed—just exactly enough to make it correspond to your measurements. Once you know what changes a pattern requires for you, you will automatically make those adjustments and forever avoid fitting problems.

C. Place Pattern on Fabric, Cut Out Your Dress. Lay pattern pieces on fabric, following pattern layout. Note also the one given on next page. Place each correctly on lengthwise grain. If slight extra width is desired over hips or bust, block this width with chalk to save basting or pin marking. Cut each piece with sharp

[41]

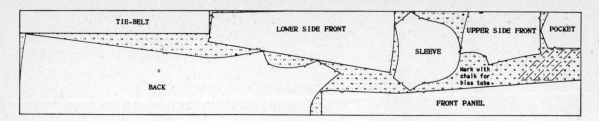

shears. Place one hand over pattern so that you will surely cut along edge. Mark for joinings, gathers and pocket locations.

Morning Dress. Thread your machine with thread matching the color of your fabric. Test length of stitch on a scrap of fabric—from 10 to 12 stitches to the inch is right for percale or light-weight cottons.

Prepare now the pieces that are later to become part of the dress; then you will not need to stop and make them when you actually begin to assemble your dress.

Bias Facings. Make bias tube, as shown, so that you can cut the required bias facing—of which you need about 1½ yards. Join small pieces of garment fabric to make this tube. First, take ruler and chalk and make lines on the fabric to mark off width the facing pieces are to be—in this case, 1⅛″. Cut the strips; and join them to form the tube, slipping down one width so that you can begin cutting on this line and cut around and around until you have one long piece of bias. Make as many tubes as necessary to obtain the required length.

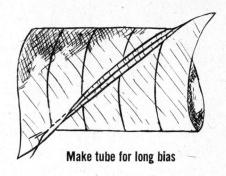

Make tube for long bias

In preparation for slip-stitching the facings when they are in place, turn one edge of facing strip over to the wrong side a scant ⅛″, and stitch.

Belt Ties. (The belt ties are made the same as the neck strap for the Work Apron.) Fold the belt ties lengthwise through center, wrong side out. Stitch across one end and along the side. Leave one end open. Clip corners, and press the seams open. Turn belt ties right side out, turning on an orange stick. Crease on the seam.

Gather Side Waist Fronts and Sleeves. To gather tops of the sleeves and the top and bottom of the side waist fronts, attach the gathering foot or machine ruffle and use the thread of matching color. Use the longest machine stitch for your gathering, so that it will be easy to adjust the gathers on the bobbin thread. Gather between the notches. Two rows of gathers at the tops of the sleeves are a help in adjusting fulness evenly.

Prepare Hems for Slip-stitching. Prepare the tops of the front panel and both pockets for a slip-stitched hem. To do this: Turn the top edge over ⅛″, and crease and stitch it. Turn the hem to the right side; then stitch at one side, as shown, continuing from one pocket to another to save your time. Turn the pocket hems over to the wrong side, and slip-stitch in position. Clip the seam at the bottom of the hem, as shown, doing this so that it can not draw. Turn the back edge and bottom of the pocket ¼" to wrong side. The front edges are caught in with the side-front seam.

Machine-Stitch Pockets in Place. Place the pockets in position on the front seam edges of side front skirt gores. Baste and stitch each pocket, stitching in the direction indicated by the arrows. Pull thread ends through, and tie.

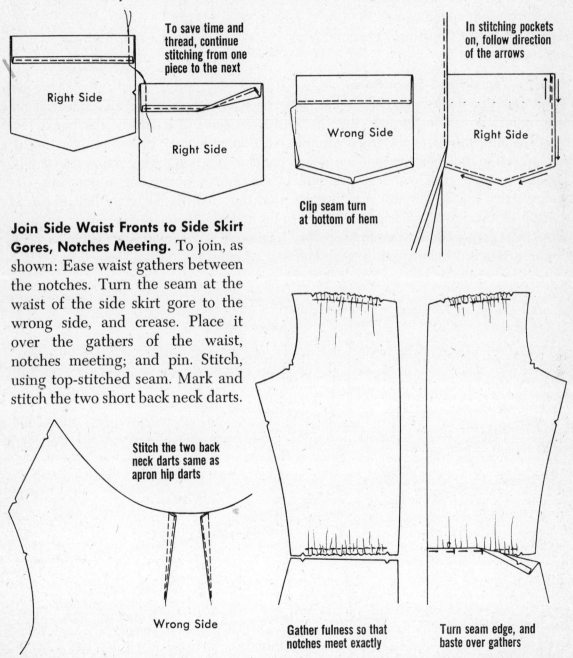

To save time and thread, continue stitching from one piece to the next

Right Side

Right Side

Wrong Side

Clip seam turn at bottom of hem

In stitching pockets on, follow direction of the arrows

Right Side

Join Side Waist Fronts to Side Skirt Gores, Notches Meeting. To join, as shown: Ease waist gathers between the notches. Turn the seam at the waist of the side skirt gore to the wrong side, and crease. Place it over the gathers of the waist, notches meeting; and pin. Stitch, using top-stitched seam. Mark and stitch the two short back neck darts.

Stitch the two back neck darts same as apron hip darts

Wrong Side

Gather fulness so that notches meet exactly

Turn seam edge, and baste over gathers

[43]

Join Forward Shoulder Seams to the Front. Crease seam edge of the yoke on the seam line. As this line is bias, take care in working with it not to stretch the line. Clip the front corners away, as shown. Slip the side front gathered sections under the forward shoulder seams, as shown, notches meeting. Pin and baste.

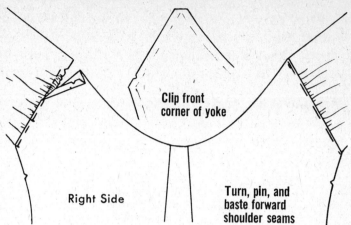

Clip front corner of yoke

Right Side

Turn, pin, and baste forward shoulder seams

Prepare Top-stitched Seam Panel.

In preparation for top-stitched seam, turn in seam edges along the sides of the front panel. Press the turned edge on both sides the full length of the panel.

Place and pin-baste the front panel in position, as shown. Place belt ties in position over the side gore waistlines. Place panel in position over the two side fronts, notches meeting. Pin panel in position, placing pins 3 or 4 inches apart. Snip the seams above and below the waistline, so that they will lie perfectly flat. Begin at the top of the front panel, and baste it in position; but leave the hem part at neckside. Take care in doing this to keep the beginning 2″ below the waistline on each line free. Stitch the skirt part of the panel, line straight and on the seam line.

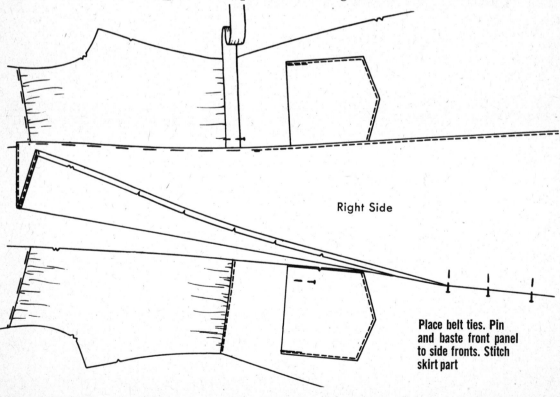

Right Side

Place belt ties. Pin and baste front panel to side fronts. Stitch skirt part

Turn dress wrong side out. Pin the underarm seams together, beginning at the armhole and pinning down on each side. Baste each seam.

Most patterns have a 2½″ to 3″ hem at the bottom. Turn and pin the hem up now, just so that you can get a correct effect in fitting.

Fit Your Dress. If you have checked your pattern carefully, as in B of your A B C's, you should need to make no major changes in this fitting. When you have the dress on, consider the following points simply for greater perfection:

If the dress looks too wide in the front neck, lay a third dart at the center of the back neck. If more than ⅜″ is to be taken in, place a dart on each side of the two back neck darts.

If the belt ties seem high, plan to drop them to the waistline. If low, lift them up half an inch or so, to where they are most becoming.

If the front panel is too wide for you, pin in the necessary amount in the center front to indicate the surplus; crowd the gathered side pieces back enough so that when pins are removed the panel will lie smoothly flat across the chest.

Remove the dress, check any fitting adjustments to see that both sides are exactly alike, and prepare to complete your dress.

Remove basting from right underarm seam, so that by having one side seam open you can have the work flat for stitching—important for top-stitching, as it must be done perfectly. Top-stitch the shoulder seams and upper part of panel.

Apply Bias Facings, and Stitch Sleeve Seams. Pin the facing piece around the neckline and on the bottoms of the sleeves, easing the raw edges so that the outside stitched edge will lie perfectly flat. For finishing, allow the facing to extend one inch at both sides of the neckline. Stitch the facing on, taking a ⅛″ seam in the facing and the seam width on the neckline and sleeves. Turn the facing down off the sleeve; bring the underarm sleeve seams together; and stitch the seam and across the facing, as shown.

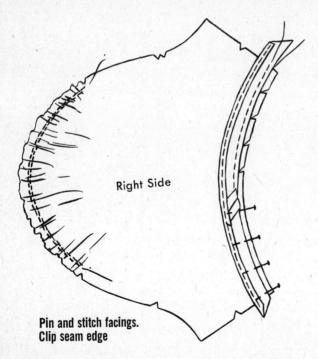

Right Side

Pin and stitch facings.
Clip seam edge

Facings, bias or fitted, are invariably used in good custom dressmaking. Once you learn how to ease them on smoothly and slip-stitch them in place, you will realize how practical they are and how professional they appear. Remember that no part of sewing is difficult when you know how to do it as a professional.

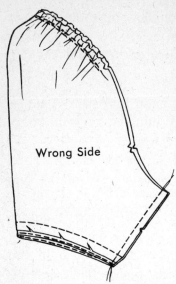

Wrong Side

Stitch the Underarm Seams. Turn dress wrong side out. Pin-baste the underarm seam that you opened, and stitch both seams. Press the underarm seams open. Clip them above and below the waistline.

For flatness on the curved lines, clip the seam edges of the neck and sleeves. Baste the facings back, basting on the edge where facing joins the neckline and bottom of sleeves. Also, overcast the underarm sleeve seams.

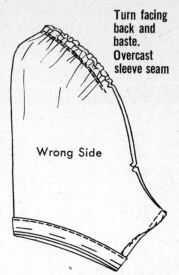

Turn facing back and baste. Overcast sleeve seam

Wrong Side

Measure for the Hem Turn. Put your dress on. Stand close to the edge of table, body erect. Hold skirt with one hand and chalk with the other, alternating hands as you turn your body slowly. Hold your dress, and press it against the chalk just enough to make a slight mark on your skirt every few inches.

Decide at this time the length you want your finished dress to be. We believe that there is a becoming length for every woman, which she should make no more than one inch shorter for the season to have her dress express the new in fashion. If, for example, 14″ or 17″ from the floor seems the becoming skirt length for your height, weight and waistline location, then compromise with fashion and make your skirt very slightly shorter or longer than fashion decrees. Then you will not be out of fashion, yet will be within the bounds of becomingness.

Remove your dress. Lay it out on your cutting board. With a ruler and chalk, true up the marks made by your chalk. Having decided the length you want your skirt to be, you now mark a second chalk line on which to

Stand close to chalk. Hold skirt with hand

For true hem line, measure even distance down from chalk line all the way around. Mark with chalk

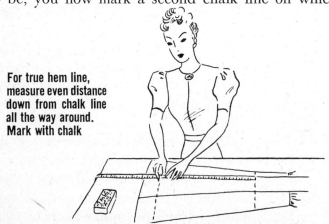

turn the hem. To do this, measure down from the first chalk line an even distance all the way around. (If, for example, your skirt length is 29″ at the side hip and your chalk mark is 9″ from the waist, measure 20″ down from the marked line.)

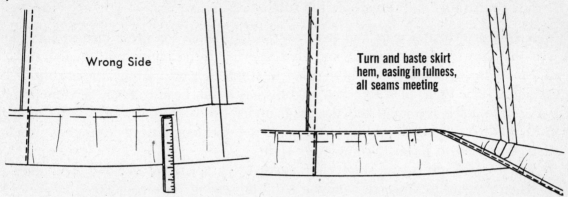

Wrong Side

Turn and baste skirt hem, easing in fulness, all seams meeting

Even up the chalk line. Then turn and crease your hem on this line. Take the skirt to the ironing board, and press the crease. Take your ruler and measure the width of the hem all the way around, marking up from the crease on the wrong side of the skirt and chalking a line at the top of your ruler as you measure. Trim the edge evenly all the way. Turn the raw edge over a scant ⅛″; and stitch on the edge, doing this in preparation for a slip-stitched hem. Use your longest machine stitch so that you can draw up the thread and thereby adjust the fulness of the hem evenly. Baste the hem in position, basting ½″ down from the stitched line.

Baste The Sleeves In Position. This dress has a forward shoulder seam, the easiest of all shoulder lines to fit. With a forward shoulder, special care is required in placing the sleeves in position so that they are beautifully balanced, with fulness evenly distributed and at the same time becoming to you. The instructions given below for positioning the sleeve apply to any dress. There is a real trick to placing sleeves correctly. It is this: First, place the sleeve in position, notches of the sleeve

and the armhole meeting exactly. Adjust the fulness across the top of the sleeve, between notches. Place pins crosswise of the armhole. When the sleeve is pinned, hold sleeves on your hands, as shown, to make sure that the lengthwise thread of the sleeve is exactly in line with the exact top of your dress—not with the forward shoulder line, but with the imaginary line that comes precisely on top of your shoulder, and which your hands indicate as you hold the dress up.

Baste always on seam allowance. When you are sure that both sleeves are right, baste them in, basting on the seam line. This latter is more important than it may seem; but, to have a garment fit, you must take up in basting the exact seam allowance provided for in the pattern.

In the basting, always try to use the normal seam allowance. When stitching, you may stitch inside the basting line to make the dress fit more snugly, or outside to make it fit more loosely. In basting sleeves in position, always keep the sleeve side toward you so that you can adjust the fulness easily.

Final Fitting. When sleeves and hem are basted, slip your dress on just to make sure that the length is correct and that sleeves are becomingly and comfortably placed. If the armhole is too loose, plan to stitch outside basting lines to make it smaller; if it is tight, plan to stitch slightly inside the basting, then clip the seam. If the shoulder is too long, slip the seam under the yoke; pin it to the becoming width, and plan to stitch on this new line. If the skirt length needs changing, decide what is needed to make it completely right.

Remove your dress, and stitch the sleeves in as you have decided they should be. Then prepare to do some handwork—"radio sewing." See page 60.

First, remove the bastings in the sleeves. Trim the armhole seams so that the edges are even. Clip the armhole seam every ½" to insure comfort. Overcast the raw edges of sleeve and dress armhole together, using an easy thread, but close stitches. Overcast the raw edges of the underarm and panel seams. Slip-stitch the neck facings and hem on front panel. In doing this, allow the facing to extend down about ½" over the yoke seam on each side. Clip through the ⅛" facing seam at the yoke line, so that it will slip under the panel hem. Use closely placed overcasting stitches at each corner, as shown, to catch the facing under the hem and make it secure.

Slip-stitch sleeve facings and the skirt hem, taking care with your slip-stitches to have an easy thread—never a tightly drawn one.

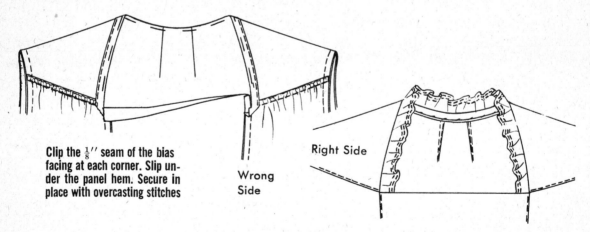

Clip the $\frac{1}{8}''$ seam of the bias facing at each corner. Slip under the panel hem. Secure in place with overcasting stitches

Wrong Side

Right Side

Neck Ruffle. Cut a strip of organdie 2½" wide and 2½ times the measurement of the neckline in length. Turn the ends in ⅛". Fold the strip through the center, the long way. Press and then stitch it, using two rows of machine stitching. Begin at an end, stitch across it toward the fold, then along fold, and across other end. Place the first row of stitching the width of the narrow side of the presser foot away from the edge. Do the second row the same way, inside the first row and the width of the narrow side of the presser foot away from it.

For gathering neck ruffle, put white thread No. 60 on your machine. Because the organdie is double and stiff, make your machine stitch as long as possible; stitch a scant ¼″ in from the raw edge of the ruffle. Slide the fabric on bobbin thread to draw it up enough to fit a lengthwise strip of organdie cut 1″ wide and the same measurement as your neckline in length. Shorten your machine stitch, and apply the binding to the gathered edge of the ruffle.

Pin the gathered and bound neck ruffle in position, beginning at the center back neck of the dress and the center of the ruffle. Overcast the ruffle to the neck facing, as shown; use stitches approximately ⅛″ long, and make sure that you catch them in the facing only. Press your dress carefully. Put it on, and wear it proudly.

Even in a wash dress, slip-stitched facings and hems are desirable. They appear nicer and make the dress look like the "better dresses." No fasteners or body darts are used in this dress, because you want the dress to open out easily for ironing and also, as it has no opening, to be large enough to slip over your head.

Afternoon Dress. A variation of the panel-front dress is to—Use body darts to fit dress smoothly in the back. Apply a slide fastener for placket closing at left side, which gives you a trimly slim waistline and also allows you to put the dress on and off easily. Finish the hem at top with seam binding, which makes it possible for you to slip-stitch hem so that top line will not show on the right side.

We want you to see these construction differences so that you will fully realize their importance; also, to see how easy it will be in the future to test the becomingness of pattern lines before you cut into expensive fabric.

Body Darts. After you have basted the neck darts, baste body darts. Do not stitch the darts until after dress is fitted. In stitching these body darts, stitch the curved line, and tie thread ends; then cut the darts open, clip edges so that they will lie flat, and overcast them.

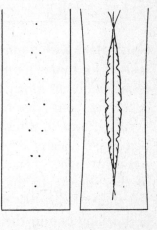

Make Slide-Fastener Placket. (Apply when you open the right underarm seam in order to do the top-stitching on the panel and yoke.) When you use a placket slide fastener that matches fabric perfectly in color, you can use simplified method of applying it to either a dress or a skirt. When your fastener does not match perfectly or when you do not wish it to show even slightly, use concealed method of application, given in detail in the instruction folder that accompanies all slide fasteners.

Simplified Method of Applying Dress Placket Slide Fastener. After the first fitting, with chalk mark off the length of slide fastener along basted underarm seam on the left side, approximately half above the waistline and half below. Stitch seam, except length measured off for fastener. Do not remove basting. Press seam open along its full length. Lay the closed fastener along unstitched part of seam on inside of dress. Be sure that the center of the fastener lies exactly over seam line, with the slider side down. Pin fastener in place, easing fabric slightly and using pins crosswise to keep it smooth and straight. Baste fastener in place, using large catch-stitches, as shown. Remove pins. Turn dress right side out.

With your stitching, make pocket at top of placket to conceal slider, as shown.

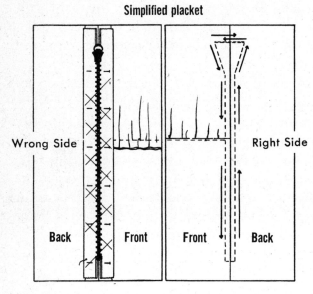

Simplified placket

Wrong Side

Back   Front   Front   Back

Right Side

To do this: Begin basting 1½″ below top of fastener and ¼″ from the seam line, and make shaped end ⅞″ wide across the top. With cording foot of machine, begin at top of fastener; stitch down to bottom, then across, up opposite side to top, across top, and then back across top again for security, following direction indicated by the arrows. Keep the stitching ¼″ from seam line or center of placket, except where you follow basting at shaped end. Pivot needle at each corner, and make square turn. Remove basting in the seam as well as from around the fastener.

Finish Hem with Seam Binding. Seam binding is used for fabric too heavy to turn under, and occasionally on flimsy fabric. When the length is correct, hem edge turned and measured and evenly trimmed, stitch silk seam binding to the hem edge, easing it on enough so that it can not draw tight; then slip-stitch the other edge of the binding to the dress, as shown, taking the shortest possible stitch in the dress fabric and a long one in the binding.

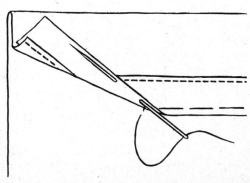

Now that you have made these two dresses, examine them carefully. If there is anything you are not satisfied with, reread the instructions to be sure that you understand the points given. Each has a definite place in your knowledge of the technique of good dressmaking. If you are not completely satisfied with results, buy a length of percale and make yourself another morning dress. As you continue with the next garment, you will see how the good work you have done here will help you there and make it possible for you not only to do more professional-looking work, but to do it more quickly.

Variations. This dress pattern has a forward shoulder; panel front; short or long sleeves, gathered or darted; and fulness in the body part of the back, which may be held in with ties or body darts, as you prefer. Here are some suggestions for finishing the neckline:

Have a bias fold of the fabric or of white pique come from each side and tie in a bow, to fill in the lower part of the square neckline.

Cut the front panel from 4″ to 6″ longer than the pattern at the top, and shirr in the extra length. If this is done, finish the extra length part with seaming ribbon on the underneath edge; and snap the top in place on one side, to give an opening sufficiently large for putting the dress on over your head. (A dress opening must measure at least 2″ more than your head measures. For example, if your head size is 22″, then the neck opening in your dress must be at least 24″.)

If you feel that a tailored band of pique would be becoming, cut a bias fold of pique 3″ wide and 18″ long. Fold it in the center the long way, right side out; and crease. Baste this around the side and back of the neck, allowing ⅝″ to ⅞″ of the pique to show. White grosgrain ribbon or velvet ribbon in color may also be used in this way to give a smart finish for the neckline. In applying trimming such as this to a neck or sleeve, plan to have as much of the trimming underneath as shows, so that it will lie flat and appear as though attached to the dress, rather than the dress to it.

If you are narrow in the shoulders, use the gathered sleeves. If you have square shoulders and desire slenderizing lines, use the sleeve with the darted top.

Separate belts may be worn with this dress, narrow ones for those over size 18, and wide ones for slender persons whose waistlines are small.

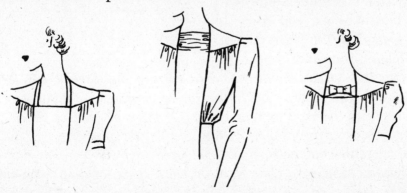

Bias-Cut Negligees

BIAS-CUT CLOTHES mold themselves beautifully to the figure and hang just as perfectly as garments cut lengthwise if they are carefully cut and handled correctly in the making. Mme. Vionnet of Paris, the greatest exponent of bias cutting, often cut her smartest dresses on the bias; again, only the skirts or sleeves.

Designers often prefer to cut plain fabrics on the bias. In this negligee you will find several fundamental principles of bias cutting and sewing, all so simple that you will realize as you sew that bias-cut fabric represents no problem when you know how to handle it.

A. Straighten Your Fabric. Lay the fabric out its full width. Pin the straightened edges of the fabric together; also, the selvages on each side. Use plenty of pins, and do this carefully so that the fabric is smooth and ready for your pattern. If using satin, pin so that the wrong side is up. If there are any wrinkles, smooth these with the iron after you have pinned the ends together. Press with the length—never across on satin.

B. Check Your Pattern with Your Measurements. Open out your pattern. Tie a string around your waist at the natural waistline. Hold the skirt of the pattern up to you. See if length is correct. Some like a dressing gown slightly longer than a morning dress; some like negligees almost to the floor; others like them ankle length. When you are checking the length of the pattern, decide the length you want your garment to be; and turn the pattern to agree with the length you desire. Measure with the tape from the waistline at center-front over the shoulder to the center-back. Check this measurement with your

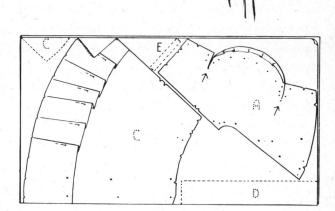

In cutting the sleeves, carefuly cut in to the inside perforations indicated by arrows, cutting pattern as well as fabric. When cutting satin, especially where French seams are to be used, cut the notches out rather than in or mark their location with tailors' chalk.

pattern. If the pattern is too long, shorten it by folding it in three places—midway across the front and back and at the shoulder. If too short, slash pattern at same points; and separate pieces to gain length.

Anyone whose figure is large in the waist and hips will find it advantageous to extend the overlap of any surplice type garment from 1″ to 3″, depending upon how much additional width her figure requires. (See diagram on page 59 for extending the front for a maternity frock.) You can extend the front overlap several inches, which means of course that in a circular type skirt, you will require a larger piecing gore in the back.

C. Place Pattern on Fabric, and Cut Out Garment. For your dressing gown, frock, or negligee, follow the layout shown for the type of garment you are making. Use plenty of pins for each pattern piece. For economy as well as for correct grain for each piece, follow the pattern layout in placing each piece of the pattern on. Leave pattern pieces pinned in place until the piecings for width are added at the back of the skirt, so that you will surely place them properly. These triangular pieces are larger when you use a 35″ cotton fabric and are usually quite small when you use 39″ rayon or silk.

For such garments, we prefer to cut the sash on the length. If you extend the front width for greater overlap, as suggested, simply make the belt shorter and the piecing gore proportionately larger. Glide your hand along the pattern line as you cut the fabric so that it can not slip. This is especially important with satin, which slides easily.

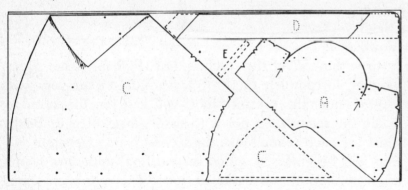

Piece Fabric for Additional Width. When cutting, you left the skirt pattern piece **C** on the fabric in order to check the seam lines after the piecing had been done for the additional width. To do this piecing, place the small piecing gore over the skirt gore, right sides together. Pin; then stitch, as shown. You have selvage edges on this seam. Clip the selvages to avoid tightness. Press the joining seam open.

Smooth the piecings out so that the skirt lies flat. Smooth the pattern out over it, and trim the edges of the piecings so that they line up exactly with the pattern. Lay a ruler or tape along this seam line, as shown; and mark with pencil or chalk to insure its being straight. Remove pattern, and prepare to make the seams.

Make French Seams on Bias Edges. To make the French seam in the blouse part, place wrong sides of two blouse pieces together. Smooth the center-back seam every few inches. Begin at the neck, and stitch down. Make a generous ⅛″ seam. Do not allow the bias to full in, and do not stretch it. You want a "long seam," as it is called in the trade, not a "fulled in seam." To make the French seam in the skirt, place the wrong sides of the skirt together, with the center-back edges in line. Smooth them out over tissue paper, and pin the seam every few inches. Begin at the waist, and stitch down.

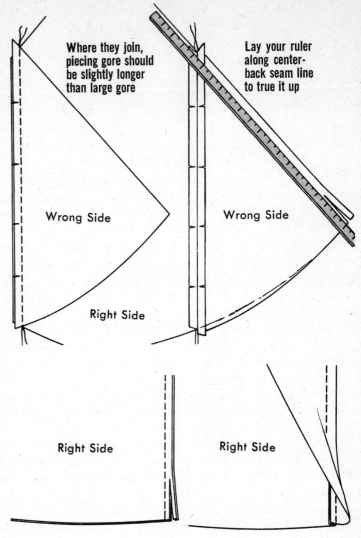

Where they join, piecing gore should be slightly longer than large gore

Lay your ruler along center-back seam line to true it up

Wrong Side

Wrong Side

Right Side

Right Side

Right Side

Trim the seams evenly to within ⅛″ of the stitching line. Pull the tissue paper away. Turn right sides together, to complete the French seam. If you are very sure of your ability to handle fabric under the pressure foot, you can pin the seam to tissue paper. Otherwise, baste the seam; then pin it to tissue, and stitch it. Begin at the neck and at the waist for each seam. Make the second seam a generous ¼″ so that all of the first seam will be enclosed within second. Join underarm seams of blouse, making a French seam. Do this on tissue as you did center-back seam. Stitch from arm-hole down. Slip waist part on to check neck and length of sleeve. If neck draws, trim at each side from ⅛″ to ¼″ to make sides lie flat.

Apply French Binding As Underarm Finish. Turn ends in and fold bias pieces, as shown. Pin them to the underarms from the right side, and baste in place. Turn the wrong side of the blouse up, and stitch the bias fold on. Continue all the way around the sleeve, turning the raw edge ⅛″ to the wrong side; and stitch it in

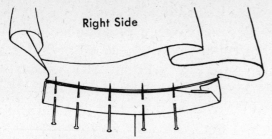

Fold French binding piece, turn ends in, and pin it across the underarm section

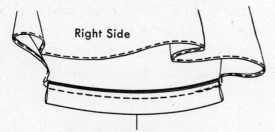

Stitch French binding on. Turn edge of sleeve, and continue the stitching around the sleeve

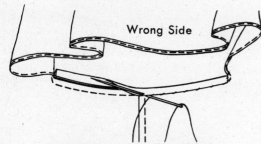

Whip binding in place along underarm, and catch ends in with close stitches

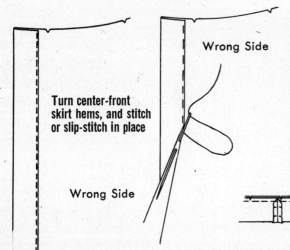

Turn center-front skirt hems, and stitch or slip-stitch in place

preparation for the lingerie hem. To complete the French binding, turn the bias fold over to the wrong side; then whip it down, and use several small overcasting stitches at each end to stay the corners.

Stitch or Slip-Stitch Center-Front Hem. Turn the center-front hems in the skirt under. (It is not necessary to turn the selvage edge under.) Machine-stitch the hems in crepe, and slip-stitch them in satin. Press the hem.

Stitch Front Edges of Blouse and Hem of Skirt in Preparation for Finish. To avoid tightening the neck edge, clip the edge around the neck curve, making the cuts ⅛" deep and ½" apart. Turn the front edge of the blouse to the wrong side. Make the turn a scant ⅛" wide—narrower, if you can turn it and catch it in stitching. Turn the lower edge of the skirt in the same way, and stitch it.

Make tiny slashes close together all around neck edge so that it will lie flat

Prepare the belt sash at this time. Join the two lengths. Press seam open. Turn right sides together, and stitch as for an apron strap or belt tie. Clip the corners and along the seam. Press seam open its full length. Turn belt right side out. Turn the edges of the open end in; then slip-stitch the opening together, using short stitches and taking them so that they do not show on the right side. Press the belt sash, and lay it aside.

Join belt pieces, and clip seam. Stitch belt lengthwise; clip seam edges; press seam open

Turn and Make Stitched, Overcast Shell Hems. This we call Radio Sewing (see page 60), because you can do it while you listen to your favorite program or even while you "visit" with friends or the family. For cotton crepe, thread a No. 3 or 4 crewel needle with size 40 six-cord thread. For satin, use matching Heavy Duty Mercerized. Use a single thread from 20″ to 25″ long. Trim up close to the stitching. Roll the stitched edge under twice. Take several stitches on the needle at one time, as shown; and pull it through. Do not draw thread too tight. Take another needle-full, and pull needle through. Continue until all stitched edges—on sleeves, blouse front, and skirt hem—have been turned and finished.

The purpose of the machine stitching is to make a firm, sturdy edge—one that will bear washing and hard wear. Crepe and satin both have a tendency to fray. The precaution of stitching and then turning the hem twice is insurance against fraying. This also gives a desirable firmness or weight to the edge.

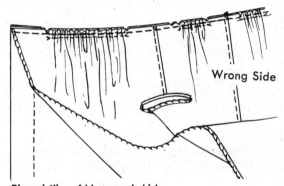

Turn stitched edge under twice; take several overcasting-stitches on your needle at a time

Put in Gathers at Waistline of Blouse. With ruffler or machine gathering foot, or with a long machine stitch, make two rows of gathers between the notches in the waistline of the blouse—on each side of the front and on each side of the center-back seam. Draw the bobbin threads up so that the waistline of the blouse fits the top of the skirt, all corresponding notches meeting. Pull the ends of the gathering threads through to the wrong side, and tie them.

Pin the blouse and skirt together. Adjust blouse fulness nicely. Baste the waistline. Slip the garment on to be sure that the waistline is just right.

Pin waistline of blouse and skirt together, notches meeting. Draw up bobbin thread; adjust the fulness

Make and Fasten the Surplice Closing. With the garment on, stand in front of a mirror. Bring the left front over to the right the distance it should be for the front hem to hang straight down from the waistline. Pin this to your slip at this point; and place a pin in the front that is to overlap this— at a corresponding point. Bring the right front over, and lap it correctly; then place a pin exactly at the edge where the overlap comes, as shown.

Pin the belt sash in place, with the folded edge up. Tie it as you want it, either at the termination of the overlapped waistline or at the underarm seam. Place it for becomingness.

Place pins at waistline to mark exact location of hooks and eyes

[56]

Remove the garment. Mark the location on the waistline where the belt sash is to come. Mark the sash also. Remove sash and prepare to stitch the waistline. If the garment is slightly long waisted, plan to take a slightly deeper seam. If it is a little short, plan a narrower seam. In sewing, you soon learn that the fit of a garment can be perfected simply by stitching inside or outside the basting lines. Stitch the waistline; then make another row of stitching near the top edge of the waistline seam, for additional strength. Trim the seam and overcast it. Sew a white hook and eye at the corresponding points of the inside lap, using Heavy Duty thread to sew hooks and eyes securely in place. To make a neat, inconspicuous closing for the outside lap, sew a white hook at the outer edge, on the underside; then make a worked eye for this as shown on page 27, using Mercerized Sewing Thread to match the fabric.

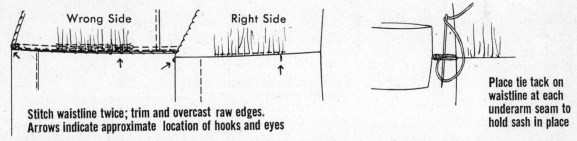

Stitch waistline twice; trim and overcast raw edges.
Arrows indicate approximate location of hooks and eyes

Place tie tack on waistline at each underarm seam to hold sash in place

Tie Tack the Belt Sash in Position. With the Heavy Duty thread, make a tie tack at each side seam, to hold the sash in place. To do this, make two stitches from 1″ to 2″ long, by catching a double thread to the garment, then through one thickness of the sash, and again through the garment. Buttonhole over the four threads, as shown, placing the stitches ⅟₁₆″ apart. These tie tacks will keep your sash always in place, yet it will not appear to be fastened and will be free enough to allow for easy pressing of the garment. When belt sash is on, press the garment carefully, pressing lengthwise just as much as possible.

Lace appliqued to the neck and sleeves of negligees adds greatly to the beauty and value

Appliquéing Lace by Hand and by Machine. If you wish to use lace to trim the neck and sleeve edges of the blouse of your satin negligee, omit the machine stitching on the edges. To determine the length of lace you require: Measure from the seam at the center-back to the waistline in the front. Measure one sleeve. Add these two measurements together, plus 6″ for ease in applying. Choose a banding lace from 4″ to 6″ wide so that you can cut it apart, as shown on next page, and thus have two lengths from one. This also gives you attractive irregular edges for the appliqué. Cut the lace carefully, cutting around the motifs, and avoid cutting the threads that form the design. When the banding is cut apart its full lengh, pin and baste over the satin, allowing the uncut edge of the lace to extend from ¼″ to ½″ beyond the raw edges of the satin.

[57]

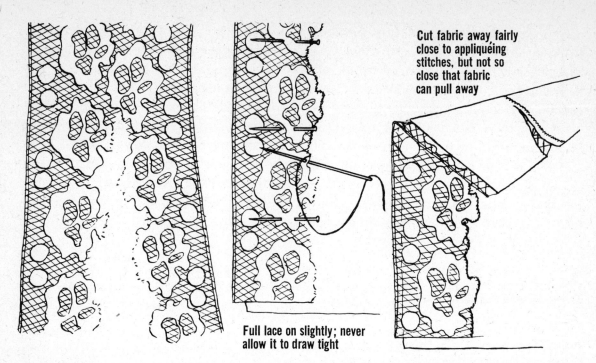

Cut fabric away fairly close to appliquéing stitches, but not so close that fabric can pull away

Full lace on slightly; never allow it to draw tight

Hand Appliqué. When the lace is in position for appliquéing, overhand the cut edges with a single thread of Mercerized Sewing to match the fabric, catching the edge securely. When all the cut edges of the lace are overhanded, trim the underneath fabric away. Take care that you do not cut any of the stitches or cut the fabric too close. Press from the wrong side over a Turkish towel, and you will have a beautifully finished edge. This same principle may be used for formal dresses, blouses, jabots—wherever lace and fabric are combined.

Machine Appliqué. There is a sewing-machine attachment called a zigzagger that is a miracle worker for appliqué, imitating handwork very well and finishing an edge quickly and securely. This attachment is comparatively expensive; but if you are one who likes lace, especially dresses and blouses of lace, then a zigzagger would be a good investment, because you can do endless seams and joinings with it and can use it for fabric appliqué as well as lace. If you are interested, go to your local sewing machine shop and have the instructor teach you how to use the zigzagger expertly. Buy one, and use it to make many beautiful things.

Variations. One may use this style pattern to make a morning dress for summer wear, one that is similar to the Hoover apron in front, in that you can reverse the fronts and thus have your dress serve as an apron. Cut your morning dress from the short version, and use an attractive print or a colored crepe. Finish the edge with rick rack or bias binding; or buy tatting by the yard; or make tatting for the blouse part.

This style garment is ideal for maternity wear. When you cut it, extend the lap almost to the underarm seam in both the blouse and the skirt part. Then as the figure requires a larger waistline, the surplice closing can be moved over. You need to

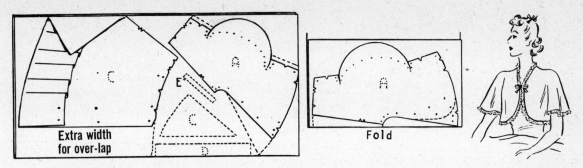

Extra width for over-lap

Fold

change only the location of the two eyes that are sewn to the waistline, in order to gain as much as 10″ additional width. Allow enough so that you have some overlap.

Use the blouse part of your pattern for a bed jacket of cotton-and-rayon challis or silk crepe. Trim the edge with blanket stitches or narrow Val lace. In cutting a bed jacket from such a pattern, place the back waistline 2″ from the fold of the material and the neckline at the fold, as shown, thus eliminating a seam at the center-back and gaining desirable fulness there. Round front edge, as shown, so that there is not so much overlap there.

Hand Finishes. Here are three hand finishes that might be substituted for edges shown in the previous pages. If any one of these finishes is new to you, try making it on a scrap of material. As you work you will see how it differs from the finishes that are familiar to you and where you will be able to put it to use.

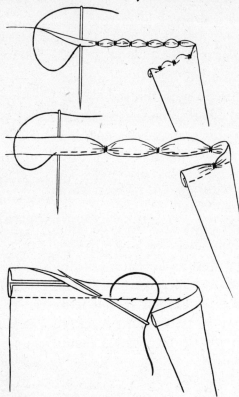

Lingerie Hem. Roll the hem toward you as you work. Every ⅛″ to ⅜″ take two stitches over the roll and draw together to form a small puff. Between the overhanding-stitches, slip the needle under the turn; do not draw so tight so as to pucker the edge.

Shell Edge. This is used on a straight edge. After creasing and basting your hem, start with 5 to 8 small running stitches. Then take two stitches over the hem, drawing it together to form a scallop. Make another group of running-stitches and then two overhanding-stitches. Continue doing this until the hem is finished.

Hand-Felled Binding. This is one of the most widely used edge finishes, because it is simple to do and gives a nice finish. Lay one edge of the bias binding to the edge to be bound, right sides together. Stitch by machine; then fold other edge to wrong side; whip it down.

[59]

Radio Sewing

SEWING, TO BE SUCCESSFUL, must be enjoyable. To be enjoyable, we must suit it to our time and not feel hurried or that we haven't the time to do full justice to the work.

In France, where skilled needleworkers took such pride in their beautiful hand sewing, the work to be done by hand was "bundled" for them. First, the cutting was done and seams or joinings made that were to be done by machine. (Many so-called handmade garments have the first seam of a French seam stitched by machine for strength and convenience, and the second seam put in by hand wholly for appearance.) Then each garment, with its facings and trimmings and threads, was rolled into a bundle; and the bundles were parceled out to the experts. Such workers often assembled in groups and listened to music or to a reader who read to them while they worked.

Long ago, I learned that handwork could be enjoyable and a surprising amount accomplished if I "bundled" my hand sewing just as though it were going to another worker—did the cutting at one time, the machine work at another, and then the handwork at my pleasure. I roll bundles up—even write little memos for myself to remind me of widths of hems, seams, etc.—and have them ready so that, when there is a little time for "visiting" or when someone has something interesting to tell or to read aloud or there is a program on the radio that I especially enjoy, I do not have to wish that I had some sewing handy. It is all ready; and I do not need to hunt for materials to complete the work, or have to stop to stitch or to cut something out.

Get the Bundle Habit. It isn't new—it is centuries old, in fact. Many of the finest examples of needlework in our museums today are the result of work planned for, assembled, and done at leisure. Women have used their leisure for sewing and for fine needlework of all kinds. They organized it beforehand—"bundled" it, just as I want you to do now. They, however, did not have the radio to speed the work and give it a rhythm that should in itself make sewing easier and more enjoyable. Let us hope that the radio may serve to bring back an interest in sewing—the kind that is practical and definitely adds beauty and value to a garment or article.

Tailoring

FOR TAILORED GARMENTS, choose fabric of firm, even weave. Sponge and shrink woolens and linens before cutting—and dampen cotton, if it is difficult to straighten for cutting.

Allow generous seam widths for tailored garments. When the pattern calls for narrow seams, allow more width. Mark the seam line with chalk or tailor's tacks, so that you will surely take in the regular seam width plus what you allow. Use chalk and tailor's tacks generously in tailored work.

Be generous also with pins and bastings. Work on a flat surface, and press each seam before it joins another. Allow seams to come together without stretching or fulling.

A tailored garment should be securely machine-stitched at all points. The stitch should be as short as is practical for the weave of the fabric. Overcasting, whipping, and slip-stitching are also essentials in tailoring. The garment should look as nice on the inside as on the outside. The parts should be blended together as perfectly as are the fingers of a glove or parts of a shoe. Because they fit so smoothly, tailored garments must always be hung on hangers—during their making and throughout the lifetime of the garments.

Garments of wool invariably are tailored. The very nature of the fabric requires that seams be dampened and pressed—that all stitching lines, edges, plaits and overlappings be pressed with a press cloth between fabric and iron. Not only should each part be pressed before it joins another, but the whole garment should be thoroughly pressed as a final finish. Use bastings abundantly when working with wool fabrics. Stretch seams ever so slightly as you stitch them so that the stitching line will never appear tight. Value your fabric and determine to have it appear as though handled by a thoroughly skilled tailor.

Never hurry when you tailor. Take time to do each part well. Tailored garments endure for several years. They should therefore be made in conservative style and of good fabric, should be beautifully fitted, and should have your very best in workmanship.

Tailored Coat and Dress

Materials. In choosing fabric for a tailored garment that is to be washed, consider the following: First, a fabric of comparatively firm weave, as pique, linen, crash, poplin. Second, a preshrunken fabric; and third, one with enough body to hold its shape, and to tailor nicely.

In unlined wash coats and jackets, rick rack proves an ideal finish for seams as it finishes the edge and at the same time decorates it.

A. Straighten Your Fabric by tearing or pulling a thread.

B. Check Your Pattern with Your Body Measurements. Open out the pattern, and separate the pieces. Check your body measurements with those given on the back of the pattern envelope. Note where changes are required, if any.

Check the length and the slope of the shoulder. If your shoulders are sloping, you may need to make the shoulder dart longer and more sloping, as shown. If your shoulders are square, you may need to allow deeper seams in the shoulder dart than your pattern calls for. This simple test will usually tell you where to add or where to take in. If one shoulder is lower than the other, simply plan to stitch the seams and dart slightly deeper for the lower shoulder.

A good line for the shoulder dart will insure the coat's hanging straight in the front. When you see a coat with the corners of the front overlapping and out of line; you know that the shoulder line needs taking up at the tip of the shoulder. If the coat spreads at the bottom, you know that there should be more length at the shoulder.

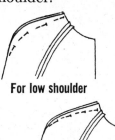

For low shoulder

For high shoulder

C. Place Coat Pattern on the Fabric and Cut Out Your Coat. Lay the smoothed-out, adjusted pattern pieces on your fabric according to this layout. The upper layout shows pattern pieces placed for a small size; the lower, for a large size. For very large sizes, it is advisable to piece the sleeves at the underarm, as indicated by the selvage-edged gores **A** and **B**. If you wish turn-back cuffs, cut your sleeves longer.

For the small layout, do this by moving the back and facings down and cutting the pockets out of the material at **C.** For large layout place under section of the collar down in **D**, to gain extra length for the sleeves.

In cutting, cut the notches outward, because you want the seam edge complete for applying the rick rack. Wide seams, as in this pattern, help an unlined coat to hold its shape and set better. Leave all pattern pieces securely pinned in place on the fabric in preparation for tailor's tacks.

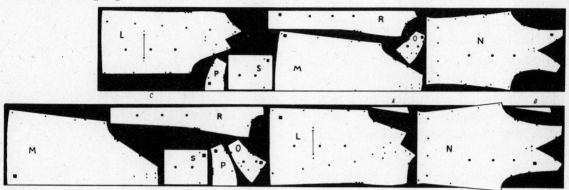

Seam Allowance. The seam allowance varies not only on different makes of patterns, but on different parts of a pattern. Remember this as you pin, baste, and stitch, so that your garments will be correct in size.

Put in Tailor's Tacks. On printed fabrics, chalk is not practical for marking perforations for darts and pocket locations. Therefore, plan to tailor tack darts and pocket locations on the front. Only a few tailor's tacks are necessary: for shoulder darts, back-neck darts, bust darts, and pockets. To make tailor's tacks, use a double mercerized sewing thread in color different from that of the coat. Take a back-stitch in each perforation, as shown; and leave a loop of thread large enough to slip a finger through. Separate the two thicknesses of fabric, which pulls the loops out straight. Clip threads. Remove pattern pieces.

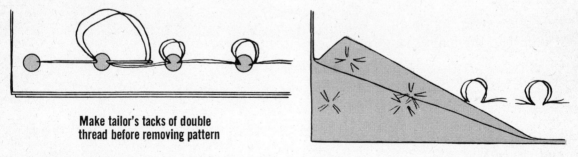

Make tailor's tacks of double
thread before removing pattern

Pin, Baste, and Stitch the Darts. Bring corresponding tailor's tacks together in the darts. Pin, then baste, then stitch darts, basting from the bottom up in each case. Stitch down from top and back again, exactly as you did the hip darts in your work apron. The darts in the center-back are pressed toward the center; in the front, they are pressed toward the side. The shoulder-seam darts are not stitched until after the first fitting. Later, these seams are clipped across near the tip of the dart, cut open, and pressed the full length. The wide bust darts are left the full width, as they serve to give weight to the front of the coat.

Baste the Coat Pieces Together. Place the front, back, and sleeves together, as shown—with all corresponding notches meeting. Pin the shoulder seams at the neck and the underarm. Place pins every few inches the full length of each seam. Baste the shoulder seams, basting from the neck down. Pin and baste the underarm and sleeve seams. Turn hems up in coat and sleeves; and pin in place, placing pins lengthwise and 3″ or 4″ apart. Slip the coat on just to be sure that it fits smartly. Study the little drawings on page 62 and see how to fit a raglan sleeve for round shoulders and square ones. Baste always on the seam line, but do not hesitate to take the seams in or let them out by stitching outside or inside the basting line if it improves the fit. Check the length at this time. Make sure that sleeve and coat lengths are becoming. Stand in front of a mirror, and turn hem of the coat under to see if a shorter length is better for you. If you are stout, no doubt it will be; if tall, then the longer length will be best.

Remove the coat, and press with the iron for the desired hem line in both coat and sleeves. Remove the basting, and open up the underarm and sleeve seams.

Stitch the Armhole Seams, Press Open, Overcast Raw Edges, Top-Stitch from Right Side. Stitch the seams, stretching them slightly as you stitch, so

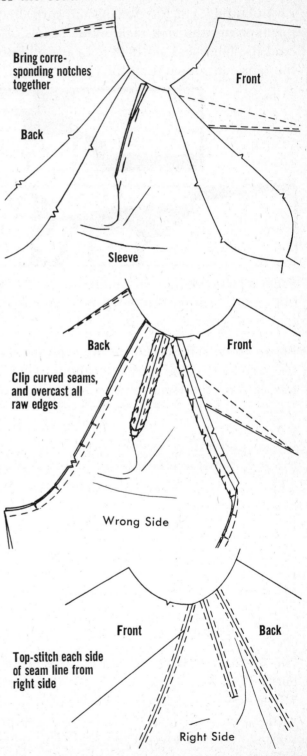

Bring corre-
sponding notches
together

Back

Front

Sleeve

Clip curved seams,
and overcast all
raw edges

Back

Front

Wrong Side

Top-stitch each side
of seam line from
right side

Front

Back

Right Side

that your stitching line will be long enough and therefore will not break in wearing. Clip the seam along the curve. Press seams open. Overcast raw edges. Do not draw overcasting threads tight. Turn coat right side up on your machine; then, with the wide side of your presser foot as a guide, top-stitch on each side of seam, as shown. Stitch out to the end of shoulder seam dart, pivot on needle, stitch squarely across, then back on opposite side. Press all seams carefully from the wrong side.

Prepare the Pockets, and Stitch in Place. First, turn the top edge over a scant ¼″, crease, and stitch. Turn hem to right side, and stitch across hem at both ends. Clip off corners, clipping diagonally and a little less than the seam's width. Turn hems to position, and slip-stitch in place. On the sides and across the bottom, turn the raw edges to wrong side; then press or baste. Place pockets in position on coat, lifting them up slightly if you have shortened your coat in fitting. Pin in place, with the sides of pockets on a true lengthwise grain of fabric; then baste and stitch. Begin stitching at the bottom of hem, and stitch up to the top of pocket; then turn and stitch down to bottom, across, up to the top on opposite side, and down again the width of hem. Pivot squarely at each corner. Keep the stitching within ¹⁄₁₆″ of the edge, which will make it less conspicuous than it would be if you stitched in ⅛″ or ¼″ from the edge.

Wrong Side

Place facing over front edge of coat. Baste in place and stitch

Right Side

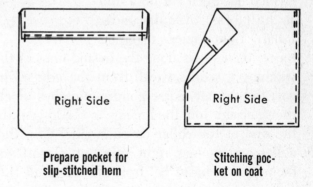

Prepare pocket for slip-stitched hem

Stitching pocket on coat

Right Side

Right Side

Apply Front Facings. Place front facings over front edges of your coat, right sides of fabric together, corresponding notches meeting. Pin-baste and thread-baste these pieces on, beginning at top and basting down. Begin at inside of lapel, and stitch out to corner; then stitch

[65]

down front edge and across bottom, as shown. At each corner, pivot on the needle to make a square turn. Clip the corners, as shown; and clip the seam every few inches. Press front seam open.

Make and Apply the Collar.

A tailored stand-up collar must have the support of an interlining to keep it erect. For this, use two pieces of unbleached muslin cut on the bias. Seam them together. Seam together the two pieces for the under collar, taking up the regular seam allowance. Press this seam open. Place the interlining and the under collar together, with the seam in the muslin directly over the seam in the fabric. Trim the muslin ¼″ smaller on all edges. Baste both together; then stitch the stand part, as shown, using the wide side of your presser foot as a guide and stitching to a depth of about 1½″.

Place the top of the collar (which has been cut on a fold of the fabric) over the under collar, right sides together.

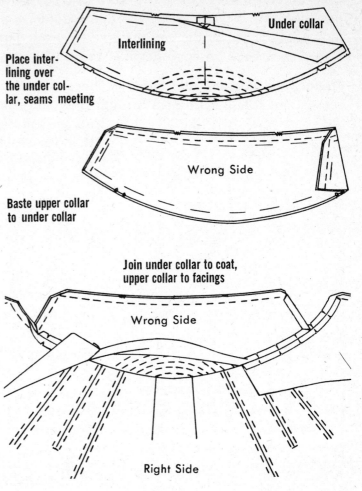

Baste; then stitch along the basted lines at the ends and across the top of the collar, stitching a seam's width from the edge. Clip the corners. Baste the under collar part to the coat—corresponding notches meeting. Clip the neckline seam, and press the seam up. Join the facings to the lower edge of the upper collar, stitching in from the end of the collar on each side. Clip the seams, and press them open. Turn the collar and facings right side out. Crease exactly on the seam edge of collar and facings, and baste ¼″ from the edge all the way around collar and facings.

Apply Rick-Rack Trimming.

Turn and press the raw edge of the upper collar in the seam's width; then, from the right side, stitch rick rack along the collar line from facing to facing. Turn the raw edge of the facings in a scant ¼″, and stitch from the neck edge of the collar to the inside edge of the facing. Stitch rick rack along the edge of the facings. Turn the raw edge of the bottom of the sleeves under also, and stitch rick rack to these.

Pin-baste and stitch the underarm and sleeve seams, beginning at the bottom of the sleeves and stitching the seams their full length. To finish these seams, begin at the bottom of the sleeves, and clean-stitch to within 1″ of the armholes; then, from this point to the end, turn the raw edges under, slip rick rack under the turned edges, and stitch.

Finish the hems of the sleeves and the coat. To do this: Turn the edges, stitch the rick rack on, and slip-stitch the hems in place. Slip-stitch the facing and the coat hem together where they meet at the lower side fronts.

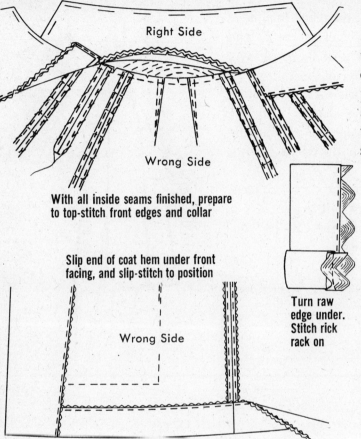

Right Side

Wrong Side

With all inside seams finished, prepare to top-stitch front edges and collar

Slip end of coat hem under front facing, and slip-stitch to position

Wrong Side

Turn raw edge under. Stitch rick rack on

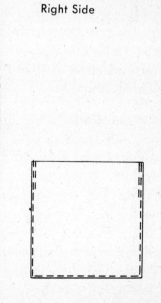

Use cloth guide to top-stitch front edge of coat and collar

Right Side

Use Cloth Guide to Top-Stitch Facing and Collar. Screw your cloth guide in place on your machine, adjusting it so that it comes ½″ from the stitching line of the needle. Begin stitching at the inside edge of the facing, and stitch to the corner. Pivot, then stitch up to the top of the facing. Pivot at the corner, and stitch in to a point opposite the notch. Pivot, and stitch up to the notch; then stitch on the collar line a distance of ½″. Then stitch around the collar. Repeat on the facing of the opposite side. Pull all thread ends through, and tie. Remove all bastings. Slip-stitch collar and front facings in place, under rick rack. Press and thus finish your coat.

C. Place Dress Pattern on the Fabric and Cut Out Your Dress. To do this: First, assemble dress pattern pieces. If you are size 18 or smaller, use upper layout. If larger than size 18, use lower layout.

For the upper layout, fold the fabric over to the width of the back gore, **H;** and place this piece on the fold. Place the front panel piece, **F,** and the front and back pieces, **A** and **B,** as shown. When you cut across the fabric at the bottom of the back piece, **B,** move the fabric forward enough to give sufficient width for the sleeves. Cut one side front gore; then move the pattern and cut the second one. Do the same with the front facings and cuffs.

For large sizes, simply place the pattern pieces on the fold, as shown; then cut out dress.

These layouts show how fabric can be conserved when laying out pattern.

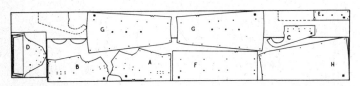

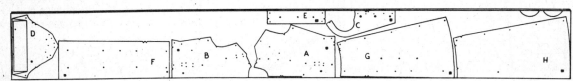

Put in Tailor's Tacks. White chalk marks will not show on white fabric, and pencil or colored chalk will soil it. Therefore, if using a white or pastel fabric, plan to tailor-tack the darts.

Make the Darts. This dress is fitted quite snugly, hence wide bust darts, and front and back body darts. There are back shoulder darts also. Many prefer these to neck darts, especially in sports clothes, believing that they give greater ease across the shoulders. Baste the darts, including those in the tops of the sleeves. Stitch

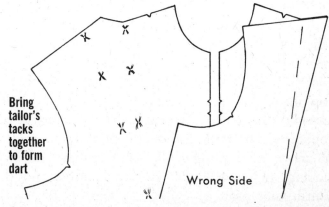

Bring tailor's tacks together to form dart

Wrong Side

[68]

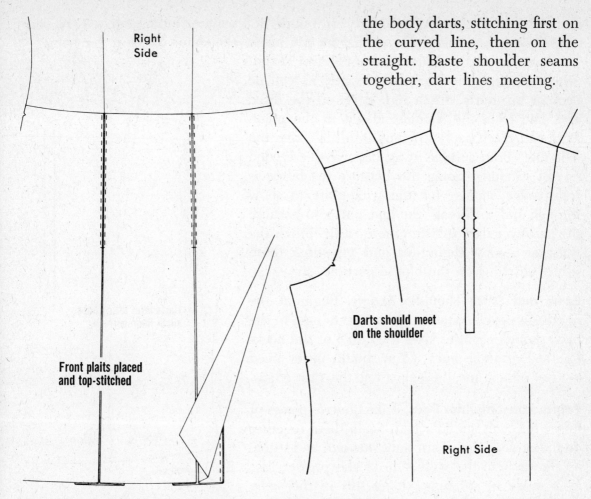

Right
Side

the body darts, stitching first on the curved line, then on the straight. Baste shoulder seams together, dart lines meeting.

Darts should meet
on the shoulder

Front plaits placed
and top-stitched

Right Side

Lay Plaits in Front of Skirt. Baste and stitch front panel in the skirt. Fold plaits in; pin, baste, and press. Top-stitch the plaits to depth you desire, beginning at the top and ending usually at a point slightly above the fullest part of the hip. Pivot, stitch across the plait, pivot, and then stitch up the other side. Repeat on each side of the panel.

Join the waist and skirt of front and back, all corresponding notches meeting; and baste in preparation for fitting. Pin underarm seams, from armhole to bottom edge of skirt; and baste, leaving a placket opening on the left side. Turn the hem allowance up, and pin-baste the hem—which you should do always when you baste a garment for fitting.

Fit Your Dress. Before fitting your dress, put on foundation garments such as you will wear with the dress; also, shoes with heels of a height you will wear. This is important. When you put on your dress, notice the darts first. Are they exactly right for you? Is the shoulder seam the right length? Should you make the shoulder and bust darts deeper or let them out slightly? Should you take in or let out the shoulder seams? Shoulders that fit perfectly are an essential of well-fitting garments.

Be careful to fit shoulders properly. In taking in a seam or letting one out, be sure to use your dressmaker pins so that no pin marks can show. Measure for hem.

Open up the shoulder and underarm seams. Stitch the back shoulder darts exactly as you do neck or hip darts. Stitch bust darts on the fitted dart line from the shoulder down to the point. Turn and stitch back, stitching a full ¼″ from the first row. Trim surplus away beyond this second row of stitching—doing this because the fabric is transparent enough for the wide dart to show through and to "break" the line, and also because the narrower dart will iron more easily. Stitch the waistline seams; then turn and top-stitch these seams, stitching on the blouse portion.

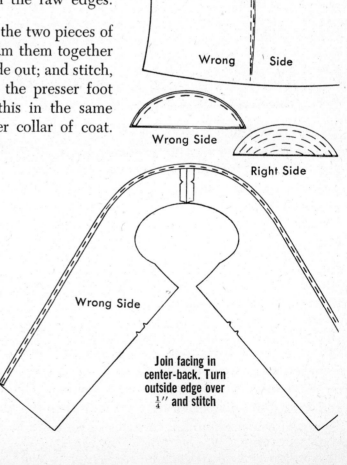

Darts form fitting lines; stitch them perfectly

Wrong   Side

Wrong Side

Right Side

Wrong Side

Join facing in center-back. Turn outside edge over ¼″ and stitch

Baste and Stitch Shoulder Seams. Begin at the neckline in each instance. Take care to ease in the back shoulder and to keep the curve of the neckline and armhole lines. (You should never need to trim either line.) Clean-stitch the raw edges.

Prepare the Shoulder Pads. Take the two pieces of fabric for each shoulder pad. Seam them together on the curved edge. Turn right side out; and stitch, as shown. Use the wide side of the presser foot as a guide in stitching, doing this in the same manner as you did on the under collar of coat.

Prepare Facing for Collarless Dress with Revers. Join the center-back seam of the front facing. Turn the outside raw edges over ⅛″; and stitch.

Place the lengthwise edges of the facing along the center-front slash, right side of facing to right side of blouse. Baste and stitch in place. Press these seams open. Clip the corners diagonally at the lower part of the center-front slash. Fold the facing so that it overlaps perfectly the full length of the

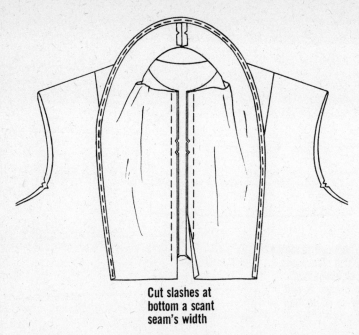

Cut slashes at bottom a scant seam's width

opening and also fills the center space. Crease, and stitch the facing to the neck edge. Clip the corners away at the neck.

Turn the facing to the inside of the dress. Crease carefully around the neckline, use your orange stick to square the corners, and baste facing carefully in position. Turn front of dress back above waistline; slip the ends of the facing down; and stitch twice across, as shown. With this done, press the facing and neck edge carefully. Begin stitching at the bottom of the facing on right hand side, follow the direction indicated by the arrows, and pivot exactly at each corner. Stitch up to within ⅜" of the neck, stitch around the neckline, down on the opposite side to bottom, then across and back again. Pivot squarely, and stitch exactly in the seam.

The stitching around neck and on facing serves to hold the facing in position without slip-stitching the facing in place, makes ironing easier, and gives more professional-looking finish.

Pin and baste underarm seams, working from armhole down. Stitch right seam; then stitch left, leaving 10" for dress placket. Press seams open, and clean-stitch.

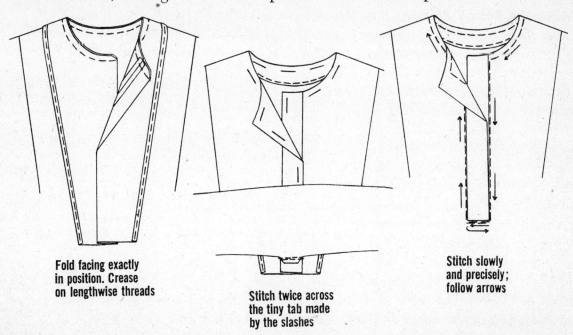

Fold facing exactly in position. Crease on lengthwise threads

Stitch twice across the tiny tab made by the slashes

Stitch slowly and precisely; follow arrows

Make and Apply Cuffs. Place right side of cuff to right side of sleeve. Stitch, making a ¼″ seam. Turn the cuff down, and press the seam toward the cuff. Bring the underarm lap sleeve seam together. Stitch from the armhole down, through the width of the cuff. Clean-stitch the underarm lap sleeve seam above the cuff line. Turn the cuff back, turn the raw edge under ⅛″, and whip it in place. Turn the cuff up to position on the right side of the sleeve, turning just below the seam line; and press it in place. Then

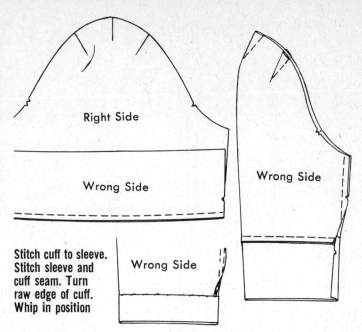

Right Side

Wrong Side

Wrong Side

Stitch cuff to sleeve. Stitch sleeve and cuff seam. Turn raw edge of cuff. Whip in position

Wrong Side

baste the sleeves in the dress, all corresponding notches meeting. Also baste shoulder pads in place across the top of the sleeve.

Slip the dress on. Check the sleeves. Adjust if necessary. Usually they are quite correct. For round shoulders, occasionally it is desirable to move the sleeves forward ¼″ to ½″ in the armhole. Remove the dress; then stitch the sleeves in, stitching the shoulder pads in place at the same time. Trim, clip, and overcast the armhole seams. Press shoulder pad out into top sleeve; press the top armhole seam in toward the blouse.

Make the Button Placket. Because the belt holds the dress at the waistline and also because you will want to wash this dress many times, we recommend that you use a placket popular in tropical countries—one that will smooth under a mangle if necessary. To make this: Cut a bias strip 1¼″ by 10″, and stitch to front edge of placket opening on right side. Cut another strip 2″ by 10″, and stitch it to back edge of placket on right side. (Take a full seam's width from

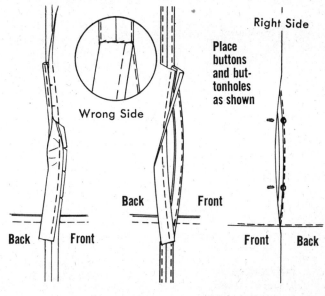

Wrong Side

Back   Front

Back   Front

Right Side

Place buttons and buttonholes as shown

Front   Back

front of placket, but only ⅛″ from the back.) Clip, and press seams open. Turn raw edge of strips under ⅛″ and clean-stitch, holding free from dress.

Baste front strip back in position. Then, ¼" beyond joining line, turn under-placket strip back; and stitch directly on this line. Press; turn dress wrong side out. Turn ends of facing strips under; whip neatly and securely to dress seam. Two buttons will hold placket securely, especially when the belt is on. For these, place the buttonholes 2¼" above waistline, and 2¼" below. If no belt is to be worn, also place a button and buttonhole or hook and eye at the waistline. (For making buttonholes, see page 24, for sewing on buttons, see page 27.)

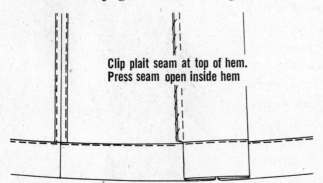

Clip plait seam at top of hem.
Press seam open inside hem

Put in the Hem. Measure the hem an even width all the way around. Turn the top edge a scant ¼", and stitch it. Press the seams open inside the hem. (In order to do this, you will have to clip the overcast seams of the front plaits at the top of the hem.) Slip-stitch the hem in place.

Make Belt Bar. At the waistline on the right side, make a vertical bar 1" longer than your belt is wide. This bar should be secure, and will serve to keep your belt in position at the waistline. One belt bar is usually quite sufficient; but you may also make another bar on the back of the placket.

Variations. We suggest a number of ways to vary this ensemble: You might make the jacket and dress of a print with a small design. Short jackets are smartly fashionable. If you cut the jacket one inch longer than the blouse front, the line of the jacket will correspond with the low waistline in the dress.

A light, unlined tweed or flannel coat is ideal for wear with dark dresses. Both could easily be made from this pattern. The seams of such a coat should be bound with seam binding in matching color. You fit, baste, and stitch a coat of wool exactly the same as for your piqué coat. As for the pockets, you prepare them, slip-stitch the hem, and then stitch the pockets in position. When pressing a wool coat, slip strips of cardboard under the edges of the side, the sleeve seams, and the shoulder seam darts, so that the seam line will not show on the right side. Do all the final pressing from the right side.

Plain silk or rayon crepe could be used for a smart ensemble, or a print for the blouse and plain for the skirt and jacket. For such, you would make the jacket short and clean-stitch the underarm seams. For the crepe dress, you would omit the body darts in the blouse and allow the small amount of fulness to ease in around the waist. Also, you would use a slide fastener for the dress placket. The dress pattern provides the bow collar. This is especially nice for a crepe dress.

Afternoon Dress and Bolero

Materials. Any firm, medium, or light-weight fabric is appropriate for this dress — cotton or rayon, silk, velvet, lace, or light-weight wool.

Piqué is a staple fabric that can snap a dull dress out of its doldrums and make it smart simply by its presence in collars and cuffs, pipings, ties, belts, etc. When it makes an entire garment, it is very chic, especially when beautifully tailored. Quality piqué wears and washes to perfection. Because piqué shrinks considerably, be sure to choose Sanforized piqué when you buy for a garment. Fabric that has been Sanforized is shrunk uniformly and permanently; and when 35″ piqué, for example, is put through the Sanforizing process it shrinks to a width of 33″ which, as you realize, would be far too much shrinkage in a garment.

When you make smart garments of good fabrics, take time; finish the seams, and do all the work nicely. Do not cheapen your work with careless stitching or pressing, and do not hurry unduly to complete your sewing— rather, take care with each part so that it fits into place in the garment perfectly and does credit to you and your own good workmanship.

A. Straighten Your Fabrics. Pull and stretch your fabric until all crosswise threads are straight. By this time, you realize how really important it is to have the fabric —both on the cross and length—straight, before you put the pattern on. Then, when you cut your garment, all matching pieces are exactly alike, and the grain of the fabric correct in each, insuring for you a garment that will keep its shape, set well, and be completely comfortable to wear.

B. Check Your Pattern with Your Measurements. Pin the fulness that is to be shirred in the front pieces of your pattern in folds so that you can pin the waist and skirt fronts together. Hold it up to you and check the length, position of waistline, skirt fulness, etc. The skirt is quite full at the bottom for the long length but just right for the short length for a skirt such as this. If you feel it is easier to handle this pattern in a short length, simply cut away the extra length, cutting on the lowest line indicated for the short length. Save the pieces you have cut off because if you wish to make a long satin, crepe, or velvet dress later on, this style will prove ideal.

Make as few changes as possible in adjusting the pattern to your measurements. Its smartness is in its simplicity, and the lines should not be disturbed except for very necessary adjustments.

If you wish shorter sleeves than the pattern calls for, lay a fold crosswise of the pattern to shorten it above the hem line. This is especially necessary in this case because of the shaped hem in the pattern.

C. Place Pattern on Fabric, and Cut Out Garment. To do this, open out the fabric. Pin the crosswise ends together, and the selvage edges at each side. Turn the pattern up at the bottom, fold and pin it, as shown on our layout, or cut the surplus length off as explained in **B.** Lay the pattern pieces on following the layout given, which is for a fabric having no up and down. Be sure that the lengthwise of fabric,

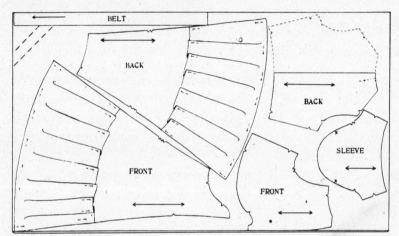

as indicated in each pattern piece, is placed directly on a lengthwise thread of the fabric. To insure this, measure with tape measure or ruler from the line indicating the lengthwise grain out to the selvage all along the pattern piece. Keep the lengthwise line the same distance from the edge throughout.

The dotted lines at the left corner of the dress layout indicate where the back neck facing is to be cut. You require only one piece, so cut through only one thickness of fabric. Cut the facing about 1½″ wide and about 8″ long at the narrow end. The back, also, is cut from only one thickness of fabric. After the skirt is cut, the fabric indicated by the dotted lines is folded back so that the back of the dress may be cut on a fold.

When a clean-stitched seam is used in finishing, as in a rayon crepe, mark all notches with chalk or pencil—do not cut them—so that all the clean-stitched seams will be true.

Seam the Center-Front of the Waist. First, baste the front hem facing from the top. Begin the stitching for this seam in the curve of the high front waistline, and stitch up to the point indicated on your pattern. Pivot, and stitch back exactly on the first stitching so that there will be no danger of the seam's pulling out. Press the center-front hem facings back, up to the neckline; then stitch them in position across the bottom to insure their being caught into the waistline seam when it is made later. These hem facings make a substantial and practical finish, as they will stay in position without stitches to hold them. When V-neck dresses are in fashion,

[75]

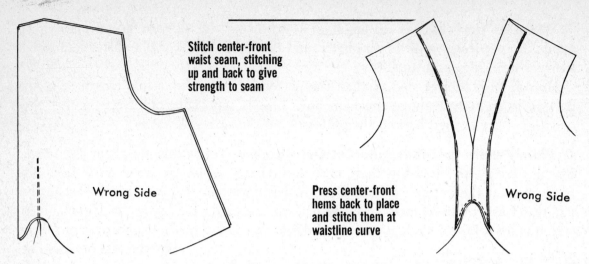

Stitch center-front waist seam, stitching up and back to give strength to seam

Wrong Side

Press center-front hems back to place and stitch them at waistline curve

Wrong Side

this is a satisfactory way to finish the neckline even when the pattern does not call for it—in which case, in cutting you will allow extra width for the hem facings.

Make Group Shirrings. Rows of shirrings are used to hold the fulness in position at each side of the front waistline and also on the top of each sleeve. (The markings on your pattern indicate the location of these shirrings.) Four rows are ideal. Stitch the first row ⅛″ in from the raw edge, using the machine gathering foot or a long machine stitch. Place the next row the width of the wide side of the presser foot away from the first—and so on, until all four rows are stitched. Pull the top threads through to the wrong side, but do not draw the shirrings up yet.

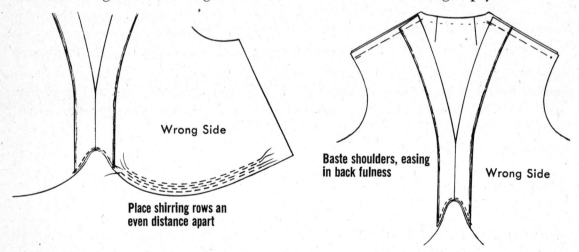

Wrong Side

Place shirring rows an even distance apart

Baste shoulders, easing in back fulness

Wrong Side

Make the Back-Neck Darts. Make these darts very narrow, stitching down and back again just as you did on the hip darts in your aprons. Stitch carefully, so as to taper the darts to a slender point; and avoid making them too wide at the bottom.

Baste the Shoulder Seams. Pin the seams in place first, with the back extending a seam's width beyond the crease in the hem facing, as shown. Begin at the neck to baste. Ease the fulness of the back in, holding the front shoulder slightly tight so that the armhole edges true up perfectly. There is an art in basting shoulders. This dress gives good opportunity to baste a shoulder so that, when stitched and pressed, it will fit without a wrinkle in the front hollow of the shoulder, yet have ample ease over the round part of the back shoulder.

Assemble Skirt. Pin the skirt gores together, beginning at the top. Stitch from the top down, stitching on the seam line. Turn the raw edges under ⅛"; and stitch, making clean-stitched seams. Press both seams open. Clip the ends of the seam away at the top diagonally, as shown.

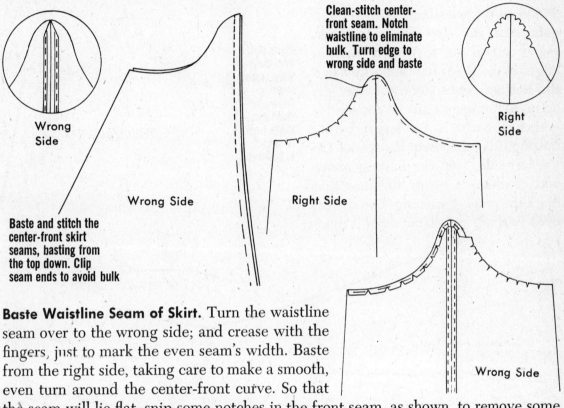

Wrong Side

Wrong Side

Baste and stitch the center-front skirt seams, basting from the top down. Clip seam ends to avoid bulk

Clean-stitch center-front seam. Notch waistline to eliminate bulk. Turn edge to wrong side and baste

Right Side

Right Side

Wrong Side

Baste Waistline Seam of Skirt. Turn the waistline seam over to the wrong side; and crease with the fingers, just to mark the even seam's width. Baste from the right side, taking care to make a smooth, even turn around the center-front curve. So that the seam will lie flat, snip some notches in the front seam, as shown, to remove some of the fulness; and clip the seam across the back.

Draw up the waistline shirring threads. Draw up the bobbin threads of the shirrings in the curve of the front waistline. Wrap the thread ends around a pin in the form of a figure 8 at each end of each group. Later, thread a needle with these thread ends; and catch them securely so that the shirrings can not pull out of position.

Make the Waistline Joining. (See illustration on next page.) Lay the waist part out on your cutting board or table. Pin the skirt carefully to it, adjusting the shirrings as required. Do the front first, beginning at the center. Then baste, using small stitches so that the curve is exactly true throughout. Next do the back, again working from the center.

Baste the Underarm Seams. To do this, lay the dress its full length on the table, wrong side up. Bring each side seam together. Pin first at the armhole and then at the waist, to make sure that the waistline seams meet exactly. On the left side of the dress, place marking pins for the 8″ slide fastener placket—4″ above and 4″ below the waistline. With the fingers, coax the skirt edges together, being careful not to stretch the bias edges in the least. It is important that the bottom edges come together exactly, so the seam must be pinned together crosswise its full length before basting is begun. Baste the seams. On the left side, stop the basting above and continue it below the pins that mark the placket opening. Use a short even-basting, and do not draw it tight.

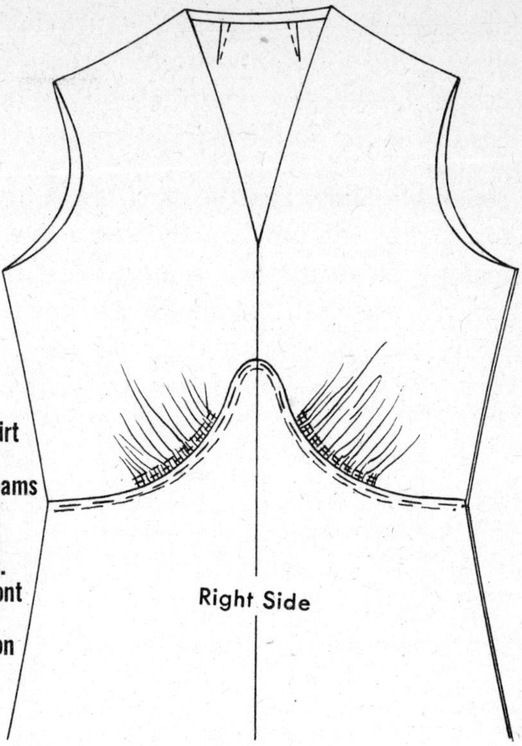

Place skirt over the waist, seams meeting. Draw up shirrings. Baste front of skirt to position

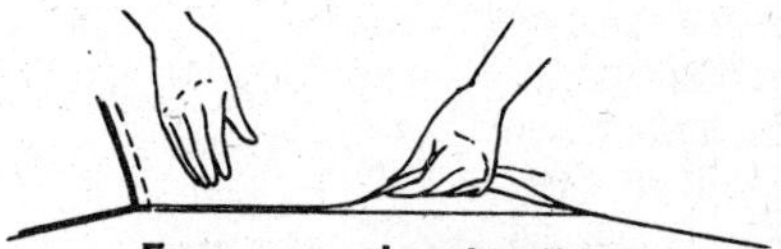

Right Side

Ease seam edges together

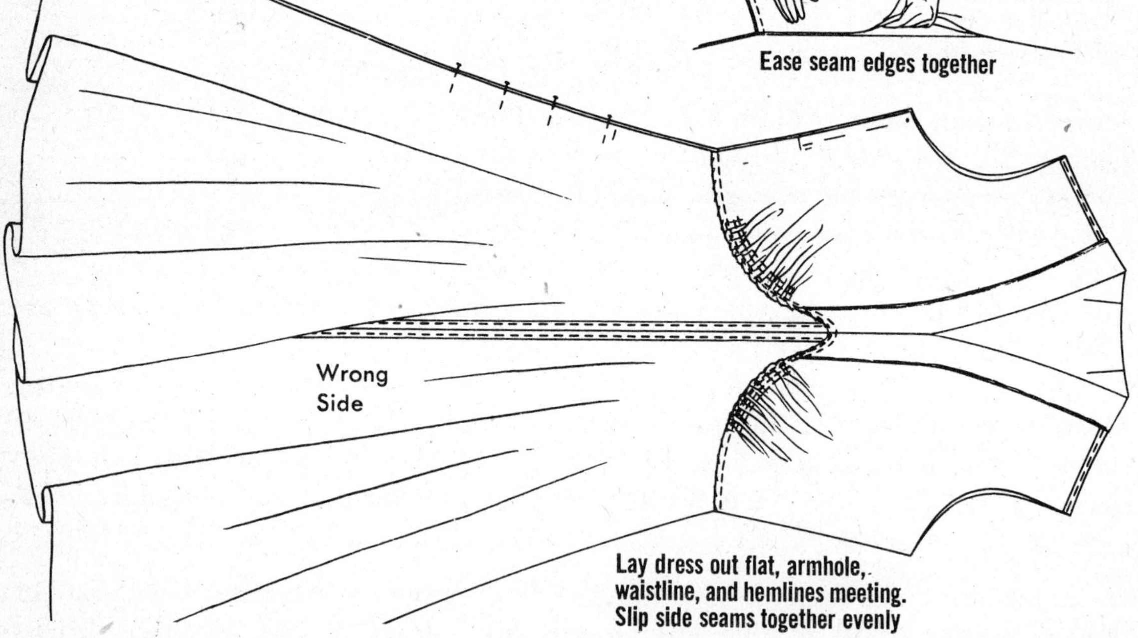

Wrong Side

Lay dress out flat, armhole, waistline, and hemlines meeting. Slip side seams together evenly

Fit Your Dress. Put your dress on. Notice the shoulders—are they smooth across the front? Is the V-neckline correct at the sides? Could you make the neck darts at the back slightly deeper? Are your shoulders the same height? Would a tiny pad under one shoulder square it up and balance the upper part of your dress? To test this, notice your waistline. Is it lower on one side than the other? Of course, the waistline may sag because one breast is smaller than the other. In that case, a tiny dart on both the front and back underarm seam will lift the low side up into position and balance the dress nicely. Or, the wearing of a bust pad on one side will bring the waistline into position. If you are full in the bust, you may want to slip the front skirt section down as much as possible to gain length there. If you are flat chested, you may want to lift the skirt front up a little. Such changes must be no more than a fraction of an inch, lest you distort the lines of the dress. When you have made the adjustments in the seams that you feel are necessary, remove the dress.

Stitch the Shoulder Seams. Begin at the creased line of the front hem facing, and stitch out to the armhole. Take the 1½″ wide bias facing piece; and pin it in place on the back neck, ¼″ in from the edge. Hold it full enough at the top so that there will be ample flare at the outside edge. Baste this on, ⅛″ down from the edge. Leave enough at the ends to bring the bias piece down over the front hem facings. Then stitch the bias facing on. Trim the ends; and whip them down over the front hem facings, to complete the neckline. Turn the free edge of the bias facing under, and clean-stitch it. Clean-stitch both shoulder seams also. Tack the bias facing to each of the back-neck darts, simply to hold it in position.

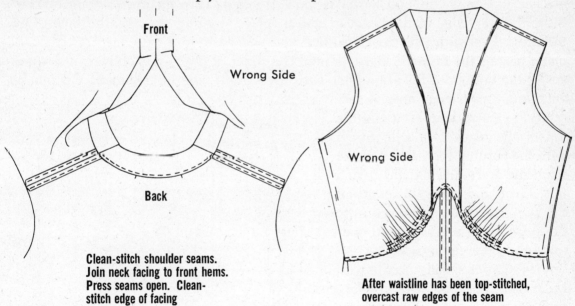

Front

Wrong Side

Back

Wrong Side

Clean-stitch shoulder seams.
Join neck facing to front hems.
Press seams open. Clean-
stitch edge of facing

After waistline has been top-stitched,
overcast raw edges of the seam

Top-Stitch the Waistline. First, open the right underarm seam from the armhole down to 6″ below the waistline, so that you can easily smooth the dress out under the presser foot as you stitch. Then begin at the right underarm seam, and top-stitch the waist and skirt together across the front. Take time and stitch carefully so as to round the curve nicely and keep the stitching line true throughout. Begin at the right underarm seam also to top-stitch the back waistline—this being done to avoid the necessity of rumpling the skirt under the arm of the machine. Turn the dress wrong side out. Stitch the waistline seams of skirt and waist together, stitching ¼" from the raw edges. Trim this seam, and overcast it neatly.

Make Concealed Slide-Fastener Placket. You have already measured for the fastener —half of its length above and half below the waistline. Stitch the seam above and below the opening, and then baste the opening. Press the seam open its full length, and remove the basting.

For a curved side seam such as this, cut a bias facing piece 1½" wide and 2" longer than the metal part of the fastener—as the fastener for this dress is 8" long, the facing will be 10". Place right side of facing to right side of dress on the front edge of the placket opening, placing on the seam allowance, ⅛" from the seam line. Pin, baste, and stitch it in place. Clip the seam. Turn the facing back into position, baste, and press. (The seam line extends ⅛" beyond the stitched line of the facing.) On the back of the placket, turn the seam edge over ⅛" to the wrong side, baste, and press. Place the closed slide fastener in position under this line, right side of fastener up, and turned edge ¹⁄₁₆" away from the metal part of the fastener. Baste. Place the cording foot on your machine; and stitch the fastener in place, stitching directly along the line of the fabric.

Lap the faced front edge of placket ⅛" over the stitched back line. Close the placket, pin crosswise, and baste. Remove the pins. Turn the dress wrong side out. Baste the free edge of the fastener tape in place, basting through the facing and the dress. Feel with your needle so that you will baste in a true line ¹⁄₁₆" from the metal part of the fastener. Baste around the slider at the top, as shown, and square across the bottom of the seam line. Turn dress right side out. Smooth the placket out. True your basting lines, if necessary, to make them even and the top of the placket smooth. Stitch with the cording foot. Begin at the seam line, and stitch in to the basted line. Pivot, and stitch the length of the opening. Pivot, and stitch in to the seam line. Pull the thread ends through to the wrong side.

Thread your sewing needle with these ends, and take several whipping-stitches in the fastener tape to give strength to the stitching line above and below the fastener.

Remove all basting. Clip away any surplus facing length above and below the slide fastener tapes. Place the placket over a bath towel,

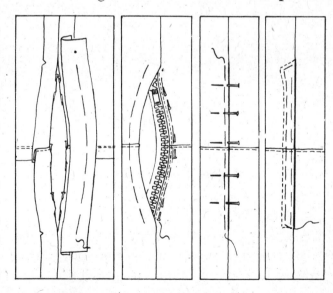

Baste and stitch facing to front edge of placket, fastener to the back edge. Baste placket together; stitch around the fastener

press from the wrong side, and your concealed placket is complete.

Rebaste and stitch the right underarm seam. Then clean-stitch the raw edges, as well as those on the left-side seam above and below the slide fastener. Press these seams as smoothly and as perfectly as possible.

Make Sleeves, and Place in the Dress. Clean-stitch the bottom edges of the sleeves. Stitch the underarm seams. Clean-stitch them, and press open. Clip away the surplus at the bottom of the seam, as shown. Place the sleeves in the dress, the armhole notches meeting. Draw up the bobbin threads of the shirrings. Wind these on a pin at each end of the shirring, in the form of a figure 8. Adjust the fulness in the armhole. Thread a needle with the shirring thread ends, and stay the end of each row with whipping-stitches. Baste each sleeve in position.

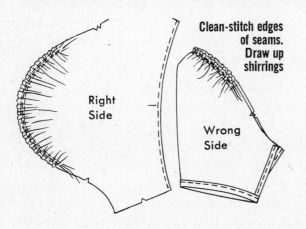

Right Side

Clean-stitch edges of seams. Draw up shirrings

Wrong Side

Hang Circular-Skirt Hem. The first essential in hanging the hem of a circular skirt is to let the garment "hang" on a hanger overnight before you turn the hem—so that the fabric can sag if it is determined to, before you turn the hem. Therefore, when the sleeves are basted in and you have the dress ready for fitting, put it on a regular hanger for overnight. Next day, put on shoes having heels of the height you will wear with the dress; and try on the dress. Notice the sleeves. Be sure the fulness is placed correctly. With your skirt marker, mark for the hem, just as you would for any other skirt. Remove the dress. Lay it out on your table right side out, folded at center-front and center-back lines. Measure the length evenly all the way across the skirt. Chalk-mark for the length. It will be necessary to trim a little off at the sides because of the sagging of the bias seams. When the length has been made even, measure the depth you want the finished hem. A circular skirt requires a narrower hem than does a lengthwise skirt. A 2″ hem—even less—is really best.

Turn the raw edge under a generous ⅛″. Clean-stitch it, using a size 24 white six-cord thread in the bobbin and a matching thread on top. Use a long stitch so that you can draw the fulness of the hem up by means of the bobbin thread. When the hem is basted and the lower edge pressed, slip the dress on again just to be sure it is even all the way around. Slip-stitch the hem in position, doing this with the skirt spread out on the table so that the hem lies perfectly in position. Use long slip-stitches, and take care that they do not show through.

Wrong Side

Clean-stitch edge of hem using heavy bobbin thread. Draw up thread and distribute the fulness evenly. Pin and baste for slip-stitching

When the hem is in, stitch the sleeves in on the armhole line, and then ¼″ outside this, as you did for the waistline seam. Trim the raw edges just enough to even them. Overcast the raw edges together.

Press your dress thoroughly, going over it carefully in the way your fabric requires. Then the dress itself will be complete and ready to wear. (Use cheesecloth wrung out of water for rayons and cottons. Use drilling for sheer wool and silk.)

This type of dress is more slenderizing when the belt is omitted. But you may wear a belt to contrast, or you may make a belt of the fabric. See illustrations and captions for instructions for making a belt of the fabric.

Make Fabric Belt. Take a lengthwise strip of firm muslin 4″ longer than your waistline measurement and ¼″ narrower than the width you desire for the finished belt. Take a lengthwise strip of fabric twice the width of the muslin plus 1″. Lay the fabric on the table, wrong side up. Center the muslin on this strip, pin, and baste together the full length. Turn fabric right side up. Decide how many rows of stitching you want in the belt. Stitch the first row on a lengthwise thread of the fabric, the distance in from the edge of the muslin that you want between the rows. For a belt 1⅛″ wide, 3 rows of stitching, as shown, made with the wide side of the presser foot will fill the space nicely. It is important to begin each row from the same end of the belt and to keep the stitching lines true. When the stitching is done, bring the lengthwise edges of the fabric together, wrong side out; and stitch, making a ¼″ seam. Press the seam open, turn the belt right side out, and press again.

For covering the rustless rings, cut two lengthwise strips of fabric 1″ wide and about 12″ long. Turn the raw edges to the center, as shown; and press. Place one end of a strip on the side of the ring, and hold between the thumb and finger. With the fingers of the other hand, wrap the folded fabric tightly around and around the ring until it is completely covered, holding the end in place all the time. Clip off any surplus length in the fabric. Turn the end in, and whip it down neatly.

When both rings are covered, hold them up on each side of your front waistline, to decide how far apart they should be. The space usually is approximately one-

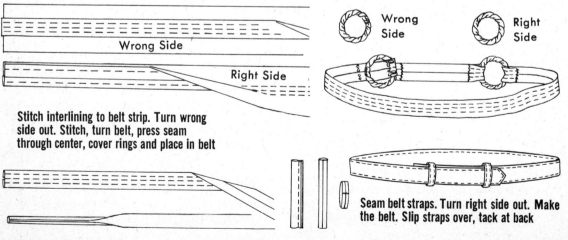

Wrong Side

Right Side

Wrong Side

Right Side

Stitch interlining to belt strip. Turn wrong side out. Stitch, turn belt, press seam through center, cover rings and place in belt

Seam belt straps. Turn right side out. Make the belt. Slip straps over, tack at back

sixth of the waistline measurement. This distance, plus 2″, gives you the length you require for the center-front piece of the belt. If the waist measures 30″, for example, you will want the rings 5″ apart; and so you will need 7″ for the center-front piece. From one end of the belt you have made, cut off the required length. Bring an end of this piece over each ring, and whip the ends down neatly and securely. Take one end of the belt, bring it over the opposite side of one ring, and whip it in place. Put the belt on, and draw the free belt end through the ring at the end of the center piece. Trim away any surplus length beyond 1¼″. Turn the raw ends in, and whip down. Sew small hooks to this end and straight eyes to the belt to complete the closing.

Ribbon may be stitched to the right side of fabric in the way the muslin is stitched to the wrong side, and thus used both for support and decoration. Fabric slide loops may be made from 1¼″ wide lengthwise strips stitched and turned. These slides may then be made into rings that slip over the belt and form slide loops for an over-lapping belt. This belt will be held in place with a hook sewed to one end of the belt and a worked eye made on the right side of the belt in a position to correspond with the hook.

Seam Finishes for Fabrics That Fray. Rayons, sheer wools, and flimsy cottons fray easily; so the seams must be stayed. To stay seams, clean-stitch or stitch and overcast them; bind with bias binding or seam binding; or cover the raw edge with a narrow net footing to prevent fraying. In any event, three things are necessary: (1) Finish the edge so that it can not fray or pull out; (2) Avoid tightening the seam—ease binding on, for example, so that it can not shorten the seam edge; (3) Avoid any finish that will give an edge so heavy as to cause a mark to show on the right side after it has been pressed.

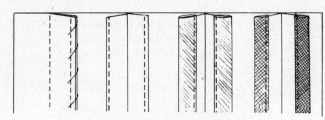

Use seam finish appropriate to the fabric and seam location in garment

Where seams overlap, as in the waistline and sleeves, stitch first on the seamline. Then trim just enough to even them; and stitch the raw edges together from the wrong side, placing the stitching line a generous ⅛″ from the edge. Overcast the raw edges together neatly and securely.

· When Cutting the Piqué Bolero. Place the straight edge of the revers facings near the selvage, as shown, so that you may use the selvage as a finish for the edge. Therefore, do not cut on the pattern line, simply leave selvages on; otherwise it is necessary to bind these edges or turn and clean-stitch them. Cut interlining for shoulder pads from unbleached muslin.

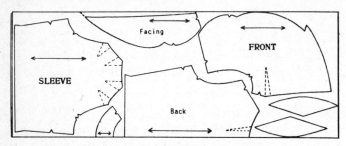

Mark, pin, baste, and stitch all the darts—at the back neck and the underarm and in the tops of the sleeves. (See illustration for marking darts.) Baste the shoulder and underarm seams. Slip the bolero on to make sure that all the lines are correct and that the bolero fits smartly. Remember that it must not be too snug; also, that there is a hem to be turned at the bottom, which will shorten the bolero considerably.

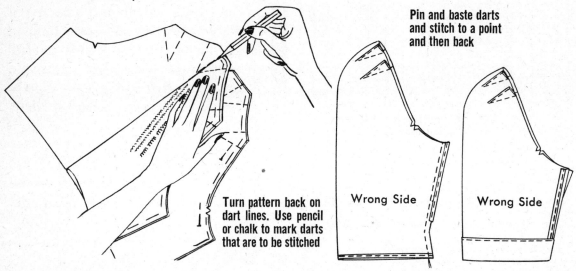

Take off the bolero. Stitch the shoulder seam. Open the underarm seams; then bind all the seam edges, including the sleeves. To avoid bulk under the neck facing and the hems, stop the binding 1″ short of the neckline, and 1½″ short of the bottom of the bolero and the sleeves. Clean-stitch the bottom edge of the bolero and the sleeves at this time. Baste, and stitch the underarm seam of the sleeves.

Make Fitted Facings for Neck and Revers. Lay the revers facings and neck facing in place, right side to right side of the bolero. Pin the facings on. Pin the shoulder joinings in a seam so that the facings fit the bolero perfectly. Baste and stitch these seams. Turn the outside edge of the neck facing to wrong side; and clean-stitch edge, keeping the stitching line in line with selvage edge of the revers facings. Baste the revers and neck facings in place, basting carefully so that they fit without the slightest stretching or pulling. Begin at **A** on the extreme outside edge of the facing. Stitch around front and neck edges. Pivot at **B** to make a sharp turn. Trim the seam to within a scant ¼" of the stitching line. Clip the seam into the stitching line at **B**. Clip around the curve of the revers and across back neckline so that when the facings are turned back the seam will lie flat.

Press the clipped seam open so that you will get a beautifully true edge. Use a sleeveboard if you have one; or wrap your press cloth around a milk bottle, and use this as a press block for this seam. Turn the revers and neck facings back into position, and press in place. Baste the underarm seams, stitch, and press open. Turn the hem up at the bottom, and slip the front edge under the facing. Baste and slip-stitch the hem; also, the sleeve hems. Slip-stitch the selvage edge of the revers facings in place, catching the hem securely where the selvage overlaps it. Catch the neck facing to the darts, using several tacking-stitches to hold it in place.

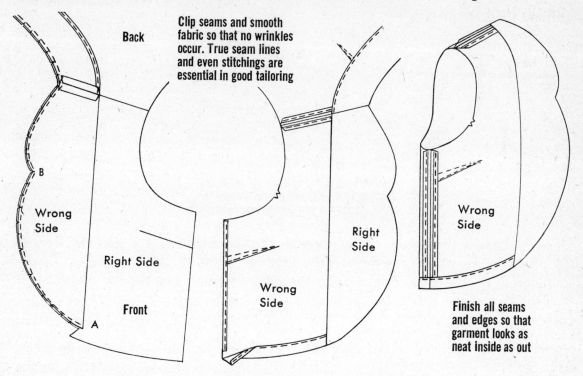

Baste the sleeves in, all notches meeting. Slip the bolero on to be sure that the sleeves are in correctly. Remove, make any necessary corrections, and stitch the sleeves in.

Bind the Armhole Seams. First, trim the seams evenly, trimming as little as possible to accomplish this. Clip the seam every ½″, to within ⅛″ of the stitching line. Press the seam back toward the garment, doing this over the sleeve board or milk bottle. The clipping of the seam allows sufficient flare for this. Baste the bias binding on, beginning just in front of the underarm seam. Ease the binding on to the clipped edge. Do not draw the least tight. Allow the binding to overlap about ½″, and make a neat joining. Stitch the binding on. Remove all bastings.

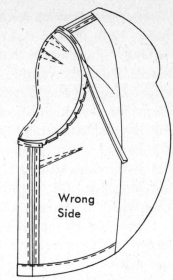

Wrong Side

Make Washable Shoulder Pads. Place three short pieces of featherbone over the muslin interlining, as shown. With a long machine stitch, stitch from one piece to another so as to avoid breaking the thread. Place the long piece of featherbone over the three short ones, and stitch it lengthwise of the interlining Place together the right sides of the two fabric pieces that are to form the covering. Place the boned interlining over this; and stitch around the pad from **A** to **B,** making a scant ¼″ seam. Snip the corners off. Turn right side out. Turn in the raw edges of the unstitched part, baste, and stitch. Continue the stitching all the way around the pad and thus complete it.

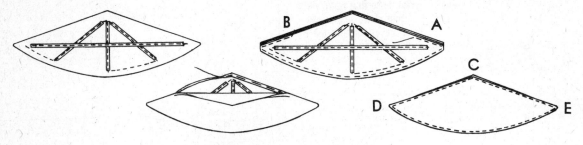

Featherbone in two or three ply makes an ideal support for shoulder pads. Is easy to stitch to position with a long machine stitch

Place the Pads in the Bolero. Pin in place on the shoulder seam so that the lengthwise featherbone comes just beyond the armhole seam. Tack the point **C** to the shoulder seam—the ends, **D** and **E,** to the armhole seam. This type of pad is practical for all types of garments. Cover with taffeta when using it in wool, velvet, or silk garments.

Variations. This style with its nipped-in waistline is slenderizing, especially when worn without a belt. We make it in the short-sleeve version because we believe the short sleeves are more youthful. Pattern, however, provides both long and short sleeves, so you may use the ones you prefer. If you make a bolero that requires a lining, see the instruction chart that accompanies your pattern.

[86]

The dress may have a removable piping at the neck and sleeves. It may have a collar cut to fit the neckline and V-front. If you are very flat in the front, you may slash the front waist section from the shoulder down almost to the waistline and separate the front enough to allow for group shirrings in the front shoulders.

The bottom edge may be faced or turned and stitched or the edge may have a French binding or have the lower edge picoted and turned back and slip-stitched. The bolero in piqué or lace would be smart for wear with a long dark crepe dress made in this style.

Hem Finishes. The hem finishes given in the instructions for this dress can be varied by using the one shown here. You may wish to make a bolero lined with contrasting fabric. The hem and facing can be catch-stitched down, thus eliminating extra bulk.

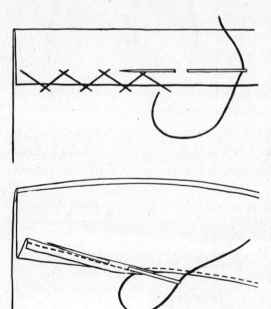

Catch-Stitched Hem. Used on firm fabrics whenever the edge is pinked or not turned under. Use a fine needle and work from left to right. Make small horizontal stitches, seldom more than ⅛″ long. These stitches should not be seen on the right side of the fabric or garment. Zigzag above and below the raw edge, as shown, thus forming a series of overlapping cross-stitches.

Faced Circular Edge. On full circular skirts or edges, it is often necessary to make a false hem. Cut a fitted facing on the same grain as the skirt, or use a true bias of the width desired. Stitch the facing to the edge, right sides together, then turn to wrong side and press carefully so that the edge will not be pulled out of shape. Turn the top edge of facing strip under and stitch; then slip-stitch it in position, as shown.

[87]

Princess Frocks

Materials. For a dress-up house-coat, choose rayon, satin, crepe, taffeta, dimity, or dotted Swiss. For a very practical house-coat, choose an 80 square percale, such as a gay percale that you know will look charming and will wash well.

A fabric having no up-and-down should be selected for a princess house-coat. For economy's sake, you must fit the pieces of the pattern carefully on your fabric; otherwise, a princess style can prove more expensive than is practical.

For a percale house-coat, three types of trimming are suitable for the collar and cuffs: a piping of piqué, an edging of rick rack, or a percale bias binding. Decide what trimming you will use before you start to sew, as trimming is applied during the making.

Such patterns usually come in two lengths. If you want a short house-coat rather than a long, cut it to correspond in length to that of a morning dress.

Pattern Layout. Place pattern on fabric, as illustrated below. For a large size, of course, you have more length; and you move the pieces down on the fabric to make room for width of each.

Center-Back Gore. Notice how fabric is cut and brought down from underneath to make room for the center-back gore after other pieces are cut.

Sleeves and Collar. If you wish a sleeve straight at the bottom, chalk a line at sides and across bottom, as indicated. If you wish a longer sleeve, measure down from the underarm seams in a straight line the distance you desire. Cut bias pieces, as indicated, to use when applying collar.

Short House-Coat. Fold pattern on line of perforations indicating short length.

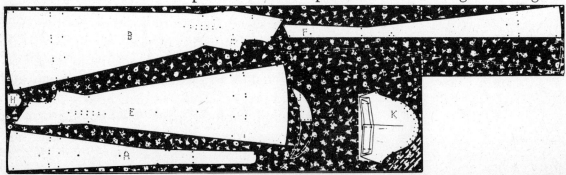

A. Straighten Your Fabric. To straighten your fabric is always essential. This is more important, if possible, when you are opening fabric up its full width, as you then need to pin the selvages together on each side to keep the woof threads even. Stretch your fabric gently but firmly on the bias. Pull diagonally; straighten; and press, if necessary, so that you have a smooth fabric to work on. The A in the A B C's of good dressmaking is to begin with a straightened fabric—never allow yourself to forget this or to assume that the fabric is straight.

B. Check Your Pattern with Your Measurements. The principles learned in fitting a princess-cut garment are helpful in fitting basques, bodices, jackets—all garments that are fitted over the bust and through the waistline.

1. If the bust is high and the pattern draws upward from the waist, slash the pattern; then insert a piece of tissue, as shown, to bring the waistline of the pattern to normal position.

2. For round shoulders, slash the pattern across the shoulder; and drop it down so that the waistline is in normal position.

3. For flat bust, where the pattern provides too much fulness from shoulder to waistline, lay a fold in the pattern to take out the surplus length.

4. Where the waistline is larger than the pattern, cut the underarm lines with less curve. Omit the body darts, or make them smaller than the perforations indicate.

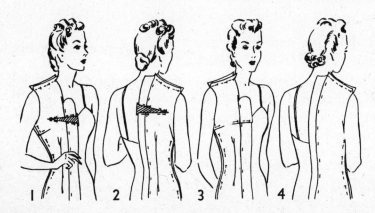

We suggest adjustments in the pattern for a high bust, round shoulders, flat bust, and large waist. If you need to make several adjustments in your pattern, make them; then cut the waist part out of inexpensive muslin or percale or an old worn sheet or pillowcase, cutting it to extend far enough below the waist to take in all the body darts. Baste this carefully, fit it to your figure, lay darts to take up excess fulness, and take care to keep the grain of the fabric correct throughout each section. Rip up this basted guide pattern, and lay it over the tissue pattern; then cut the upper part of your house-coat from this, marking notches just as you would with the tissue pattern.

C. Place Pattern on Fabric, and Cut Out Garment. When laying out a long princess-cut garment, especially for large sizes, it is sometimes an economy in fabric to turn back the corners of the back gores on a lengthwise thread and piece these gores. The piecing will come mostly in the hem. In any case, it will show very little when joining is made on a lengthwise thread and seam is carefully pressed open and overcast. In laying out a princess-cut garment, check each piece a second time to be sure that perforations for lengthwise grain are correctly placed. Correct grain is important for all garments, and doubly so for a close-fitting garment that has many sections.

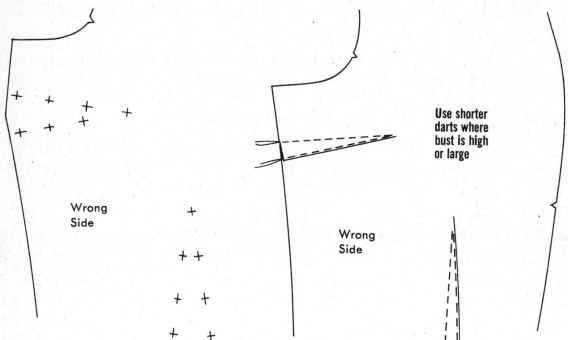

Use shorter darts where bust is high or large

Wrong Side

Wrong Side

Mark for the Underarm and Body Darts and the Sleeve Plaits. Use a lead pencil, and mark perforations on wrong side of fabric. There are two ways to do this: Place a pin through each perforation, catching both thicknesses of fabric so that you can mark both sides alike with your pencil. Or, on the top sleeve, make a pencil mark in each perforation; then remove pattern piece, pin it to the under sleeve, and mark perforations on it in the same way.

Put in the Underarm and Body Darts. If you are quite sure that your pattern size is correct and that you have adjusted it to your measurements, you can safely pin, baste, and stitch underarm and body darts at this time. If you are not sure, do not stitch darts until after the first fitting. Crosses are shown where dart lines should be pinned together.

Stitch the underarm darts in from the edge, then out again so that there are no thread ends to tie—exactly as you did hip darts in your aprons. Stitch the body darts on the dart line and then on the outside line—one each in the side-backs and side-fronts. If the bust is low, make the front body darts narrower and shorter above the waistline. If waistline is large in proportion to hips and bust, it may be advisable to make very slender darts or omit them entirely. Measure your waistline and your pattern to make sure about this before you stitch the darts.

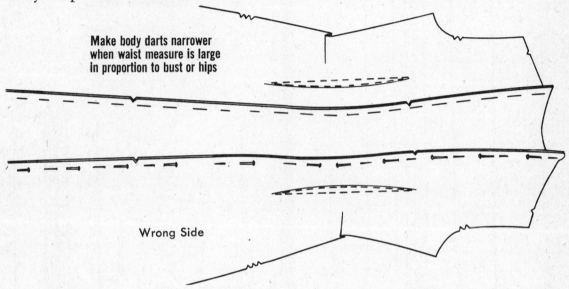

Make body darts narrower when waist measure is large in proportion to bust or hips

Wrong Side

In joining the sections of the house-coat together, pin up and then down from the waistline. Begin at the waistline of the center-back. Pin and baste the center-back panel to the back side gores, as shown.

Measure and Mark for the Slide Fastener. To do this: Place together the right sides of the two pieces that form the center-front. From **A,** measure down the length of the metal part of the slide fastener you are using—16″ is a good length in this case—and make a tiny notch. (See illustration on next page.)

Apply Slide Fastener to Center-Front. Pin-baste the center front seam below the notch, and stitch from notch to bottom of skirt. Clip a diagonal line through the ½″ seam allowance, as at **B;** then clip exactly ³⁄₁₆″ beyond this, to provide room for metal part of fastener. Do this clipping precisely, or the space will be too wide. Press center-front seam open below the slash, with the notched edges down, as at **C.** Press the edges back evenly above the slash—these seam edges are now ¹¹⁄₁₆″ wide (½″ plus ³⁄₁₆″). From right side, place fastener under open section, with the tiny bar at bottom of fastener exactly against the slashed end, as at **D.** Pin the fastener in place, taking care to keep the creased edges of the fabric an even distance from the metal on both sides of the fastener the full length; then baste. Remember that you never draw a fastener tight when basting it in place, and that you use the cording foot on your machine when stitching. Begin at top of fastener, and stitch down to **D.** Pivot, and stitch across to **E.** Pivot again, and stitch up to the top. As you approach the top, remember to pull the slider down past where you have stitched—out of the way, so that it will not interrupt your true stitching line.

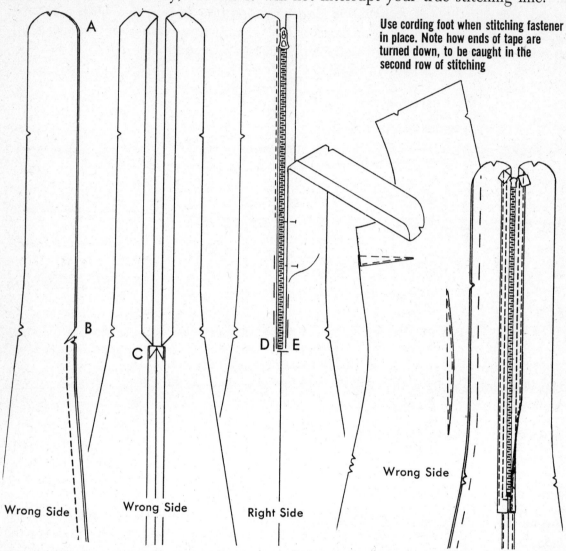

Use cording foot when stitching fastener in place. Note how ends of tape are turned down, to be caught in the second row of stitching

Secure the Slide Fastener Tape. To do this: Work with the wrong side up. Turn back the tape ends at the top. Stitch the outside edge of the tape to the seam edge on both sides of the fastener, turning the fabric edge under ⅛″ and holding the seam allowance free from the garment. This not only secures the seam and gives a finish to the edges, but serves to hold the tape back and makes it practically impossible for it ever to get caught in the teeth of the fastener.

[92]

Apply Rick Rack. If you are making the short house-coat that is illustrated, baste the rick rack in place first, so that it can be caught in the seams when they are basted and stitched. If there is to be a collar on house-coat, baste rick rack on the side front, as shown, from top to bottom; if there is to be no collar and rick rack is to continue around the neck, baste it, as shown, on each side of the front section.

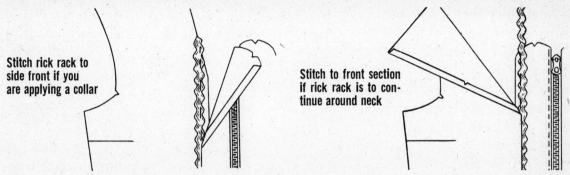

Stitch rick rack to side front if you are applying a collar

Stitch to front section if rick rack is to continue around neck

Pin Together and Baste the Front of the Princess-Cut Body. Because there is considerable curve in the waistline and over the bust in a princess-cut garment, care must be taken in joining the front sections to begin at the waistline and pin up and down and then to baste in the same way. This enables you to ease in any slight fulness over the bust and to do it so skillfully that no tiny plaits or fulness will form there when you baste the front. Join the underarm seams at this time, pinning and basting them up and down from the waistline. Pin and baste the shoulder seams: Begin at the neck; stretch the front shoulder slightly, and ease the back shoulder in so that the neckline and armhole lines are true.

Place Plaits in Top of Sleeve. The tiny pencil marks made on the fabric through the perforations of the sleeve pattern will guide you now in laying in the plaits. The single dot, **A**, indicates the top of the sleeve. Lay two plaits in the back part of the sleeve and three in the front, turning all the plaits toward **A** as you are working on the wrong side of the fabric. Pin the plaits; then baste or stitch across them to hold them in position.

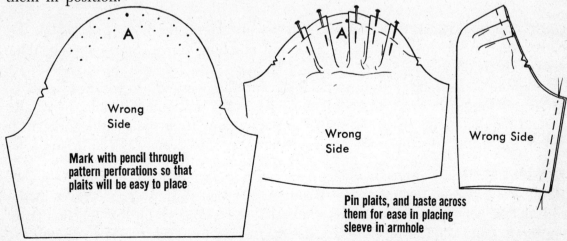

A

Wrong Side

Mark with pencil through pattern perforations so that plaits will be easy to place

A

Wrong Side

Wrong Side

Pin plaits, and baste across them for ease in placing sleeve in armhole

Make Hem Cuff. Apply Trimming. Pin the underarm sleeve seams, stitch, and press open. At the bottom of each sleeve, turn the edge up ¼″ on the wrong side; then turn the hem up 2″, and stitch it. Turn the hem back 1⅜″ on the right side —this gives you a cuff that is easy to make and can be turned down for quick ironing. Overcast the sleeve seam above the cuff. If you are trimming with

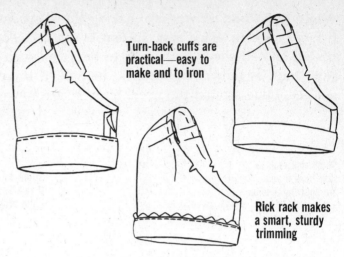

Turn-back cuffs are practical—easy to make and to iron

Rick rack makes a smart, sturdy trimming

rick rack, stitch the rick rack to the top of the turn-back cuff, holding the cuff free from the sleeve, of course. Pin the sleeves in the house-coat, corresponding notches meeting. Hold the garment on your hands to make sure that the plaits are right and the sleeves correctly positioned in the armhole, as illustrated on page 47. Baste in place.

Fit Princess-Cut Garment. Slip the garment on to make sure that it fits perfectly. Remember: You have half-inch seams; you can let them out slightly by stitching outside basting line if garment is tight, or make seams deeper by stitching inside basting if garment should fit more snugly. If shoulders droop, use a little shoulder pad to lift them up. If one breast is flatter or lower than the other, stitch a tiny pad to the side front seam on that side. It will do wonders to make the sides appear uniform. Perhaps two tiny neck darts will make the garment fit better across the back of the neck. Do not hesitate to put them in if they do. Just remember that if you take two darts in the back neck, each ¼″ deep, you will need to snip ½″ off the end of the collar so that it will fit the neckline. Mark for the hem at this time.

Stitch, Clip, and Finish Fitted Seams. When you take off the house-coat, stitch the body seams, beginning each at the neck and stitching down. Stitch the shoulder seams. Stitch the sleeves in.

Clip the body seams in the curves, as shown. Clip every ½″, to within a scant ¼″ of the stitching line. Press all body seams open. Clip the armhole seams, especially around the underarm curve. Overcast the body seams from the shoulders down to below the waist; then overcast or clean-stitch the skirt seams, as you desire.

Finish the Scallops. Pin the small facing pieces to the top of the center-front section, right sides of fabric together; then baste. With a pencil, draw good curves at the top so that you will have nicely shaped scallops; and stitch on the penciled lines, as shown. Cut away the surplus fabric. Clip the seams. Turn facing to the wrong

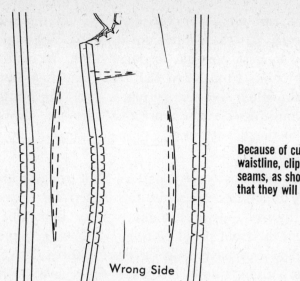

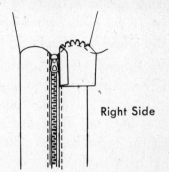

side. Whip the front edges down over the fastener tape (the edges nearest the metal), leaving the outside edges of the facing free until the collar is applied.

Because of curve in waistline, clip all seams, as shown, so that they will not draw

Wrong Side

Right Side

Make the Collar. Fold a 1″ wide piece of bias lengthwise through the center, right side out. This will form the piping. Press it; and pin it on the right side of the under part of the collar, as shown. Baste it on, making a ¼″ seam and easing the piping around the curve so that it can not possibly draw. Baste the top part of the collar over this, right sides of fabric together. Stitch all around the outside edge, making a ⅜″ seam. Notch the seam at the curves, as shown. Turn the collar right side out; top-stitch, and press.

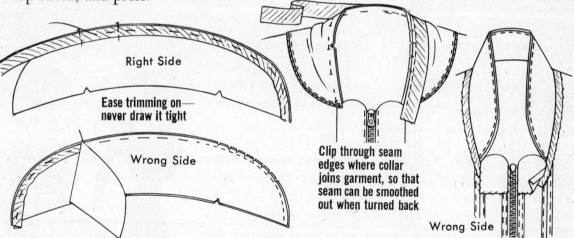

Right Side

Ease trimming on— never draw it tight

Wrong Side

Clip through seam edges where collar joins garment, so that seam can be smoothed out when turned back

Wrong Side

Apply the Collar. Pin the collar to the neckline of the house-coat, corresponding notches meeting. Baste the 1″ bias facing in place, making a seam that takes ⅛″ from the facing and ⅜″ from the neck edge of the garment, and easing the facing on so that it will lie smooth on the outside edge; then stitch this on. Turn the outside edge of the facing under a generous ⅛″, and crease; then whip it down all the way around on the wrong side, as shown. Slip the ends under the facing pieces of the scallops; then whip the facing pieces over the ends to hold all securely in place. Overcast the bottom edge of the small facing pieces.

[95]

Measure and turn the hem evenly, and crease on the hem line all the way around. Turn the top edge over a scant ¼"; then stitch on the edge, holding it free from the garment and using the longest possible machine-stitch. Draw the bobbin thread of this stitching up at points from 8" to 12" apart, and distribute the fulness of the flared hem evenly. Slip-stitch the hem in place. Press the housecoat, and it is ready to wear. When you press or iron a princess garment, always press the body seams open, as much of the beauty of the garment depends upon the smooth perfection of the seams.

Variations. Many variations are possible with this type of pattern. If a princess line is becoming and you enjoy wearing it, do not hesitate to use this pattern for several garments; and make them in different fabrics and ways to gain variety. Remember, if you do not like a low neck, simply cut the front panel pieces from 2" to 6" longer at the top than the pattern requires. You can have long or short sleeves. If you wish three-quarter sleeves open at the bottom, simply chalk out the sleeve at the bottom, as shown. Then make a deep hem and have an open sleeve that you can turn back to form a cuff.

Make a beautiful princess hostess gown of satin or taffeta or flannel—any fabric you like, in fact. Use plaited lace or ribbon for the neck and a plastic slide fastener for the front, and you will have a garment that is smartly slim and ever so practical for dress-up.

Make a morning dress of percale trimmed with rick rack. Omit the collar if you like, and extend the rick rack around the neck. Use rick rack also with a bias facing at the bottom of the sleeves.

Make a business dress of silk or rayon or wool crepe. Use piqué for the collar,

and possibly for piping the cuffs of the long or short sleeves; and have a trimly narrow belt.

Make a cool, flattering negligee of dotted Swiss or of rayon sheer, with a flounce ruffle from 7" to 10" deep. Hem the top and bottom edge of the ruffle, and gather the top edge 1" below the hem to make a 1" heading. Use self-fabric or lace for the ruffle at the neck and sleeves, and self-fabric or ribbon for the tie sash.

Sheer Dress with Slip

Materials. Dresses of sheer fabric may be of organdie, voile, sheer crepe, georgette, chiffon, triple sheer, lace or net. A sheer dress should have a slip made for it. Sometimes this is cut from the pattern of the dress so that the body lines are the same; and, with the skirt fulness in accord, the slip and dress will drape together when one sits down. A well-fitting bias slip that is not too narrow will prove quite satisfactory, especially when the length is right for the dress.

A. Straighten Your Fabric. To straighten sheer fabrics of net and lace (which rarely, if ever, can be pulled to straighten), square one end with that of your cutting board—the fold of the fabric in line with the edge of the cutting board at the side. Georgette, chiffon, and organdie should be torn and the torn edges pinned together. Very limp chiffon should be pinned to tissue paper for cutting, to make sure that it is cut true with the pattern lines.

B. Check Your Pattern with Your Measurements. Decide on the style of dress and slip you will have. Take measurements for the skirt length. If you are using the short length, fold the pattern back at the line of perforations. Shorten or lengthen the pattern crosswise of the pattern. Decide whether you will have long or short sleeves. If short, decide the length you want them; and fold the sleeve pattern in from the bottom to give you the length you require. Take time at the beginning to have the lengths correct in all parts of your pattern. Use your tape measure to make sure, and save your time as well as your fabric.

C. Place Pattern on Fabric; Cut Out Garments. Three layouts are given on page 103. Both the long and short versions are illustrated for double-width net. This is called 72″ net; but, because of shrinkage in finishing, usually it actually measures only from 68″ to 70″ in width. This has a center fold. Lay it out, with the fold toward you, as shown. In the long version, dash lines show how you can put more fulness in the bottom of the skirt if you desire it. To do this, pin your pattern on; then lay your yardstick or tape down, and draw a line outside the pattern lines.

Begin these lines up near the hip in every case so that the line will be straight from the hip out. In the layout for a long net dress, cut out all the pieces except the back and the strings; then separate the two thicknesses. Use one to cut the strings; the other, the back—as illustrated by the pattern and the dash lines. The third layout shows 39″ fabric folded and the pattern laid out for a short dress. Follow this layout if you are using crepe or allover lace. The strips cut along the selvage (marked **P**) are for the placket.

Stitching on Tissue Paper. Save obsolete tissue patterns and tissue paper that comes in packages, and use under sheer fabrics when you sew. The stitching cuts through the paper and makes it practically self-removing. Tissue insures a seam that is not tight. To prove this to yourself, take a piece of tissue and scrap of lace, net, georgette, or chiffon. Stitch a few inches with the tissue between your fabric and the feed plate, and then the same amount without the tissue. You will quickly see what a great safeguard the tissue is, and you will surely use it when stitching any fabric that is sheer or limp.

Seams for Sheer Fabrics. Four types of seams appropriate to sheer fabrics are illustrated here.

Double-Stitched. The simplest is the seam that is stitched twice. It is appropriate for use on any sheer fabric. Stitch first on the seam line, then ⅛″ outside it. Trim away the seam allowance fairly close to the second row of stitching. If the fabric is inclined to tighten with the stitching, stitch the first row on tissue. Remove the paper because, if you stitch both rows without removing the paper, some may catch between the rows and be tedious to remove. Now stitch the second row, also on tissue paper.

Lapped Seam. This seam is often used in bulky net and in closely patterned lace with a small motif. Overlap the edges on paper, the amount of the seam allowance; and stitch on the seam line. Trim away the surplus edges of the seam on both sides, as shown. If the fabric is lace and the motif medium in size, sometimes it is advisable to cut wider seams than the pattern calls for, overlap the gore at the seam line, and stitch around each motif—following the motif just as you would for lace appliqué. Trim away all surplus edges, of course.

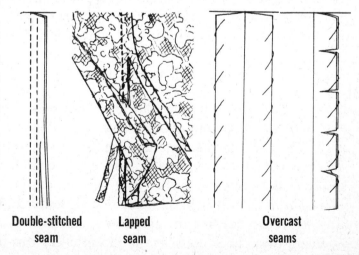

Double-stitched seam

Lapped seam

Overcast seams

Overcast Seams. Make a plain seam. Press it open; and overcast, as shown. This seam is the most satisfactory for triple sheers and light-weight crepes. For heavy nets, the next type of seam shown is often quite satisfactory, especially for shoulders and arm-holes. Make a plain seam; clip, as shown; overcast the raw edges together.

Hems for Sheer Fabrics. The fabric you use determines the hem finish. For chiffons, georgettes, and organdies, use a rolled or picot hem.

Rolled Hem. Place the fabric over tissue paper; and stitch the evenly trimmed edge, placing the stitching ⅛″ from the edge. Roll the stitched edge in to make a narrow hem, and slip-stitch the roll in position. Take care to have the stitches as tiny as possible on the right side of the fabric.

Italian Rolled Hem. Make Italian Rolled Hem by turning edge ⅛″. Begin in this turn with a knot. Do a stitch in the turn, catch a thread in the fabric, continue for 2″ or 3″. Draw up thread and repeat.

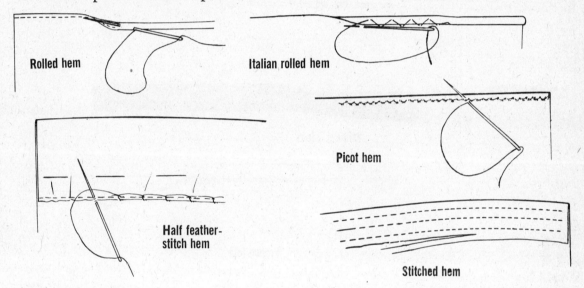

Rolled hem

Italian rolled hem

Picot hem

Half feather-stitch hem

Stitched hem

Picot Hem. Pin the fabric to paper. Baste on the line that is to be picoted, and have the hemstitching follow the basted lines. Cut the hemstitching through the center. Turn the picoted edge to the wrong side of the fabric, and slip-stitch it in position.

Half Feather-Stitch Hem. Clean-stitch the hem edge by hand. Baste it in position. Catch up a thread of the fabric of the skirt; then catch the needle in the hem edge, bringing the needle out over the thread, as shown. This stitch is used so that the thread line can not show through to the right side. If the hand-run clean-stitching shows through, remove it when you take the bastings out.

Stitched Hem. Often in net or lawn or very crisp fabric, the hem can be stitched with three or more rows, as shown. Turn the hem allowance to position, and baste. Place tissue on the wrong side; and stitch from the right side, making as many rows of stitching as you desire. Pull the paper away. Trim off any surplus in the hem width above the last row of stitching.

Edge Finishes for Sheer Fabrics. Three types of edge finishes are shown here. All are appropriate to sheer fabrics.

Tucked Hem. For a crisp fabric (such as net or maline) where a narrow edge is desired, make a tuck slightly narrower than you want the finished edge to be—$\frac{1}{16}''$, $\frac{1}{8}''$, or $\frac{3}{8}''$. Make the tuck far enough away from the edge, so that you can fold it in to form a simulated binding, as shown. The tuck illustrated is a scant $\frac{1}{8}''$ wide; so it is made $\frac{3}{8}''$ from the edge. Catch the hem in place with small even-basting-stitches, as shown.

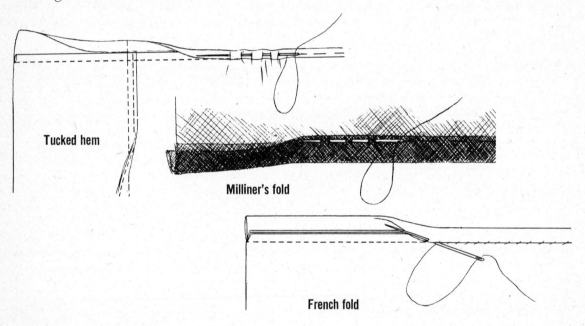

Tucked hem

Milliner's fold

French fold

Milliner's Fold. Decide how wide you want the fold in a net dress. A fold from $\frac{1}{4}''$ to $\frac{3}{8}''$ wide is about right for sleeve edges and for the lower edge of a long dress. Turn the net to the right side, a little less than twice the width desired for the finished fold. Make a second turn, the width of the fold, bringing the folded edge up to cover the raw edges. This will give you four thicknesses on the right side. From the wrong side, catch through three of these thicknesses, using an uneven-basting-stitch—and matching thread, of course. This will give a fold that serves as decoration and finish for the edge.

French Fold. A French fold is often used, especially in georgette. To make: Take a true-bias length of fabric, four times as wide as you want the finished fold. Fold the bias through the center. Stitch the raw edges to the edge of the garment on the right side, in a seam slightly narrower than the finished fold is to be. Whip the folded edge down over the stitching line on the wrong side, as shown.

The Slip. Use a pattern for a bias-cut slip. Check your bust and hip measurements and also the length. Adjust the slip pattern as you would a dress pattern, to have it correspond to your measurements, both in width and length.

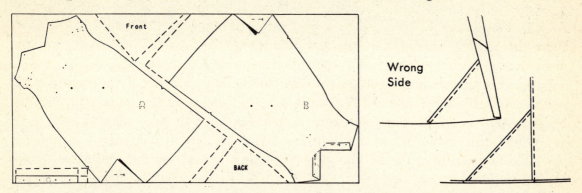

Make Daytime Slip. A shaped top is usually preferred for a sheer dress, as it gives a becoming bodice line, more protection, and a more comfortable garment. Open out the fabric. Place the pattern pieces on, as illustrated in the layout for a daytime slip. The shoulder straps and the bias for the fold that is to be fagoted to the top edge should be cut at this time. Note the piecing of the gores, which is done as in the bias-cut negligee. If the fabric has a plain selvage that is not tight, piece the gores on the selvage. If it is a wide selvage that might tighten, trim it away; and join the pieces in a narrow French seam.

Put in the bust darts at the front underarms. French-seam the underarm seams. Make a very narrow rolled hem at the top of the slip. (A rolled hem is also used at the bottom, after the length is determined. When a slip is made for a sheer dress, the length is decided when the dress is fitted.) Stitch the shoulder straps, and turn them right side out. Press.

Make Fagoted Edge. Join the pieces of bias, doing this with a diagonal joining. (See "Piecing Bias," page 10.) Turn the raw edges of the bias in toward the center, and press. Then fold again, so that you get a bias binding similar to a ready-made folded bias. For the fagoting, baste the bias folds together. Baste the top edge of

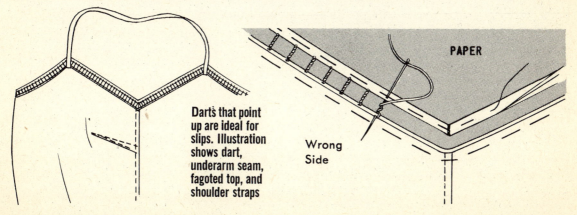

Darts that point up are ideal for slips. Illustration shows dart, underarm seam, fagoted top, and shoulder straps

the slip to a piece of wrapping paper. Baste the bias fold above this, with the open edge down, as shown. Place it from ¼″ to ⅜″ above, depending upon the open space desired for the fagoting-stitches. Fagot this bias to the slip, using a bar fagoting-stitch. To do this, place the needle in the top edge of the rolled hem of the slip; then bring it up to the bias, and catch through the two edges of the fold. Twist the needle around the bar that this makes, and bring the needle out just above the first stitch. Slip it inside the rolled hem for a distance of from ⅛″ to ⅜″, and repeat until you have secured the bias to the slip. Finish off the thread with several back-stitches. Join the bias neatly where it meets on the underarm. Pin the straps in position. Sew them securely in place after you have determined their correctness during the fitting of the dress. After the length has been determined, the rolled hem made at the bottom, and the straps sewed securely in place, press the slip to finish it.

Make Evening Slip. An evening slip differs from a daytime slip in that it is longer, often higher in the front and lower in the back, and usually has no trimming whatsoever. Determine how low you want your slip above the waistline in the back, and mark your pattern for this line. The line should be just high enough to cover your foundation garment—2″ reduction in the back is usually satisfactory. Lay the slip pattern on the dress pattern, and decide how much you should add at the bottom to make the slip the correct length for your dress. Chalk this out on your fabric, as indicated on the diagram for pattern changes and for placing pattern on the fabric. Join the bias pieces to the skirt. Put in the bust darts. Baste the side seams of the slip and fit it.

An evening slip should fit, not snugly, but should shape to the curves at the underarm. French-seam the underarm seams. Make and turn the shoulder straps. These may be wide or narrow, depending upon the width of your shoulder and the sheerness of your dress. Sometimes a slightly wider strap, say ⅝″, is more becoming to large figures than a strap that is too narrow, say from ¼″ to ⅜″. Rolled hems are used at top and bottom of the slip. The length should be determined when the dress is fitted; and the straps are pinned in position at that time and checked for length and comfort. In an evening slip, straps should be placed nearer the center-back, to help them to stay in position on the shoulders.

The Dress. (Illustration on page 97.) By this time you have determined the fabric you will use and the length your dress is to be. And, having read all the foregoing, you will have decided the seam, edge and hem finishes that you will use. Proceed then with the actual making of your dress.

Darts are seldom used in dresses of sheer fabric, because the dart lines show through and often distort the normal lines of the dress. That is why shirrings and tucks are preferred for shaping a sheer garment inside the pattern lines. When choosing a pattern for a dress of sheer fabric, always look under the recommended materials on the pattern envelope, to see if the designer has considered lines appropriate for sheer fabric.

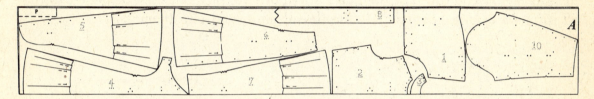

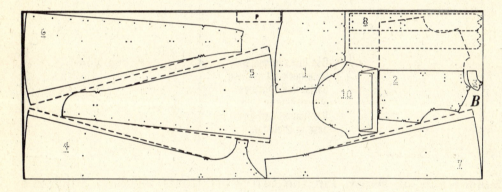

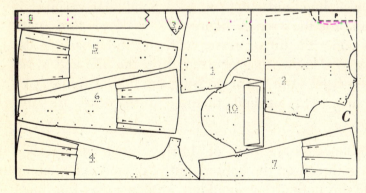

For a short dress with long sleeves, cut from fabric 35″ to 39″ wide. Fold fabric in center lengthwise. Turn pattern up at line of perforations indicating short length. Pin pattern pieces on, center-front and center-back of skirt and back waist on fold. Place other pieces on as in Layout **A**. Be sure to fold out of the way or cut away the center-front tie. Layout **B** shows double-width sheer net with width of skirt increased, indicated on layout by dash lines. Cut out all of dress except back waist and ties. Separate thicknesses and cut these as shown by dotted lines. Layout **C** shows how pattern for short-sleeved daytime length is placed on double-width net.

Make Cluster Tucks in Back Neck. In your Dress-Up Apron, on page 37, you used cluster tucks in place of darts. The same type of tuck is now used in the back neck of this sheer dress. This is to give ease through the shoulders and to prevent the dress from being too plain across the back. Some fulness in a sheer dress is always desirable. Since the tucks—three on each side of the center-back line—are used in this case more for fulness than for decoration, make them on the wrong side of the fabric. Crease on the chalk lines you marked through the perforations; and stitch a tuck on each crease, making it a scant ⅛″ deep and as long as the line of the perforations. The tucks should all be exactly the same length. To insure this, draw a chalk line on the fabric through the last of the perforations. Use this line as a guide in stitching. If you run past the line a stitch or two, pick out the extra ones, so that all rows are even to a stitch. Tie the thread ends, and clip them.

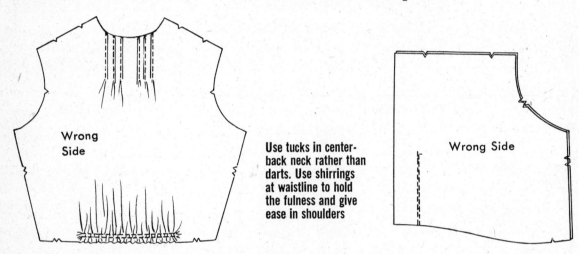

Wrong Side

Use tucks in center-back neck rather than darts. Use shirrings at waistline to hold the fulness and give ease in shoulders

Wrong Side

Seam the Center-Fronts of Waist. Pin the two waist fronts together. Stitch the center-front line. Begin at the waistline, and stitch up to a point that you feel is becoming—6″ above the waistline for the average figure, 6½″ to 7″ for those with prominent bust. Turn the fronts under the lifted presser foot, and stitch back on the first stitching line—doing this, as you know, to give strength to the line and avoid tying thread ends. Press the center-front seam open, pressing the fold of fabric back on each side up to the shoulder line. (The top ends of these "turn-backs" are later joined to the back neck facing.)

Make Group Shirrings. Mark the lines for the rows of shirring, either with crayon chalk or by creasing. With coarse thread on the bobbin, put in the rows of stitching that are to form the shirrings. Do this in the front shoulders, stitching over the "turn-back" of the center-front seam. Shirr the front and back at the waistline, and the tops of the sleeves. If you are using long sleeves, shirr them also at the elbow, as shown. Draw up the bobbin threads in preparation for the final adjustment in the seams; but do not clip the thread ends or tie the rows of shirrings until the seams are joined.

Baste Shoulder Seams. Lay the front and back together. Pin the shoulder seams, notches meeting, adjusting the top row of shirring by drawing it up until the front shoulder is from ⅝″ to ¾″ shorter than the back. Ease the back shoulder on. Remember, it should extend out ½″ (or width of neck seam) beyond the front edge at the neck, as shown, with the lines meeting exactly at armhole. When basting sheer fabrics, use short stitches to hold the seam true for fitting.

Think of seams as the supporting lines of your dress. This will help you to take care in cutting, basting, fitting, stitching, and finishing so that the seams are always true and even. If you take pains with seams, you will never slight the finishing of any garment.

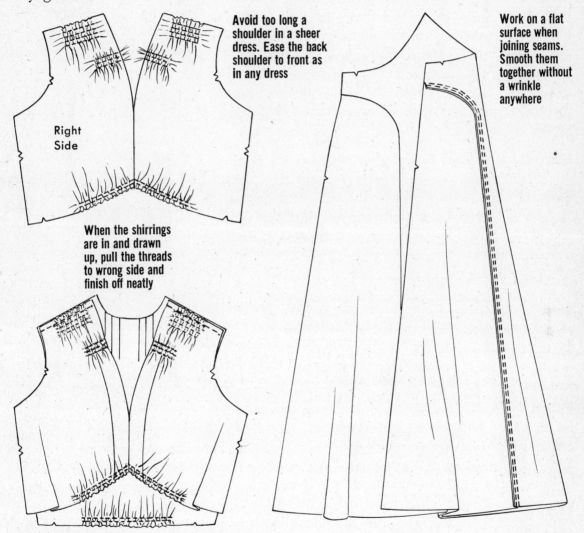

Right Side

Avoid too long a shoulder in a sheer dress. Ease the back shoulder to front as in any dress

Work on a flat surface when joining seams. Smooth them together without a wrinkle anywhere

When the shirrings are in and drawn up, pull the threads to wrong side and finish off neatly

Join Godet Gores to Center-Front Panel. This may be done in two ways: by top-stitching or by joining in a plain seam. For either, clip the seam allowance of the center-front panel around the curve so that it will lie flat when basted in place. If top-stitching is to be used, turn the edge to the wrong side the seam's width.

Baste it; then overlap the panel over the side-front gores. If top-stitching is not to be used, baste the panel to the gores in a plain seam, basting carefully around the curve so that it will lie perfectly flat. Always work on a flat surface when fitting any seam edges together, especially seams such as these, because both edges must be eased together so that neither can draw or full the least little bit.

Baste the Dress Together. When the godet gores are joined, baste the high waistline of the skirt to the front of the waist, basting this in the same manner as the skirt seams. Baste the back panel of the skirt to the side-back gores in the same way; then join to the back of the waist at the waistline. Baste the under-arm seams from the armhole down, waistlines meeting. Leave a 7″ placket opening at the left side. Determine what edge finish you will use for the bottom of the sleeves. Finish the sleeve edges. Stitch the underarm seams of the sleeves. Baste the sleeves in the armholes.

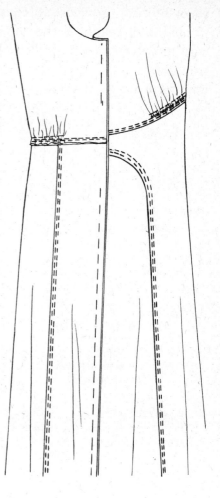

Make the Sash Ties. Fold the tie right side in. Begin at the fold, stitch around the point, and then continue the seam to the end. Clip the seam at the point, as shown. Press the seam, turn the ties right side out, and press again. Pin the ties to the waistline at each side of the dress.

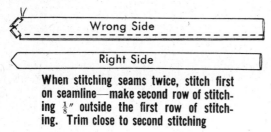

When stitching seams twice, stitch first on seamline—make second row of stitching $\frac{1}{8}$″ outside the first row of stitching. Trim close to second stitching

Fit the Dress. Put on the slip, which you have finished, except for the length. Put on the dress. Bring the sash ends together, and tie in a bow at the left side or at the center-back. Test the correctness of their location. The sash ties may be lifted or lowered as much as ½″ to give a longer or shorter waistline. Consider this in front of your mirror, and pin the ties as you desire them to be. Notice the shoulders. You can shorten them slightly by drawing up the shirring threads. Notice the sleeves. Do they set correctly? Mark for the skirt hem. It is a good idea to turn the hem (at least in front) to try for the most becoming length. A dress of sheer fabric should be made slightly longer than a dress of heavier fabric, because the heavy weight will make the dress appear longer than one made of very light-weight materials.

Remove the dress, so that you can mark the slip. Measure and make it slightly shorter than the dress—usually 1″ shorter. Remove the slip, finish the hem, attach the straps, and proceed to finish the dress. Clip the basting of the right underarm seam at the waistline. Open it just enough to slip the sash end inside, so that it will be caught in with the underarm stitching. Rebaste the seam.

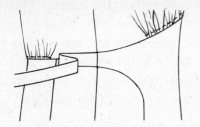
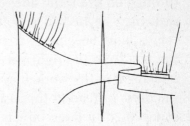

Tie-sash is sewn in seam of the right side of dress. Left side of dress shows tie-sash attached to front of dress inside placket strip

Stitch the seams—stitch the front and back panels of the skirt, the waistline, the shoulder, and the underarms, stitching above and below the placket opening on the left side. Stitch the sleeves in. If you are stitching the seams twice, place a second row of stitching ⅛″ outside the first in the seam allowance of each seam. Trim all seams up to within a scant ⅛″ of this second row of stitching. Lay the dress out on the table. Measure for the hem. Turn it evenly all the way around. If a hem is used as recommended for the short version, press the top edge; and clean-stitch it by hand, to hold the fulness in and to give you an edge in which to place the stitches. When the hem is slip-stitched in place, remove the hand-run clean-stitching thread if it shows through on the right side. If the fabric of the dress is very sheer, you may prefer to use a half feather-stitch to secure the hem rather than to slip-stitch it.

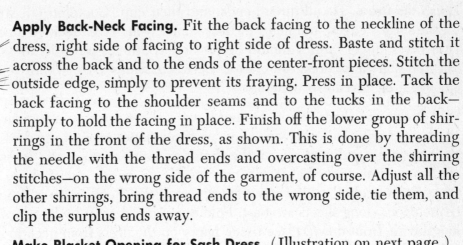

Apply Back-Neck Facing. Fit the back facing to the neckline of the dress, right side of facing to right side of dress. Baste and stitch it across the back and to the ends of the center-front pieces. Stitch the outside edge, simply to prevent its fraying. Press in place. Tack the back facing to the shoulder seams and to the tucks in the back—simply to hold the facing in place. Finish off the lower group of shir-rings in the front of the dress, as shown. This is done by threading the needle with the thread ends and overcasting over the shirring stitches—on the wrong side of the garment, of course. Adjust all the other shirrings, bring thread ends to the wrong side, tie them, and clip the surplus ends away.

Make Placket Opening for Sash Dress. (Illustration on next page.) A fitted waistline makes a placket necessary; but, in this case, the sash that is fastened to the front of the dress serves to hold the placket together and makes fasteners on the placket unnecessary. To make the placket, take two lengthwise strips of fabric, 8″ long and 2″ wide. Simply bind the seam allowance on each side of the placket, using a strip for each side.

Insert the end of one sash tie between the seam and the binding on the front edge, as shown; and catch it in with the stitching. To make this secure, turn and stitch back over it at least once. When the binding strips are in place, catch the ends together at top and bottom of placket. Use overcasting-stitches, so that none show through on the right side. (The sash on the opposite side is caught in the seam.) The sash may be tied in a bow at the center-back or on the left side—whichever you feel is most becoming. If you do not wish a bow, omit the tie at the left side; bring the one from the right side across the back, and hook it to the front of the left side, hooking it in the worked eyelets, as shown. Soft velvet ribbon ties may be sewn into the dress instead of the sash ties, and in the same way. They are decidedly effective, especially if a large bow is desired at the center-back.

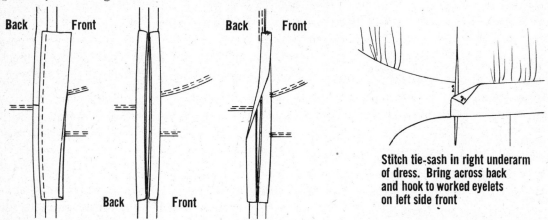

Stitch tie-sash in right underarm of dress. Bring across back and hook to worked eyelets on left side front

Finish the Dress. Tie all thread ends, and then clip. Complete all stitchings. Finish all the seams, edges, and hems in the manner you have decided upon. Then press your dress. Sheer fabrics should be pressed as little as possible. Press the seams, but not the shirrings. Press the fabric between seams only where it is necessary to smooth it or to remove wrinkles.

Fold Dresses of Sheer Fabric. Do not hang a sheer dress on a regular hanger. Cover the hanger with half a dozen sheets of tissue paper to hold the dress out enough so that it can not pull and sag on the shoulder seam; or place the dress in a large box or dresser drawer so that it can not wrinkle or stretch out of shape. To lay a dress away or to pack it so that it wrinkles very little: Begin with a generous supply of tissue paper—long sheets are best. Fold one-piece dresses by first spreading them out lengthwise, front down. Place tissue paper on the dress from neck to hem. Fold each side of the dress in toward the center, its full length, folding in accordance with the width of the box, suitcase, tray, or drawer in which it is to be placed. When the dress is folded, the sleeves will naturally lie almost diagonally across the body of the dress. Turn back long sleeves, keeping them smooth at the shoulder; and place so that the sleeves lie parallel to the edges of the dress, at sides. Next, fold the dress at a point a little below the waistline, bringing the neck of the dress toward the hem, and keeping your hand within the folding line to prevent the belt or any dress parts from slipping. If the dress, double folded, is still too long or too wide to fit into the container, fold at the bottom. Do not make an extra fold at neck or shoulders. Wrap a piece of tissue paper around the dress; and place it in its container, which you have lined with tissue.

If you are packing the dress in a wardrobe trunk, simply slip the upper part of the folded dress over the wardrobe hanger so that there is no danger of its falling off. Pin a tape around the dress just to prevent its slipping, and hang it in its place in the trunk.

Variations. This dress may have a long or short skirt and long or short sleeves. The front waist fulness may be shirred in or laid in folds. The skirt may be made more full or less full than the pattern specifies. It may have a wide or narrow flounce. If made of net, the skirt is attractive when finished with three ruffles arranged in tiers. The waist may be made of chiffon or lace; the skirt, of crepe or velvet. You may make a vestee to wear with the dress. The dress may have buttons and loops at the center-back opening; or it may be made without an opening, as this one is. The sash may be tied at the left side or at the center-back. It may be of self-fabric, or velvet, or ribbon, or even of organdie. Sheer dresses lend themselves to contrast in trimming —for example, piqué, velvet, and satin, being opaque, make ideal trimmings for sheer fabrics.

This dress can be as simple or as decorative as you desire. It gives excellent opportunity to express your individuality. Before you cut your dress, study the designs shown here. Consider which is best for you and which will help you to "Make the Most of Yourself." Now choose that interpretation, with its appropriate slip. Take time to make the dress and slip attractively—daintily, really, as sheer fabrics require delicate handling to have them emerge from the making without the appearance of having been handled overmuch.

Dressmaker Dress Ensemble

Materials. A dressmaker suit is unlined, and is usually made of cotton, linen, silk or rayon or very light-weight wool. It is soft in line and not obviously tailored; but, even so, tailoring is necessary to give it the trim, smartly-put-together look that such a suit requires.

Many silks and rayons have a spongy crepe effect to imitate wool. These are often used for dressmaker suits. Linen and gingham are also used satisfactorily, and are especially suitable for this dress and jacket.

A plastic slide fastener may be used at the center-front of the dress for an effective closing— but also quite as much for decoration. In pressing, take care not to touch the fastener with the iron, lest you damage the composition of which it is made.

A. Straighten Your Fabric. In a dressmaker suit— any garment of good material, in fact—it is imperative that the material be straight before you start to cut it. Fabric manufacturers really try to roll 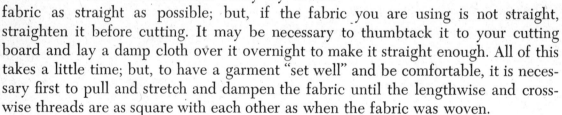 fabric as straight as possible; but, if the fabric you are using is not straight, straighten it before cutting. It may be necessary to thumbtack it to your cutting board and lay a damp cloth over it overnight to make it straight enough. All of this takes a little time; but, to have a garment "set well" and be comfortable, it is necessary first to pull and stretch and dampen the fabric until the lengthwise and crosswise threads are as square with each other as when the fabric was woven.

B. Check Your Pattern with Your Measurements. By this time you should know how much you need to shorten or lengthen your pattern—and where—to make it the correct length for you. Measure, and make any adjustments that you know are necessary so that your garments fit you perfectly. Have your pattern as near right for you as possible before you place it on your fabric.

C. Place Pattern on Fabric, and Cut Out Garments. For this dress, you use a long length of fabric. It is a good idea to place the front and back gores on, and see how much length you require to cut these. Sizes 12 and 14 will need the pattern length plus ⅛ yard; sizes 16, 18, and 20, the pattern length plus ¼ yard. For larger sizes measure for the front panel only. For all sizes tear or cut the required front length off from the long length of fabric and lay the pattern on this piece separately, simply for convenience in handling. Fold the remaining yards of the fabric, selvage edges together. Pin the crosswise ends together, then the selvages; and square both with your cutting board. For larger sizes place the pattern pieces farther apart, to allow enough width for the pieces. Measure from the fold or selvage to the large perforations, and line them up so that the lengthwise grain will be correct in each piece. The dash lines indicate bias neck facing for the dress and a belt.

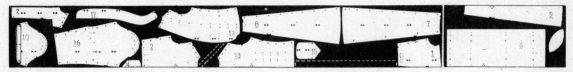

There are four practical ways to finish the front panel in the skirt of your dress: (1) Overlapping box plaits. (2) Knife plaits turned toward the center. (3) Plain center-front gore. (4) Shirred gore for center-front or center-back.

Join Side-Front Gores to Front Section. (1 and 2) If you are to have box or knife plaits in the front of the dress, baste and stitch the front gore in place between the side-front gores. (3) If you are using a plain gore without plaits: To avoid fulness in the front, simply cut a plain front gore, using the pattern piece for the center-back as your pattern; baste the gore in place in the front of the skirt in preparation for fitting; later—and only in this case—press the seams open. (4) If you are shirring the fulness, use elastic thread, if obtainable; and make five rows across the top part of the front gore—one on the waistline seam; the others, ⅞" apart. Wind the elastic sewing thread on the bobbin, and use matching thread on top.

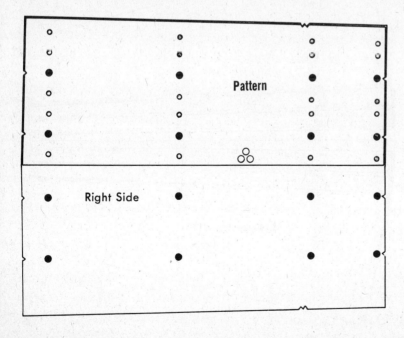

Pattern

Right Side

Make Box Plaits. Fold the front panel through the center, lengthwise, right side out. Place panel on the ironing board; and, with press cloth over it, press a center-front line. Pin the pattern piece on, and cut short notches at top and bottom in line with the large perforations. With a white piece of crayon chalk, mark each small perforation. With a colored piece, mark each large perforation. Remove the pattern, and turn the folded panel over; place the pattern on this half, and mark the perforations on it the same as before. To insure true lines in plaits, mark perforations carefully and take the time to measure and baste each plait its full length.

Fold the plaits on the line of white chalk marks, and bring them over to the colored marks. Keep the lines for the plaits as even as possible, pin, and baste. Baste the center-front plait first; then the two box plaits nearest you, as shown. You will find that the plaits overlap considerably at the waistline, as shown at **A**—to keep the lengthwise grain of the fabric correct in each plait, and yet to draw in the fulness in a way to get the right flare at the bottom of the skirt.

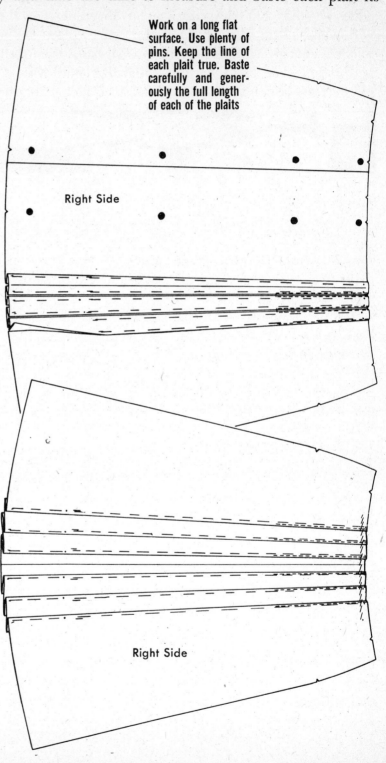

Work on a long flat surface. Use plenty of pins. Keep the line of each plait true. Baste carefully and generously the full length of each of the plaits

Right Side

Right Side

A

Knife Plaits. Mark the plaits the same as for box plaits. Fold them to panel the center, as shown. Bring the side gores over the front to form a plait at each side. This conceals the seam joining, which really becomes the inside edge of the last plait. In making knife plaits, you will find that the last plait at each side is ½″ narrower than the others. This difference is not important. Use short diagonal-basting across the top to hold the fulness securely.

Make Shirrings. For shirrings, mark your fabric for the number of rows desired. In this case, mark rows across the front gore of your skirt pattern which—when the shirrings are in—becomes the back gore in your dress. Place fabric right side up. Take a ruler and draw a delicate crayon line along the edge of ruler and across the top of the gore ⅜″ from the edge. Draw four or five lines below this, each about ¾″ apart. Use matching thread on top and size 24 white or black six-cord on the bobbin. Lengthen the machine-stitch and shirr the crayon-marked rows. Because this gore is wide and you need to shirr it into a narrow space, the long-stitch gathering is best. Draw up the bobbin threads to have them correspond to the width of the back gore. Place this gore in the back of your skirt and fit it just as though it were plain.

When shirrings are used in the skirt, shirr the tops of the sleeves, stitching through the lining and the dress fabric. Extend the rows of shirring 2″ beyond the dart lines on each side in the top of the sleeve.

Baste the Skirt for Fitting. Crease or baste a line down the center of the center-back gore. Lay the pieces of the skirt out on a table; ease the edges together; baste each seam, beginning at the waist and basting down. To allow for the placket opening, begin to baste the left skirt seam 3½″ down from the waist.

Turn the hem up on the wrong side, and pin it. Place the pins on the right side of the skirt, straight up and down, with the heads up. When the hem is turned, it is much easier to determine the becoming length if the pins are placed on the right side; for, while you are trying the skirt on, you can lift your skirt yourself and true up the hemline as required.

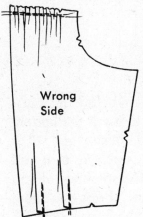

Wrong
Side

Gather Top of Side Waist Sections. Darts are used almost exclusively in fitting this dress. The only gathers are across the top of the side-front sections. Make two rows of fine machine gathers from the notch in to the front edge—one row on the seam line; one, ¼″ above. Later, these threads are to be drawn up to fit the yoke section of the blouse and these thread ends tied.

Make Fulness Tucks. There are eight fulness tucks on the blouse portion—two on each side of the back, two on each side of the front. These tucks are made on the inside, to give a trim waistline and yet give ease through the blouse part of the garment. Pin and baste the tucks at the waistline, basting the depth indicated in the pattern. If you are short-waisted, make each tuck ½″ shorter. To avoid tying thread ends, stitch the tuck from the waist up the desired distance; turn and stitch back. Baste and stitch neck darts in both dress and jacket backs.

Make Tailored Corners. Tailored corners are used to enable you to square a corner perfectly; also, to give strength to the corner and prevent fraying. They are ever so simple once you understand them. There are two corners to tailor. These come at the corners of front shoulder yoke and the front of the dress, as indicated by the arrow.

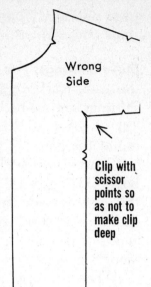

For the stay pieces, take two tiny selvage pieces 2″ long and 1″ wide. Clip the corner in diagonally, as at **B**—¹⁄₁₆″ less than the seam allowance. Open up this little clip, and stitch the selvage edge of one of the little stay pieces to it. Make the seam ¹⁄₈″ wide at the ends, but only ¹⁄₁₆″ at the inside point of the clip, as at **C**. To insure flatness at the tailored corner, notch the applied piece, as at **D**. Press the stay piece back in place. Turn the edge of the yoke and side of the front to the wrong side ³⁄₈″, and baste. Trim away the corners, as at **E**.

Wrong Side

Clip with scissor points so as not to make clip deep

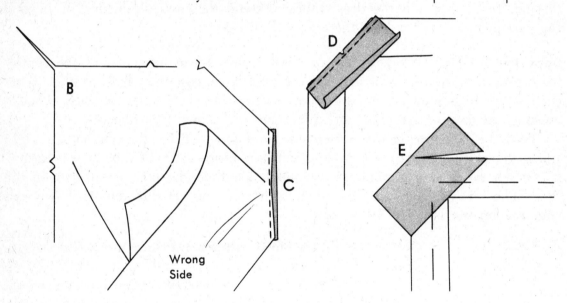

Apply Plastic Slide Fastener. Measure ½″ down from the neck edge on the center-front of your dress, and place a pin at this point. Lay the fastener—below this pin—along the center-front edge, place a pin in the edge of the dress to mark the bottom of the plastic part of the fastener, and then lay the fastener aside. Baste, and stitch the center-front pieces together. Begin 2″ below the second pin; stitch up to it and then down to the waistline, making a ³⁄₈″ seam. At the top of the stitching, clip in a diagonal line exactly ½″—that is, ¹⁄₈″ beyond the stitching line. Press the seam open. Turn the edges of the front (above the stitched seam) to the wrong side ½″. Baste in a true line. Lay the fastener under the opening, right side up. Baste it precisely in position. Put the cording foot on your machine, and stitch along the sides and across the bottom of the fastener. Pivot at the corners. Do all with the

[114]

same care that you applied the enamel fastener to the Princess Frock, and remember when necessary to lift the presser foot and move the slider out of your way as you stitch. Turn to the wrong side; and stitch the fastener tape to the seam allowance, stitching twice down each side so that the fabric will not fray.

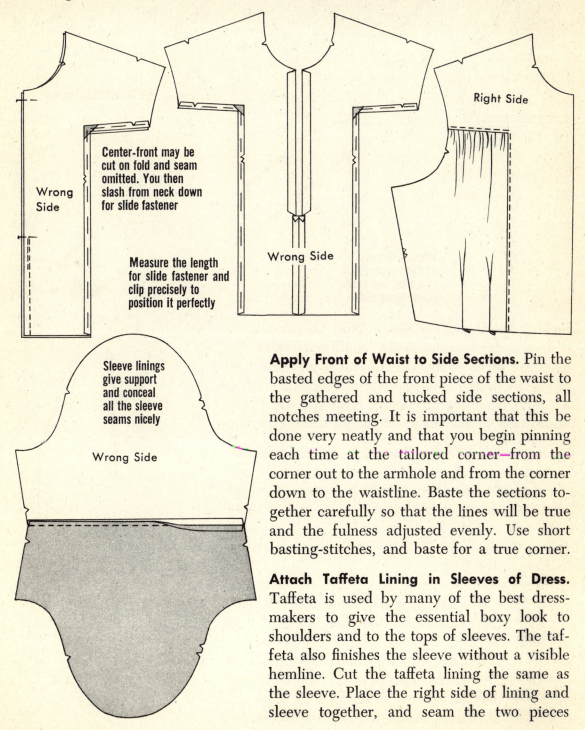

Wrong Side

Center-front may be cut on fold and seam omitted. You then slash from neck down for slide fastener

Measure the length for slide fastener and clip precisely to position it perfectly

Wrong Side

Right Side

Sleeve linings give support and conceal all the sleeve seams nicely

Wrong Side

Apply Front of Waist to Side Sections. Pin the basted edges of the front piece of the waist to the gathered and tucked side sections, all notches meeting. It is important that this be done very neatly and that you begin pinning each time at the tailored corner—from the corner out to the armhole and from the corner down to the waistline. Baste the sections together carefully so that the lines will be true and the fulness adjusted evenly. Use short basting-stitches, and baste for a true corner.

Attach Taffeta Lining in Sleeves of Dress. Taffeta is used by many of the best dressmakers to give the essential boxy look to shoulders and to the tops of sleeves. The taffeta also finishes the sleeve without a visible hemline. Cut the taffeta lining the same as the sleeve. Place the right side of lining and sleeve together, and seam the two pieces

[115]

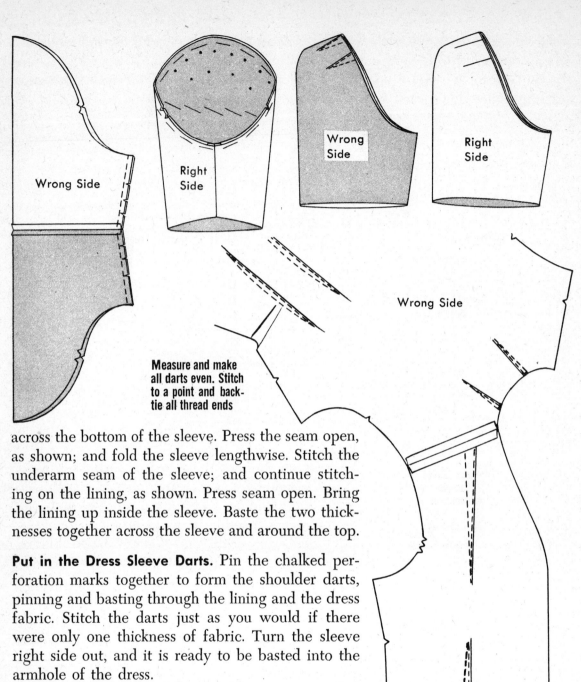

Wrong Side

Right Side

Wrong Side

Right Side

Measure and make all darts even. Stitch to a point and back-tie all thread ends

Wrong Side

across the bottom of the sleeve. Press the seam open, as shown; and fold the sleeve lengthwise. Stitch the underarm seam of the sleeve; and continue stitching on the lining, as shown. Press seam open. Bring the lining up inside the sleeve. Baste the two thicknesses together across the sleeve and around the top.

Put in the Dress Sleeve Darts. Pin the chalked perforation marks together to form the shoulder darts, pinning and basting through the lining and the dress fabric. Stitch the darts just as you would if there were only one thickness of fabric. Turn the sleeve right side out, and it is ready to be basted into the armhole of the dress.

Baste shoulder seams and underarm seams of dress. Place the front shoulder seam over the back shoulder seam, right sides together, neckline and armhole lines true. Pin and baste together, stretching the front shoulder slightly and easing the fulness of the back shoulders into place. Use short basting-stitches so that the fulness can not plait in when you stitch the shoulders. Baste the underarm seams—

basting, of course, from the armhole down. On the left seam, end the basting within 3½″ of the waistline to allow for the placket opening.

Join waist and skirt of dress. Turn the skirt wrong side out. Place the waist of the dress inside the skirt—right sides together. Pin the waistlines together, all notches meeting. Baste. Hang the dress up, ready for fitting.

Put Shoulder and Body Darts in Jacket. (Illustration on opposite page.) Lay out the back and front sections of the jacket on the table—wrong side up. To form the darts, bring together the markings made for the perforations. Pin them all as evenly as possible, baste, and stitch them. Cut away the lower part of the front body dart, as shown, to avoid bulk later under the hem.

Baste shoulder seams and underarm seams of jacket. Baste these seams with the same care as you did those in the dress, especially the shoulder seams. Turn the hem at the bottom of the jacket. Pin it up so that you can better judge the becomingness of the length later on when you fit the jacket.

Consider the Pockets. The pattern calls for three pockets. If you are large in the bust, omit the breast pocket. If you are large in the waist, use either welt or bound pockets at the waistline (see pages 28 and 29) instead of flap pockets.

Make Flap Pockets. If you are using flap pockets (as the pattern calls for), lay the flap facing over the taffeta, as shown at **F**. Stitch, making a ¼″ seam. Turn the facing to position and press, thus concealing the stitching line. Place the right side of the fabric over this, and baste the pocket and the lining together. Stitch, beginning at **G** and continuing down one side and around the curved bottom line to **H**. One side is left open from **G** to **H** so that the pocket may be turned right side out. After the stitching, clip the corners away. Notch the curved edge to avoid bulk. Turn the pocket right side out, and slip-stitch the open side together. Stitch the flap, stitching ¼″ from the edge; and continue the stitching all around the edge of the pocket. Pivot on the needle at each point to make a nice turn. (This is the way Schiaparelli made pockets. A long back-stitch is used on the wrong side to attach the pockets to the garment.)

Pin the pockets in position on the jacket in preparation for fitting, putting a pin at each side of the top so that, if necessary, you can quickly change the location of the pockets to a more becoming one when you fit the jacket.

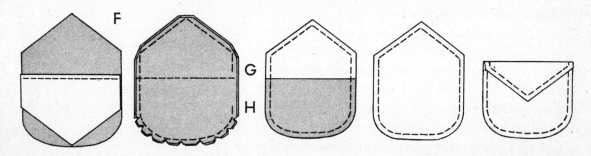

Wrong Side

Right Side

Make the Shoulder Pads. These are really shoulder rolls. Fold them lengthwise, jacket fabric inside, lining outside. Stitch across the ends, as shown. Clip the corners. Turn right side out. Pad with strips of cotton batting slipped inside. Slip-stitch the open seam edges together.

Put in Elbow Darts, and Baste Long Sleeves. The pattern calls for one deep dart at the elbow; but, in making the dress, we found that to divide the large dart into two darts distributed the fulness better. Therefore, mark your sleeves for the one large dart, and use this to place your two ¼″ darts. Use the top dart line for the basting line of one dart, and the bottom dart line as your guide in basting the second. Stitch these darts to a point and back again, just as you did the hip darts in your aprons and the back-neck darts in your dress. Baste and stitch the darts in the top of the sleeve, making them slightly deeper than required by the pattern. Baste the underarm sleeve seam. Do this on your cutting board or table, so that both sides of the seam meet exactly at the armhole and wrist, with any fulness in the back eased in.

Wrong Side

Baste sleeves in. Turn the basted sleeves right side out. Pin the sleeves in the armholes, notches meeting. Hold the jacket on your hands to test the sleeves, as explained on page 47. Your eye will tell you if they hang correctly from the shoulder. Moving a sleeve forward or backward ¼″ in the armhole makes a great deal of difference in the way it hangs. When you are sure the sleeves are correct, baste in position, using short even-basting-stitches. Turn the hem allowance at the bottom and pin, placing the pins on the right side of the sleeve so that it will be easy to adjust the length during the fitting. Pin the shoulder pads in place across the top of the armhole seams.

Fit the Dress. Put on the foundation garments you will wear with this suit. Put on shoes with heels of the height you will wear. Put some face powder on—and lip rouge if you use it. Put on your dress and stand in front of a mirror, with your pin box handy. First, be sure that your dress is on your body straight, with the armhole seams turned in toward the dress. Close the slide fastener. Close the placket opening, and pin it. Now, consider the fit across and over the shoulders. Could the darts at the back neck be slightly deeper? Do the shoulders fit smoothly and without wrinkle? If your neck muscles are large (indicated by a comparatively large neck measurement), you may find it advisable to open the shoulder seams slightly at the neck to ease the garment there and allow it to fit down on your shoulders as it should. If your shoulders slant, use a shoulder pad in the dress as well as in the jacket. Notice the underarm seams. Does the blouse seem too full or too scant? Should you stitch inside or outside the basting lines? Sometimes plaits pull a blouse down at the waistline. For this reason, a fairly snug waistline and hipline are desirable, as they serve to hold the plaits in position and prevent dragging down.

Determine the skirt length. Even though you have pinned your skirt hem in position, mark a line with your skirt marker—to check for an even length. Remember not to make your skirt too long. Wear your skirts as short as becomingness allows, especially in a trimly fitted suit such as this.

Fit the Jacket. When you have adjusted and pinned your dress and are satisfied that, in stitching, you can perfect its fit to your satisfaction, slip your jacket on. Square it at the shoulders. (When you have shoulder pads, it is necessary to straighten them nicely over the dress sleeves each time you put your jacket on.) Lap the center-front line as it should be for an easy fit. Any alterations you have made in the shoulders of your dress will need to be made also in the jacket. Notice the length of the shoulders, the fit of the underarm, the elbow fulness of the long sleeves. Bend your arms up toward your chest, and check the sleeve length. A long sleeve will shorten from ½″ to ¾″ in wearing, so do not make it too short. Notice the length of the jacket. The usual length of suit jackets is to the hip bone or slightly below. If a longer length is more becoming to you, you can lengthen the jacket as much as the hem and then face it. You can shorten the jacket as much as is practical without giving it a bobbed look. After the jacket length is decided, consider the flap pockets and their location—for becomingness to you. Do not hesitate to unpin the pockets and lift or lower them until you find their best location. Be sure that the grain of the fabric in pockets and jacket agree.

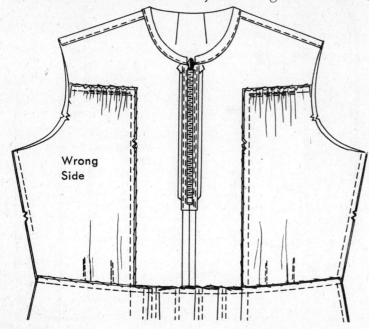

Wrong Side

Remove the jacket and the dress. If necessary, baste any adjustments you have made in fitting, so that you will surely perfect them in the stitching.

Remove the jacket sleeves, and open the underarm seams.

Stitch the body seams. Stitch the shoulder seams of both the dress and the jacket;

then clean-stitch. Stitch the waistline; also, the underarm seams of the dress. Overcast the waistline.

Apply a 1″ wide clean-stitched bias facing to the neck edge of the dress; catch the ends down over the slide fastener tape at the top of the center-front, as shown.

Apply the Placket Strips. Because you are using a slide fastener that opens the dress low in the front, a 6″ or 7″ placket at the left side is long enough. This you can close easily with two snaps and a hook and eye at the waistline. To finish the placket, cut a selvage strip of taffeta 1″ longer than the placket opening and 1¼″ wide. Stitch the raw edge of this to the placket edge at the back of the dress, on the right side of the fabric. Cut a second strip of taffeta the same length and 1″ wide. Stitch this to the placket edge at the front of the dress on the right side of the fabric, as shown. Turn each strip over to form a binding for the seam edge. Baste, and stitch along the bound edge, as shown. The surplus width in the strips serves to stay the placket and to give firmness for the stitches that hold the snaps. Baste the strips in place so as to hold them until the fasteners secure them permanently. Tack the

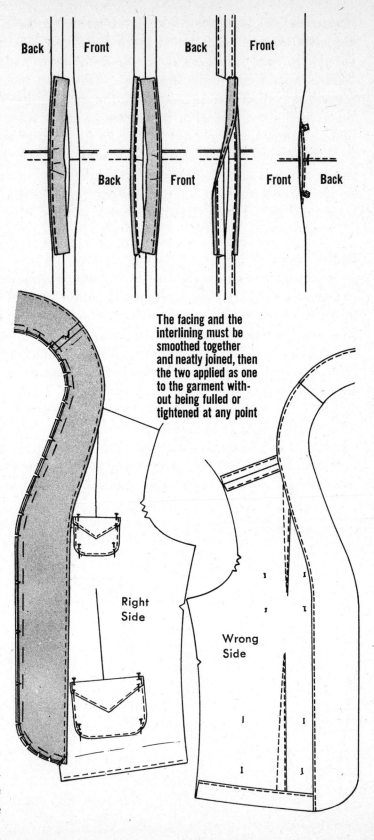

The facing and the interlining must be smoothed together and neatly joined, then the two applied as one to the garment without being fulled or tightened at any point

bound edge of 'the front of the placket seam to the waistline seam. This gives a short, soft, flat, inconspicuous placket that is easy to make.

Apply Front Facing to the Jacket. Seam the front facing pieces at the center-back. Press the seam open. Lap the interlining pieces on the seam line, as shown; and stitch. Lay the interlining over the right side of the facing piece, smooth, and pin carefully. Stitch on the outside edge, making a ¼" seam. Turn right side out, baste on the turned edge, and stitch ¼" in from the edge. Lay the facing along the front edges of the jacket, right sides together. Smooth out flat, pin, and baste all around the edge. Stitch ⅜" in from the edge. Remove all bastings. Notch the seam, as shown, about every 1" on the curves and about every 3" on the center-front line. Press the seam open. Turn the facing to the wrong side. Baste—first on the edge, then half the facing width in from the edge. Catch the stitched edge with tacking-stitches to hold the facing in place, tacking it to the back-neck darts and the shoulder seams. At the bottom of the jacket, slip the hem under the facing; and whip the joining.

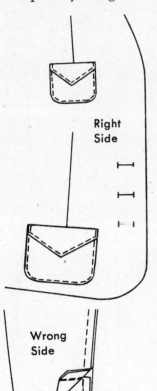

Right Side

Wrong Side

Make Bound Buttonholes. Make three crosswise buttonholes. Cut them ½" longer than the diameter of the button. If you have not made bound buttonholes our way, turn to page 25. In a suit as nice as this, you must make the bound buttonholes as skillfully as possible; so you should take some scraps of firm fabric and practice making two or three buttonholes so that you know how carefully they must be measured—how precise you must be in the cutting, stitching, and finishing.

Complete the stitching. Baste and stitch the underarm seams, and clean-stitch them. Turn the edge of the hem under, clean-stitch it, and slip-stitch it in place

Finish the Jacket Sleeves at the Bottom. Turn the hem to the right side, and clean-stitch the hem edge. Stitch through the hem on each side of the sleeve seam. Clip the seam corners, turn the hem to the wrong side, and slip-stitch it down. Stitch the sleeve seams, stitching down to the top of the hem. Turn and stitch back a few inches on the seam so that it will not rip out. Clean-stitch or overcast the seam.

Baste the sleeves in your jacket. Bind the armhole seams, clipping the seam first, the same as you did in your bolero on page 86.

Clean-stitch the underarm seams of your dress. Overcast the seams of the back gore and the side-front gores—their ⅜" width will not permit their being clean-stitched.

Even the hem. Clean-stitch the edge, baste it, and slip-stitch in place. Rebaste the plaits that you necessarily have opened up in the hem so that you can press them finally and perfectly in place. Complete the stitching wherever necessary. Take any slip-stitches or tacking-stitches that are required. Clip any thread ends. Remove all bastings. Press both the dress and the jacket.

Mark and Place the Fasteners on the Placket. Lap the placket seam precisely, and pin securely. Turn the dress to the wrong side. With chalk, mark the location of the three fasteners ⅜" in from the seam line—the hook and straight eye at the waistline; the snaps 2½" above the waistline and 2½" below. Sew these in place, as shown on page 27.

Prepare and Make the Collar. The collar has rounded corners, Peter Pan style. Two types of collars are practical for this dress—one, a fagoted collar, the other cut from two thicknesses of piqué. Stitch these together from wrong side, as shown. Notch the curved edge. Turn right side out and top-stitch outside edge. Bind inside edge.

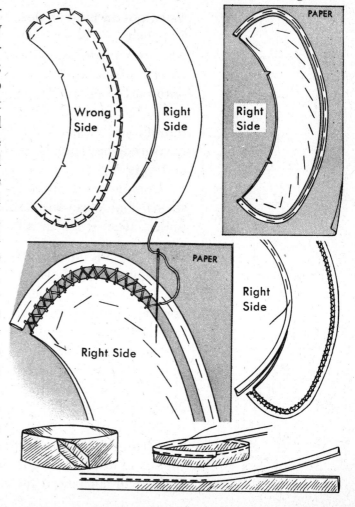

To make the Peter Pan fagoted collar, as shown: Trim away the seam allowance on the outside edge of the collar pattern; then use pattern to cut two thicknesses of piqué. Place right sides together; and stitch around the outside, a scant ¼" from the edge. Turn right side out, and press. Baste the collar to a piece of firm wrapping paper; and around it, ¼" from the edge, baste a piece of No. 5 bias fold binding. Catch this binding to the collar with fagoting-stitches, as shown. (The enlarged diagram shows how the stitches are placed close together and how they cross from the binding to the collar to hold both edges securely.)

When the fagoting is complete, bind the neck edge of the collar with bias; and turn the ends of the binding neatly over the fagoted bias.

Make and Apply Washable Pipings. Often with a dress of this kind, especially one having a removable collar, piping of the same fabric as the collar is desirable for the sleeves. To make these: Cut a true bias of the collar fabric, 1½″ wide. Measure the bottom of the sleeve; and join the piping strip on the bias, as shown, so that it will measure about ⅛″ less than the width of the sleeve at the bottom. Fold the bias through the center; and bind the top edge, taking off less than ¼″ from the width of the fold. Turn one end of the bias under where it meets, to make a neat overlap. Pin these bands in the sleeves, with ⅛″ showing below the edge. With basting-stitches, catch the bias binding to the sleeve lining or hem. Such pipings are easy to remove for washing and to replace afterward; and they not only give a finish to a sleeve or a neck edge, but serve also to keep it clean. Illustrated also is a long strip of bias appropriate as a piping for a V neck or for the neckline of a tailored suit.

If you wish belt of self-fabric, place strip of lengthwise interlining over one half of belt as explained on page 82. Stitch in straight lines or in points as shown. Finish ends of belt and close with a slide, or hooks and eyes and snaps.

Variations. Many variations are possible with this type of dressmaker suit. One is to use a print fabric for the dress and a plain light or dark fabric for the jacket. The jacket may be made with short sleeves. If you like, you may use buttons and button-holes instead of slide fastener.

To hold the fulness in the side section of the waist, pin tucks may be used on the wrong side rather than gathers. A slide fastener that extends to the waistline may be used. Both styles of collars are shown here. Choose the one that you feel is most becoming to you. If you are in doubt, cut both collars from muslin; and try them on when you fit your dress. We also show the piqué bolero worn with this dress. The plain front shown is made by using the back gore of the skirt as a pattern to cut the front as well as the back section of the skirt. Don't overlook the possibility of reversing the position of the front and back gores of your skirt, so that the elastic shirring gives fulness in the back. Because of the tucks at the waistline, a narrow or fairly narrow belt is best.

Dinner Ensemble

Materials. For a really nice ensemble such as this—whether made for evening or daytime wear—use fabrics of especially good quality with enough body to hold in shape and even enough in weave to give satisfaction in wearing. Choose a conservative color; as you will wear such garments many times. They make an ideal background for white or colorful accessories.

If you make the sleeves short, you will need enough taffeta or light-weight muslin to line them —⅓ of a yard—enough taffeta to make the triangular-shaped shoulder pads, and cotton batting for padding.

If you make the short version of the dress and use allover lace for the waist part, you will require a length of 39″ fabric equal to your measurements—over your shoulder from waistline in front to waistline in back, which will be from ⅞ to 1⅛ yards—with ½ yard added to this measurement if you are making long dress sleeves.

The top for the dress may be made of lace, velvet, satin, or taffeta, as you prefer. Lace is appropriate for dress-up wear, and it is in keeping with the silhouette lines of the ensemble. Some like the blouse top even when the skirt is long.

A. Straighten Your Fabric. The most important part of handling fabric, cutting, fitting, and sewing is to have the warp and woof straight, exactly at right angles to each other. This straightening must be done before you begin to place the pattern pieces on the fabric. Remember, no matter what you sew, straighten the fabric first. Cut on a thread when practical. Learn to have definite respect for fabric grains—lengthwise, crosswise, and true bias.

B. Check Your Pattern with Your Measurements. Choose a classic style. One that will be smartly wearable for several years. If you feel it advisable, cut a muslin bodice (or waist, whichever you are making) and jacket. Fit these to your figure, and then cut out the fabric from this muslin guide pattern. Now that skill in construction is yours, concentrate on greater perfection in fitting. A classic ensemble, such as this is, depends for much of its beauty and gracefulness upon the way it fits you through the body—especially around the hips and waist and in the shoulders. Just the right fit will insure a skirt that hangs trimly, one that will fall nicely no matter whether you are sitting or standing. Well-fitting shoulders and sleeves in a jacket are as essential to smartness as comfort in wearing.

C. Place Pattern on Fabric, and Cut Out Garments. When you know that your pattern is adjusted right for your measurements, take a piece of tissue paper and cut a duplicate of the front piece of the jacket and also of the back of the peplum. If you are making the bodice, cut duplicate patterns of the front and back, as there are to be two thicknesses throughout. By this time, you have decided whether you will make a long or short skirt and long or short sleeves. If you are making the long dress, fold the pattern back a seam's width inside the selvage. Cut a tissue of this folded-back section, and use it as a pattern piece for the small gore, **A.**

Adjust your patterns to the lengths you prefer. See how these pattern pieces are arranged on the fabric in the layouts. Two are given—one for the formal dress and short-sleeved jacket; one for the short dress with a blouse top and long-sleeved jacket. (The first layout is shown above and the second layout is shown on page 135.) The blouse (front, back, and sleeve) is illustrated laid out on lace. For this dress, the pattern should be turned back above the waistline at a point in keeping with the high waistline in the skirt. Fold the lower edge in on the front of the pattern, as shown; and slash the lower edge of the back, as shown—so that both will lie flat when in place on the fabric. The dotted lines show: (1) where the back-neck facing is cut—use the top of your back waist pattern for this; (2) where a true bias facing 2¼″ wide is cut for the short sleeves.

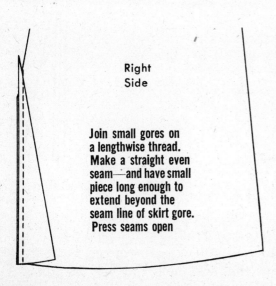

Right
Side

Join small gores on a lengthwise thread. Make a straight even seam—and have small piece long enough to extend beyond the seam line of skirt gore. Press seams open

FORMAL DINNER DRESS

Piece Gores at Center-Back. In using any material, it is necessary to know when it is practical to piece it and how to make an inconspicuous joining. You learned on page 53 how to piece the bottom of gores to make them wide enough. That is what you do first in making this long skirt. Join the two piecing gores to the bottom of the back skirt gores in a plain seam. Press the seams open. Overcast the raw edges.

Baste the Center-Back Seam, then Stitch. Begin at the top, and baste the center-back seam. Measure down from the top of the seam the length of the placket fastener plus the waistline seam allowance—½″ in this case. Place a pin at this point. Begin at the pin, and stitch from there down. Clip the surplus seam ends at the top of the pieced gores. Clip the seam, press it open its full length, and overcast the raw edges. The reason for overcasting the raw edges rather than clean-stitching is that no seam-line marks should show on a dress of this kind, just as no top-stitching shows. If you are using a fabric that does not fray readily or curl on the edge, then you may save time by cutting the dress with pinking shears. Overcast seams are safe in any case; and, with only three seams in the skirt, they may be done very quickly.

Apply Slide Fastener to Center-Back Placket Opening. A simplified placket is best for a center-back opening such as this. Simply place the skirt placket fastener the seam allowance down from the top of the skirt—½″ in this case—right side of fastener to wrong side of skirt, and the metal line precisely over the seam line. Pin in place; then baste with large catch-stitches from the wrong side. Attach the cording foot to your machine; and stitch the fastener in place, stitching on the right side of the fabric. Stitch down one side of the fastener; pivot on the needle at the end, and stitch across the end; pivot, and stitch up the side. Remove the basting, and the fastener will be securely in place.

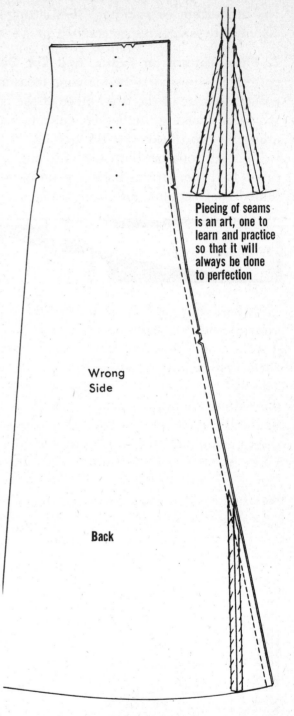

Piecing of seams is an art, one to learn and practice so that it will always be done to perfection

Wrong Side

Back

Baste the Body Darts and the Side Seams in the Skirt. Pin the body darts in both the front and the back gores evenly and smoothly. If your waist measurement is large in proportion to your bust and hips, baste the darts slightly narrower than the pattern indicates. If your waist is small in proportion to your other measurements, baste the darts slightly deeper. Use short basting-stitches that will hold the line in fitting.

Place the front and back, side seams together. Lay the gores flat on your cutting board, and ease the seam lines together without stretching or pulling. Baste, beginning at the top. As the skirt is now ready for fitting, fold it carefully across the top; place it in a trouser hanger; and hang it up so that the lower edge can sag (if it is inclined to) while you make the bodice.

This bodice is double, the purpose of the double section being to give firmness across the top and, consequently, a trim, smooth line. This is an important factor in all formal dresses. The bodice must have enough body to set without a wrinkle and never be so thin as to look like a slip. If crepe is used, make the inside of the bodice of the same fabric as the outside. If velvet is used, make the inside of sheer fabric.

Baste, Stitch, and Press Darts in Front of Bodice. The bust darts in the bodice are short. If you wear an uplift foundation or brassière, it is safe to baste and stitch them. Otherwise, baste in preparation for fitting. When these darts are stitched, they should be stitched twice, up and back on the same stitching line—to give a firm seam, to make overcasting of the seam unnecessary, and to provide strength enough so that you can cut the darts open to within 1″ of the top. The darts can then be pressed very flat, as shown.

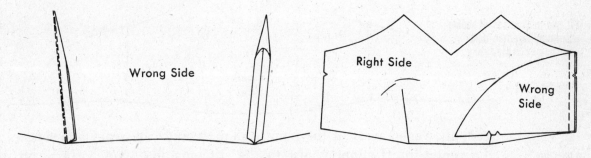

Join Underarm Seams of Fronts and Backs. You have two thicknesses of bodice cut exactly alike. Baste the back and front of each of the underarm seams in preparation for fitting. Pin one of these around you. Make sure that the back pieces meet at the center-back and that there is just enough fulness in the body so that it "sets" easily on your figure. Stitch the underarm seams. Clip them, and snip the ends away to avoid bulk. Press the seams open.

Join the Two Thicknesses of the Bodice, and Stay the Edge. (Illustration on next page.) Lay the two thicknesses of the bodice flat on your table, right sides together. Beginning at the point in the center-front, pin the edges together across the top, as shown. Measure this top edge to find the amount of seam binding required to form a stay to prevent the edge from stretching out of shape. Take the seam binding—half of the measurement—and cut it lengthwise through the center. Baste this to the top seam line of the bodice, as shown. Baste in a true line. Turn the corners nicely. Stitch across the top of the bodice, stitching directly through the center of the half width of seam binding.

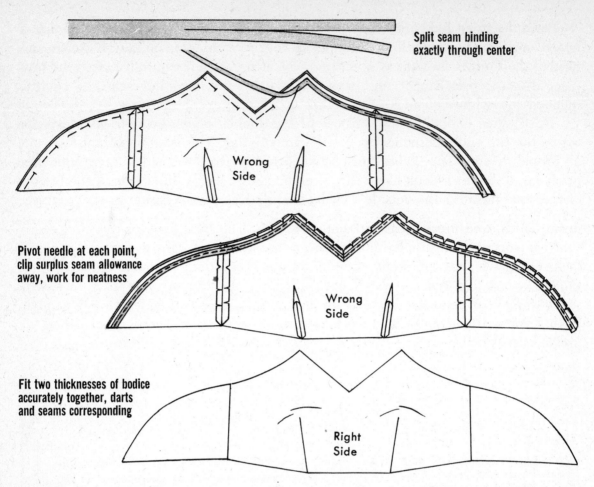

Split seam binding
exactly through center

Wrong
Side

Pivot needle at each point,
clip surplus seam allowance
away, work for neatness

Wrong
Side

Fit two thicknesses of bodice
accurately together, darts
and seams corresponding

Right
Side

Clip the seam allowance away at the points. Clip through the seam allowance precisely in the center-front, clipping just to the stitching line. Notch the seam allowance all the way from center-back to center-back. Press the seam open, using a sleeve board or padded milk bottle. Turn bodice right side out. Press with great care, always pressing down from the top. When the bodice is turned, you should have three true points, as shown—two up, and the center one down. The curves at the back must be true and line up perfectly, one with the other.

Make the Straps. Do you remember how you made the neck strap in your first apron? Well, you make these shoulder straps in the same way. Turn right sides together. Stitch the full length of each strap. Clip the seam. Move the seam to the center of the strap, as shown. Press the seam open. Stitch across one end. Turn the straps right side out and press again. Look at your bodice pattern, note location for the straps in the back, and pin one end of each strap in position in preparation for fitting.

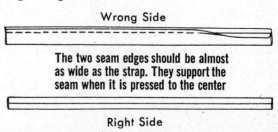

Wrong Side

The two seam edges should be almost as wide as the strap. They support the seam when it is pressed to the center

Right Side

Baste Bodice and Skirt Together. Beginning at the center-front, pin the bodice to the skirt, as shown, leaving the lining free; then baste. (Side seams of bodice and skirt should meet. Top of the front body darts should be in line with the dart lines in the bodice.) Do this work on a flat surface so that the joining will be smooth and without a wrinkle. Bring the free edge of the inside of the bodice down over the seam; baste to hold it in position for fitting.

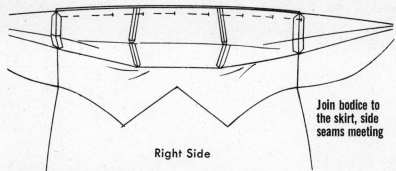

Join bodice to the skirt, side seams meeting

Right Side

Fit the Formal Dress. Put on shoes that have heels of the height you will wear with this dress. Put on your best foundation garments. (No slip should be worn with a dress of this kind. A long petticoat cut from the same pattern, but slightly narrower, is ideal.) Put the dress on. Close the slide fastener. Adjust the dress on your figure. Make sure that it is straight at center-front and center-back. Smooth the skirt and bodice around the body so that not a wrinkle is visible. Bring the free ends of the shoulder straps over the front. Pin them directly under the points in the front of the bodice—straight, secure, and exactly the right length.

Determine the length you want your dress to be. Some who wish to look as tall as possible make the skirt a scant half inch from the floor. Some who dance a great deal turn theirs from one to two inches above the floor. Others make the skirt ankle length. Consider fashion's dictates and how you will wear your dress; then make the length one that you know is practical as well as becoming. When the length has been determined, remove the dress. Take out the bastings that hold the lining of the bodice in place. With crayon, mark the location of the straps and their lengths. Remove the straps until all stitching is complete.

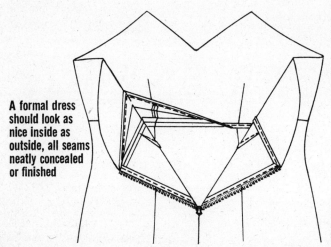

A formal dress should look as nice inside as outside, all seams neatly concealed or finished

Complete All Stitching. Stitch the body darts in the skirt. Stitch the side seams. Stitch the skirt and bodice together, clip the seam, and press it open. Stitch seam binding to the bottom of the bodice.

Slip the tape ends of the slide fastener up inside the bodice. Bring the seam binding over; and catch it to the fastener tape on each side to make a neat, secure finish. Slip-stitch the binding over the bodice seam.

Finish the Seams and Hem. Overcast the side seams in the skirt. Turn and crease the hem. Even it by making the hem the depth all around that it is in its shortest place. Stitch seam binding to the turned edge. Slip-stitch this in place, taking care to make short, easy stitches and to ease the binding on so it can not draw in any place.

Attach the Shoulder Straps. Pin the straps in their correct position. Conceal the unfinished ends by turning them inside the straps. Catch the straps to the lining with double thread and whipping-stitches. Do not allow any stitches to catch through to the right side. Sew tiny stays to the shoulder straps on the underside, to catch over your lingerie straps.

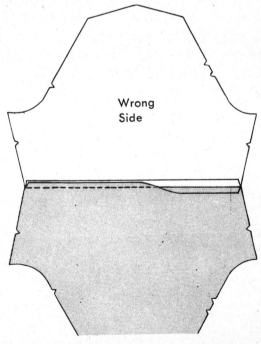

Make shoulder straps as wide or narrow as are becoming to you. Stitch and turn right side out: Attach four ends neatly and securely

When your dress is finished, make sure that there is not a thread end anywhere. Place the dress on your press board. With your drilling press cloth, go over it carefully, sponging the cloth and pressing so that the seams look as if they had grown together and there is not a bulge or ripple or wrinkle anywhere. To hang your dress up, place a piece of fabric over your dress hanger; and pin the straps to this, pinning from underneath so that no marks will show on the right side. If necessary, fold the dress around toward the back so that no wrinkle can form in the front while the dress hangs, waiting for your wearing.

JACKET

Taffeta Lining in Short Sleeves. If you are having short sleeves, cut the taffeta lining for them. Stitch the lining to the bottom of the sleeve, and press the seam open. Baste the underarm seams; and stitch, as shown. Bring the taffeta back in position inside the sleeve. Baste to the top, just as you did in making the Dressmaker Dress.

Wrong Side

Place Darts in Back Neck and Sleeves. Fold the pattern back; and draw chalk (or pencil) lines to mark the dart lines on the back of the neck and in the top of the sleeves—as you did for Bolero on page 84. Baste the darts with short stitches in preparation for fitting.

[130]

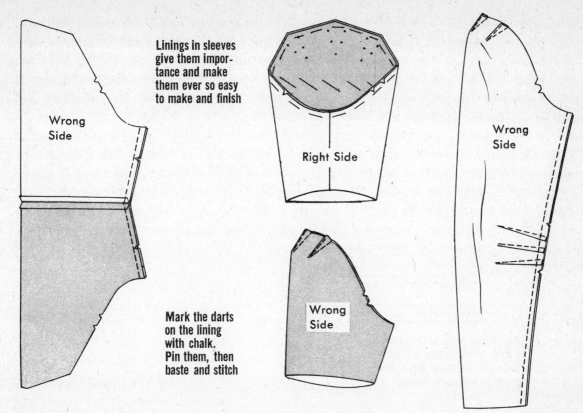

Linings in sleeves give them importance and make them ever so easy to make and finish

Wrong Side

Right Side

Wrong Side

Wrong Side

Mark the darts on the lining with chalk. Pin them, then baste and stitch

If long sleeves are to be used, mark and baste the darts at the elbows also. Pin the sleeves together—first at the bottom, then at the top—and baste from the armhole down.

Shirr Side Fronts. With coarse thread in your bobbin, matching thread on top, and a medium-long stitch, make three rows of shirrings on each side between the notches.

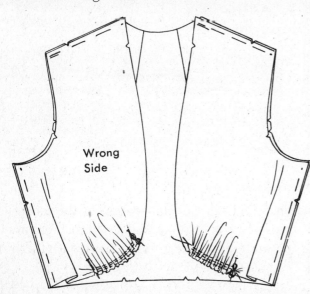

Wrong Side

Pull top thread to wrong side, draw up the bobbin thread, and wind the ends in a figure 8 on a pin.

Baste back and side fronts together. Baste the shoulder and underarm seams. In doing this, remember to stretch the front shoulder seam slightly and to ease the back on to it.

Make Loops, and Place in Center-Front. Take the ¾" strip of bias. Fold over a cord—wrong side out. With the cording foot on your machine, stitch along the cord; and stitch twice or three times across the end, through fabric and cord. Then turn this tubing right

[131]

side out, as shown. When the cord has been pulled out, slip it off as it is not used further. (Its purpose is to keep the tubing an even width and to make it easy to turn it right side out.) Mark the jacket on the right side for the buttons. First, measure and mark halfway on the peplum, as indicated by the dotted line. Beginning there, make a chalk (or pencil) mark every ¾″, continuing as far up as you want the buttons to come—16 loops are right for the average, 14 or 15 for the small, and 17 for the large figure. Lay the tubing so that it will form a small loop (as shown in the large diagram) with both ends inside the ¾″ marks and ¼″ allowed at each end of the loop for stitching it in place. Cut the amount off the tubing, and use it in measuring and cutting the number of loops required. Pin and then baste the loops in place, so that they will be even in size as well as an equal distance apart. Stitch along them, as shown, stitching slowly and lifting the presser foot frequently, if necessary, to keep each loop in position.

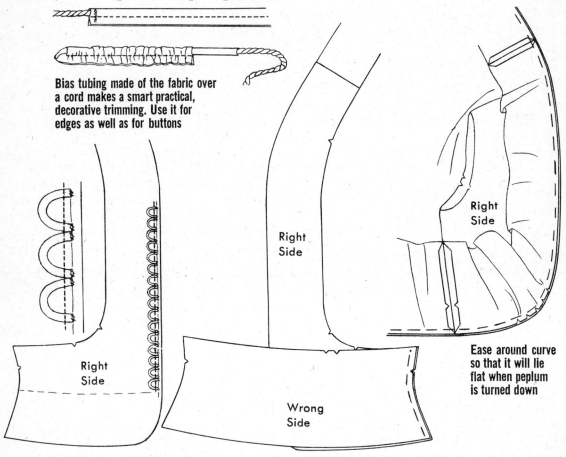

Bias tubing made of the fabric over a cord makes a smart practical, decorative trimming. Use it for edges as well as for buttons

Right Side

Right Side

Right Side

Right Side

Ease around curve so that it will lie flat when peplum is turned down

Wrong Side

Join the Fronts and the Back Peplum Section. (We will call the section of the jacket that extends down the front and around the waist the "Fronts and Peplum.") Baste the back of the peplum to the front at the underarm seams. Baste the front pieces together at the neck in the center-back. Prepare the facing also, which should be exactly the same as the top.

[132]

Baste Fronts and Peplum to Sides and Back of Jacket. (See illustration on opposite page.) Lay the fronts over the blouse part of the jacket, all notches meeting. Pin, adjusting the shirred fulness carefully between the notches; then baste. Clip the peplum seam around the curve, as shown, so that it will smooth out flat. (Underarm seams of peplum and blouse part should meet exactly.) Baste all the way around. Clip the seam so that it can not draw. Baste sleeves in jacket. At this time, in preparation for the fitting, baste the sleeves in position, all notches meeting.

Fit the Jacket. Put on the dress (which you have completed), and fit the jacket over it. Remember that the fronts overlap only ¼" at the center. The facing piece that forms the collar stands up on the neck in the back. The center of the peplum should come at the normal waistline or slightly below it. Make any necessary adjustments in fitting. Do not fit the front or peplum too tightly—as they are to be faced. This facing will take up some fulness. Remove the jacket. If you have made any fitting changes in the seams of the jacket, baste them also in the facing piece as it must fit the top perfectly.

Stitch Seams and Darts, Press Seams Open, and Finish Them. Stitch the back-neck seam of the front and the facing. Stitch the back-neck darts and the sleeve darts, the shoulder and underarm seams, and the underarm seams in the peplum. Press all seams open. Bind the shoulder seams and the underarm seams of the blouse part. If short sleeves are being used, stitch them in. Clip and bind the armhole.

Long Sleeves. If you are using long sleeves, remove them from the armhole. Stitch the seams; press them open, and overcast them. Lay the sleeve flat, and cut a 2½" slash on the fold opposite the seam, as shown. Stitch a 2¾" bias facing to the bottom of the sleeve. Clip the corners away. Turn facing to the wrong side, stitch binding to the top edge, and slip-stitch it in place.

If you wish the sleeve fitted more closely at the wrist, dart it in when fitting, as shown. Cut away half the amount pinned in; then apply the 2¾" bias facing.

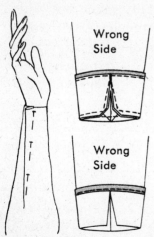

Wrong Side

Wrong Side

Leave an opening deep enough to get the hand through. Fasten this with two or more small snaps. When the sleeves are finished and pressed, baste them in the jacket. Slip it on to be sure they are correctly placed. Remove the jacket, stitch the sleeves in, and clip and bind the armhole.

Stitch the Fronts and Peplum to the Jacket. Apply the Facing. (Illustration on next page.) Begin at the center-back neck, and stitch the fronts and peplum in place all the way around. Keep the stitching line even. Lay the facing over the fronts and peplum, and pin carefully in place all the way around. Make sure that all seams meet; also, that no part is stretched or pulled in. Baste all the way around as shown. Begin at the center-back, and stitch all the way around. Press this seam open, doing this over a sleeve board.

Clean-stitch the free edge of facing; and baste it back in position in the jacket on all edges, except along the side where the buttons are to be.

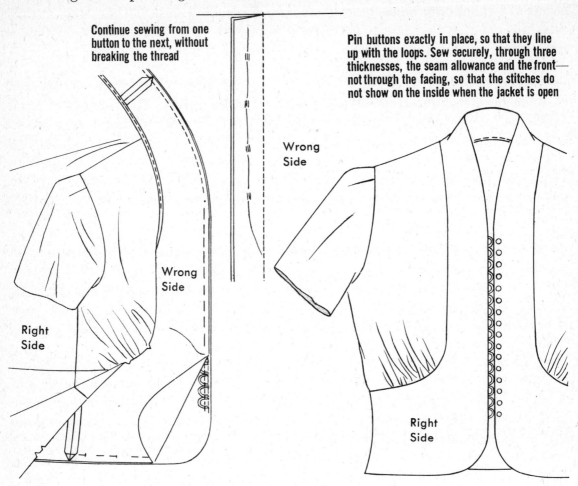

Continue sewing from one button to the next, without breaking the thread

Pin buttons exactly in place, so that they line up with the loops. Sew securely, through three thicknesses, the seam allowance and the front—not through the facing, so that the stitches do not show on the inside when the jacket is open

Wrong Side

Wrong Side

Right Side

Right Side

Sew the Buttons on, Using a Continuous Thread. Pin the buttons exactly in position on the left of the jacket, ¼" in from the front edge. Begin at the first button, using a long double thread. Work from the wrong side. Put your needle under the facing; and sew the button to the seam allowance and to the front, so that no stitches show on the facing side. Take several stitches. Do not break the thread, but continue to the next button. Carrying the thread from one button to another gives strength to all the buttons, helps you to line the buttons up more evenly, and makes the sewing go much faster as you do not break the thread and begin again with each button. When the buttons are all sewed in place, slip-stitch the facing in place all the way around.

Press the Jacket. Go over the jacket, clip thread ends, and press every part carefully —and remember the difference between ironing and pressing. Hang the jacket up.

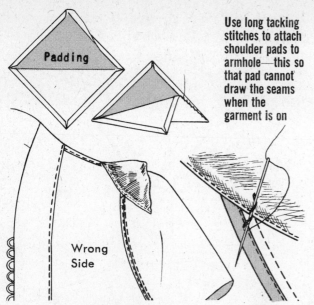

Use long tacking stitches to attach shoulder pads to armhole—this so that pad cannot draw the seams when the garment is on

Padding

Wrong Side

Make and Attach Shoulder Pads.

The shoulders of a soft dress jacket such as this is should be padded softly—not mannishly. Take a 5" square of taffeta, turn the edges in ¼" on all sides, and press. Take a 4" square of cotton batting, and cut it diagonally through the center. Place the cotton triangle on the taffeta, fold the taffeta over it to cover the cotton, and stitch on two sides. Place these finished pads in the shoulders of your jacket; and tack them in three places—two at the armhole seam and one at the shoulder seam, as shown.

FORMAL AFTERNOON DRESS

Use Two Patterns. Often when you sew, you like one feature in one pattern and something else in another. Learn to combine these features to express your individuality and your own good taste. For example, take the front, back, and sleeve of the blouse of the Afternoon Dress shown on page 74. This pattern can be folded over in line with the high waistline of the skirt of the formal dress, and, as shown in the layout below, cut from lace or formal fabric. This can be sewed to the top of the skirt (in a daytime length), and thus you make a formal afternoon dress.

To shorten a skirt and yet avoid having it too narrow at the hem, take off half the amount by turning the skirt up at the bottom; and take up the remaining half by folding the pattern, as shown.

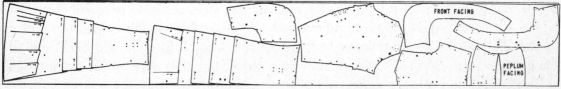

FRONT FACING

PEPLUM FACING

To make such a dress, put in the front shirrings—three rows, as shown. Stitch the center-front fold, and press it in place. Baste the shoulder and underarm seams, and stitch. Press them open. Make the skirt as already described, except that you stitch and finish the center-back seam completely, instead of allowing for a placket there. Join the back-neck facing to the center-front turned-back edges. Complete the neck. Stitch the bias facings to the sleeves. Stitch the sleeve seams, and continue through the facing as shown on page 46. Slip-stitch the facing in place. Gather the sleeves, and stitch them in the armholes. Overcast all seams. Join the blouse to the skirt in a plain seam. Overcast the raw edges, and press the seam toward the skirt. Put in a simplified dress placket at the left-side seam. Press all carefully, and the dress is finished.

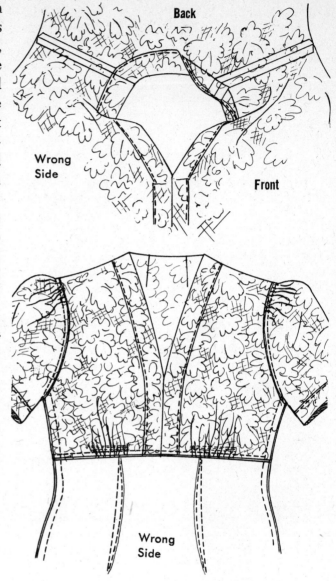

Variations. Few ensembles have as many practical variations as this one—which make it possible for you to individualize your ensemble and at the same time have it smartly becoming. You can, for example: Make the dress with a lace blouse. Make the jacket of lace and satin or of velvet; or make it of crepe, and embroider it. Use a plastic fastener up the front, rather than buttons or bows. Make long or short sleeves. If a square neck is practical for you, cut the neck square across at a becoming line. Plait or gather the tops of the sleeves. Pipe or cord the inside edges, as shown. Make bows of velvet, and sew a band of velvet around the bottom of the skirt. Make the skirt long or short. If you want fulness in the back, cut the back gores from 5″ to 7″ wider; and shirr the fulness in across the center-back. (Illustrations on opposite page.)

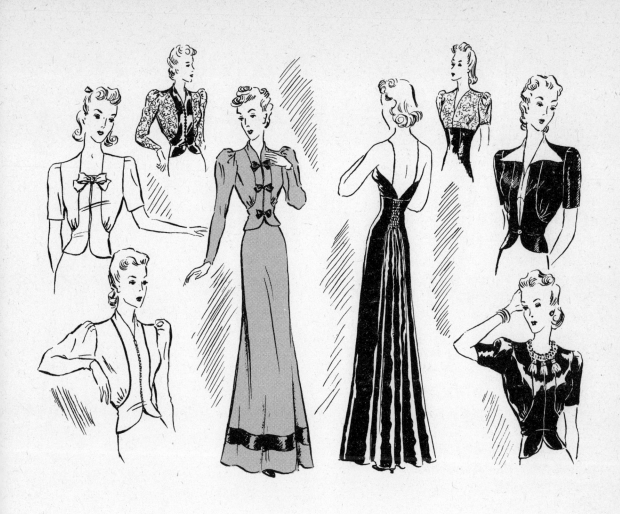

Decorative Machine Stitching

DECORATIVE MACHINE STITCHING can be made with matching thread or with buttonhole twist or yarn, but for cotton frocks the #30 crochet cotton is best, because it is strong and comes in many attractive fast colors. Such thread washes and irons beautifully and is just right in weight to make an effective stitching line.

Use it for the hems of ruffles, for applying bias binding, for groups of three to seven rows of decorative stitching. Use it to outline collars, belts, pockets, even to outline floral motifs stamped on the fabric from embroidery patterns.

As explained in machine smocking on page 174, if you use crochet thread, you simply wind the crochet cotton on the bobbin, use a mercerized sewing thread on top—and stitch from the wrong side of your fabric. To insure accuracy in this, it is well to baste or mark with a tracing wheel exactly where you will stitch so that all lines and corners will be well turned and true.

We have given only a few examples here, but every fashion book will provide you with designs on which you can use this method of trimming effectively. This provides a quick and easy means of decorating children's wash clothes and every-day household linens.

Cloth Guide Top Stitching

PRACTICALLY EVERY SEWING MACHINE has its own cloth guide. Many women push it aside again and again, little realizing how helpful it is in top stitching a garment, especially when rounding corners or stitching through irregular thicknesses, as on collars, cuffs, belts and pockets.

The cloth guide screws to your sewing machine a short distance to the right of the needle. Your machine instruction book tells you just how to adjust it to the width of stitching you want. You simply hold your fabric close to this guide and stitch; it prevents slipping and insures an even stitching in all places throughout the stitching line. Get your cloth guide out and use it right away. You will soon realize what a real friend it can be.

We have given only a few possibilities here for stitching, but any garment having top stitching calls for the cloth guide. Nearly all tailored garments have top stitching in their construction. If you want two or more rows of stitching, simply move the guide a presser foot's width away from the needle, and make a second row. If your thread breaks, always pull threads through to the wrong side and begin again with the last stitch; never overlap on the stitching.

Appliqué

APPLIQUÉ CAN BE DONE by hand and by machine—with visible whipping-stitches, running- or machine-stitches, or blanket-stitches of crochet thread or yarn, also, with liquid thread. The suggestions given opposite are simply by way of illustration to hint at the possibilities of this interesting form of decoration. Choose the motifs and the colors that you like and that are completely appropriate for your material and the design of the garment or article. Cut your motifs precisely so that there are no uneven edges. Use small, sharp scissors or a razor blade.

Prepare the cut-out motifs for application by turning under the raw edges and basting or pressing them back. Special care must be given to this in wash fabrics so that there will be no frayed edges. Felt and very firm woolens and ribbons do not need to have edges turned under, but practically all other fabrics do, unless, of course, you are using very close stitches or the sewing-machine zigzagger, when no edges need to be turned.

Always pin, then baste a design in position before beginning the securing stitches. Very often a motif can be cut from the fabric of either the skirt or blouse to provide decoration of the other. Again, pieces of print may provide the pattern from which to cut motifs of other fabrics. Wallpaper is an excellent source of design. Use its motifs as a pattern in cutting.

Appliqué for Home Furnishings. Appliqué is a practical decoration for many types of home furnishings—for the ends of draperies, for valances, on quilts and coverlets, on scarves, cushions, table linens, towels and other decorative articles.

Beautiful table linens can be made with an organdy base and chintz or cretonne flower motifs appliquéd to the organdy. Place the designs at corners or at each end of the cloth, and put a smaller motif on each napkin. A panel of motifs can also be made through the center of the cloth. Turn the raw edges in and baste; then whip them down or sew from the wrong side.

In valances and heavy draperies where effect only is desired, it is possible to appliqué the motif with liquid thread. This also is ideal for applying a fabric design in appliqué effect on a mirror or picture frame.

It is important with appliqué, either for clothing or home furnishings, to decide how much service is to be expected from the article in question, and let that determine the method of finishing. Appliqué done on a quilt must be done very neatly and very perfectly, because quilts are often washed and stand much wear and last for many, many years. Some people appliqué scrolled designs of taffeta or satin to blankets. Since the blanket is washed very carefully in lukewarm suds, usually the appliqué will come through satisfactorily if it has been carefully whipped on by hand. Sometimes a gathering thread is put around the seam line of the appliqué and the appliqué gathered in slightly to give a puffed effect for the motifs.

A VARIETY OF SUGGESTIONS for shirring apparel are given here. You need to allow for shirrings one and one-half times or double the finished length if the fabric is sheer. You can shirr fabric, then use a plain pattern to cut a garment to fit the figure. Trimmings, as illustrated here, may be made from pieces of the fabric.

Finger your fabric and decide whether it will shirr beautifully, hang well after shirring, be limp or bouffant as you desire. Then proceed to shirr according to your desires. Hand shirring is beautiful, but not too practical from the standpoint of the time it takes to do. (See page 39.) Therefore, for speed, use your sewing-machine ruffler or gathering foot, or use your cording foot over a large or small cord, as you prefer. Draw up the cord to space the fulness appropriately. To make shirrings even on a cord, gently and firmly pull and seesaw shirrings crosswise of the stitching, doing this the full length of the cord.

In normal times there is available an elastic thread that is excellent for shirrings. This is wound on the bobbin and used with a matching sewing thread on top. It is a time-saver. Full instructions for using it accompany each roll of thread.

Always remember, in using the ruffler or gathering foot, to use a strong thread, such as size 24 or 36 six-cord on the bobbin, so that it will hold when you draw it up or let it out to adjust the fulness as required.

Group shirrings are not recommended for wash garments, because they are too difficult to iron, but for velvets, taffetas, sheers and sheer wools, they are decorative and effective and economical as trimming. Always practice on a scrap of the fabric. Shirr a small piece exactly as you intend to have it in whatever you are making to be sure you will get the effect you have planned before you actually begin on a section of your garment.

Shirrings for Home Furnishings. The method of doing shirrings for home furnishings is the same as that for dresses, except that your fabric is often heavier and, therefore, you use a longer stitch on your machine. If you are using cording for the shirring, the cord will doubtless be larger.

The same care in shirring that is given to garments is necessary for home furnishings—the same matching thread, evenness of stitching and spacing, the same care in finishing off, whether it be stitching back on the corded line or whipping the corded end under to hold it securely. Remember to secure every end of shirring so that it will not pull out.

Entire valances are made of shirring; edges and inserted bands for bedspreads and pillow shams are made of corded shirrings. Cushions often have inserted all around the edges a band made with three or more rows of shirring. When desiring to make such articles, see suggestions for them in the home furnishing departments of stores or in smart decorating magazines, and then adapt an idea to your purpose.

Ruffles, Ruffles, Ruffles

RUFFLES LIKE RUCHINGS, picoting, pinking and lace are decidedly feminine, and women seem to adore fashions that favor ruffles—no matter how hard they are to iron or expensive to clean.

There are occasions when ruffles seem to be completely in order—confirmation, graduation, weddings. Ruffles are ideal for flattering necklines and for dress-up aprons. Modes and manners tell us that ruffles on a maid's apron were an indication that she had put aside her work apron and had time to serve us. With all America doing its own housework, it is indeed a good sign when the housewife can boast a ruffled apron.

In making ruffles cut all but shaped ones either on the true bias or crosswise. The more sheer your fabric, the more full your ruffle must be. It takes one-and-one-half times the length for skimpy ruffles, twice for moderately full ruffles and three times for billowy ruffles. One-and-one-half times means that for each yard of ruffle you need 1½ yards of ruffling. See page 39 for instructions on piecing ruffles.

The appearance of your work is greatly enhanced if shirring is evenly spaced. The space to which the shirring is to be sewn should be evenly divided and marked with pins, notches or chalk. Divide and mark portion to be gathered into the same number of spaces. After shirring threads are drawn up and fastened around a pin, put marks together. This will help you to distribute the fulness evenly through the length of the ruffle. Allowance for fulness is usually indicated on patterns. For home furnishings, add twice the finished length for fulness. More is needed for limp fabrics, less for bulky ones.

Use a strong thread for hand gathers and a running-stitch with a knot to begin. Use the ruffler or the gathering foot on your machine. Test on a scrap of fabric and adjust the stitch so that the desired fulness will be shirred up. You can always pull up the bobbin thread if necessary to make gathers more full, but if the gathering line is too short, break the gathering line, shorten your stitch and gather the edge again and thus avoid broken gathers.

Make gathers more full around an outside curve so that the outside edge of the ruffle will lie flat and not cup. Crowd gathers at a corner so the outside edge will be smartly square.

To prevent a square-cornered ruffle from cupping along the bottom or outside edge, more fulness is necessary than on a curved edge. Allow as much fulness as can be drawn into the corner. A flat fell seam will be most practical in applying a ruffle on a square corner. If bias trim is appropriate, bring the seam to the right side and bind with bias binding. Clip seam edge of ruffle so it will lie flat.

Bows, Bows, Everywhere

BOWS may be used in so many ways for decorative effect that they are always in fashion in some forms. They may be very small, flat, and tailored, large and softly draped, crisp and perky. They may be just tacked on, as in the evening dress illustrated at the lower right, or actually be a part of the construction of the garment, as in some of the waistline effects shown here.

The suggestions given here are only a few, simply to suggest possibilities. Fashion always decrees the size of the bow, its frequency of use in a garment, and its color and material. Sometimes bows are used to give an interesting fabric combination; for example, velvet bows on wool or lace. Then again there may be contrast in color or fabric if a large bow is lined with fabric of a lighter weight, a different color, or a different texture.

Bows, whether of ribbon, velvet or lace, need a light touch in the tying, assembling, or arranging and placing, and some fingers are more adept than others at tying bows. If your fingers are not deft, it would be better to find some other method of trimming. Also, if you are the tailored type, think twice about the effect of a bow before deciding to use it on your dress.

Usually a bow is nicest if it is cut in sections and then assembled with needle and thread. Then each part can be placed as desired and made secure within the bow.

A shows how a tailored bow is assembled.
B a bow of velvet ribbon.
C shows a crushed-center tie-around.

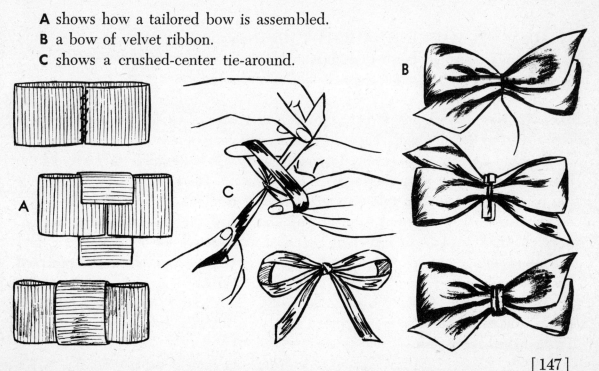

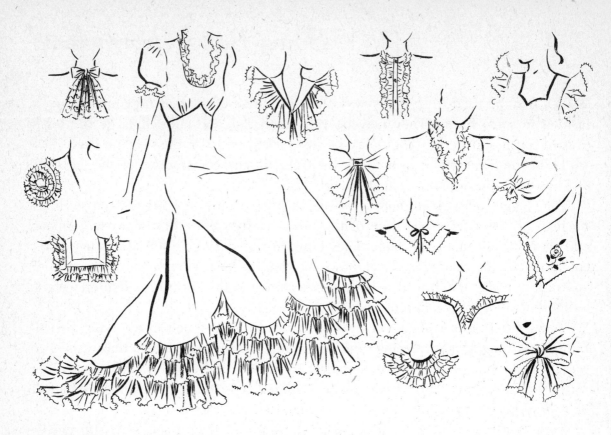

Machine Picoting

PICOTING IS MACHINE HEMSTITCHING cut through the center. This gives a sturdy inconspicuous finish to each edge. It is an especially practical finish for organdie, lawn, net, chiffon—all sheer and semi-sheer fabrics.

There is a shop in almost every town and city that does hemstitching by the yard. The shop people insist that you baste or crease or chalk line exactly where you want the hemstitching. They do the hemstitching; then you cut through the hemstitched line for the picoting. In making ruffles it is desirable to mark off the fabric, making the ruffles twice as wide as you want. Have these hemstitched, cut the picot apart, and then fold the ruffles in half and cut. Then gather these raw edges. In this way you make use of both halves of the cut-apart hemstitching, have only half as much hemstitching cost and an effective lot of ruffling. Picoting has an advantage over pinking in that it washes perfectly and therefore is practical for neckwear and for sheer frocks that are tubbed often.

The illustration shows the picot edge used in a variety of ways—on collars, jabots, ruffles for all sorts of purposes. Your own material and style will suggest further ideas for its use.

[148]

Pinked Edges, Seams and Decorations

ORIGINALLY WE HAD pinking irons which we used to notch edges with; now we have pinking machines that notch edges for us. Many women use their scissors and clip notches one by one. Notching and pinking are one and the same and make an ideal edge finish for fabrics that do not fray easily as taffeta, chintz, organdie, flannel or broadcloth.

Pinked edges are widely used in home furnishings, where effect rather than permanence is the goal. When weight is desired on an edge, two or three rows of fabric may be used, often of different colors. Ruffles and valances for curtains and bedspreads often are finished by pinking. Pinking is rarely used on cotton wash garments, simply because the edge will roll and prove difficult to iron.

A skirt, belt, bag and suspenders are shown made of a peasant-type chintz with felt trimming. Taffeta is shown in rosettes, bows, double and multi-effect ruffles for bags, muffs, neckline and so on—even for plain collars of felt. Many women prefer to notch the seams of their dresses rather than overcast them, hence the dress illustration. Test your fabric first before you pink it. Its attractiveness, flatness, all will tell you whether or not such a finish is right for your purpose.

Edge-Stitcher

MOST SEWING MACHINES have an edge-stitcher. The instruction book showing its use illustrates insertion and narrow edging being sewn together. The edge-stitcher is a real time-saver. It holds lace, insertion, or both, or ribbon or braid without drawing it tight or holding it full. It helps in following a marked line and it holds edges together so that both are easily caught together with one row of stitches.

Anyone using the edge-stitcher for the first time should avoid corners and curves and should practice using it with scraps of the fabric to "get the hang of it" before beginning on the garment itself. Another precaution is to stitch over newspaper so that delicate or sheer fabrics cannot catch or be retarded by the feed plate of the machine. Paper often speeds machine stitching and is a great protection, especially on light-weight fabrics.

Upon reaching a corner that is to be mitered with the edge-stitcher, try to stitch the outside edge first, pivot on the needle, fold the miter carefully, then proceed with the new row. Never skimp or slight a miter. Always allow plenty of fabric and time for a neat corner.

The edge-stitcher is a wonderful time-saver when rows and rows of lace or insertion are to be stitched together to make, say, a jacket, such as the one illustrated on the opposite page. In such a case it is usually advisable to stitch the many rows together first, then to place the pattern on and cut out the garment just as you would from a fabric having a prominent crosswise stripe.

The examples shown here of the practical uses of the edge-stitcher are only a bare indication of its possibilities. You have but to put this gadget on your machine and practice for a quarter of an hour to realize how it can enhance and speed your work. Not only can you use the edge-stitcher for joining lace and insertion and for applying lace along an edge as illustrated here, but you can also join rows of ribbon for making such things as purses and hats. This attachment is a great convenience when you want to stitch any narrow trimming along an edge—as piping, for example. With one stitching it helps you to do what would take several operations without it.

  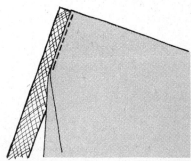

Cording

THE CORDING FOOT is one that you usually need to buy as it does not come with a set of attachments. But do buy one and learn to use it. Practice cording a simple pot holder, then doing a slip-cover for a plain chair and so on until you can use any size cording and produce any fashion effect you desire.

Elsewhere we have shown you how to cover a cord with a piece of bias. Here we show how covered cord, i.e. cording, is used for decoration. Cording may be made of self-fabric or of contrasting fabric or color or both. Just don't use it unless you are willing to take the time to cut a true bias. Join your strips on the lengthwise grain, using a short stitch. Then cover your cord carefully, using a cording foot on your machine or basting the covering on so that the basting hugs the fabric tight to the cord. Stitch or baste the cording to one edge before joining it to another. Cording gives weight to a garment. It emphasizes design and trimming lines and makes an effective, inexpensive (except for the labor) trimming.

Overlap cording at square corners, as at **A;** do not try to square it. Ease it on curves so that it won't hoop. You do this by pulling the cord slightly inside the bias so that you have enough fabric to ease in around even sharp curves as in a heart-shaped pocket, bound all around, as in **B.** Overlap ends as shown. Clip the bias at intersections of scallops, as in **C.**

When cording meets, as around a band, overlap it as at **D.** At ends, separate the strands of cord, flatten it down and stitch or whip the ends.

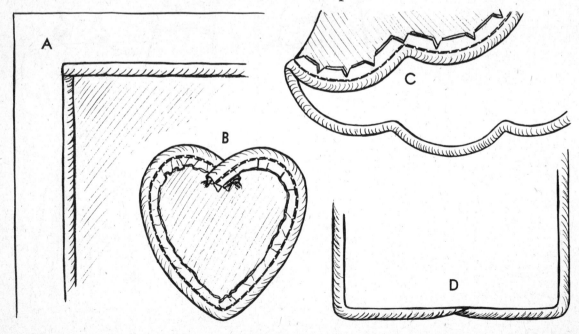

Quilting

QUILTING IS ONE of the most interesting of the needle-crafts, and it is indeed practical because it provides warmth in garments, it provides bulk when that is desired, and it can make truly beautiful decoration.

Our space here allows for only a very few examples, but your imagination can tell you at once how interesting this craft is when applied to home furnishings.

When you quilt you must begin with three things: (1) fabric and padding that quilt beautifully, thus justifying your work; (2) a plan or design for your quilting so that the right effect is assured; (3) determination to put every stitch, every row in perfectly without haste or carelessness. Quilting is an exacting type of work.

For block quilting for a coat interlining, you need your fabric and your padding, which for warmth should be of wool interlining that you can buy by the yard. The interlining is usually stitched to cheesecloth backing. This you baste to the wrong side of your fabric. You quilt from the right side unless you are following a transfer design, as in the boleros or shawl collar coat. In these cases you transfer your embroidery design to the cheesecloth and quilt from the wrong side. Care must be used in doing this; you have to look at the underside frequently to insure its smoothness, perfection of stitching, etc.

A coat such as the box coat in the center may have, say, satin or velvet on both sides. For this, the interlining is put in between, the yardage quilted, and then the garment cut out by a pattern. The seams are bound with ribbon or fabric and the coat is made so that it is reversible. In such an interlining as this, if quilting is done by machine, fabric should be attached to two sufficiently long sticks, so that material can be rolled and thus kept out of the way as the quilting proceeds. If the quilting is done by hand, then fabric should be stretched in frames exactly as for a bed quilt.

All-over quilting may be purchased ready-made. This often is very effective and inexpensive. Chintz, calico, satin, taffeta are fabrics most often done in ready-made quilting and are available in drapery departments. Some stores have a service which enables you to have fabric of your own selection quilted, for which you are charged by the yard.

A few of the illustrations show the use of floral or leaf designs. For this type of quilting, you obtain the effect in a different way from that used for all-over quilting.

To do such designs: Get wool or cotton wadding and stamp the chosen design on it. Lay the wadding on the wrong side of the fabric with the design up. Stitch the outline of the design. Then cut the padding away around the outside of the design, leaving it under leaves, petals, or scrolls that are to stand up in the finished garment. After lining or facing is applied, the puffed effect will be apparent.

[155]

Bands and Straps

FASHION EVER SO OFTEN decides that straps and bands of self- or contrasting fabric, of ribbon or insertion or braid, are in order. When nicely applied, such trimmings are effective and really not difficult if you follow a few simple rules. If they are to be of self-fabric, use a firm thin fabric, also cut on the bias, inside so as to keep a true edge. Cut carefully, and baste and stitch with equal care so that the strap is even in width throughout. See **A.**

When placing strap on garment lay it on with garment out flat. Never draw or pull a strap on. It must be so easily and smoothly put on that it seems to belong precisely there.

We give here a variety of attractive, practical applications of bands and straps. Study these and let them help you when next you trim a garment in this manner. Remember that your stitching on such trimmings must be just as perfect as top stitching. Some bands have edges catch-stitched to the garment. No matter how attached, do not use bands unless your time allows you to apply them perfectly.

This type of applied band may also be used in mending garments if they are worth the time. It allows you to patch a hole so that it looks like trimming.

Braiding

TRANSFER PATTERNS FOR BRAIDING often accompany a pattern design. Or you can easily make your own if you use designs as simple as those we have illustrated here. Transfer the design to your fabric or trace it on. Sew the braid on by hand or use the braiding foot or the underbraider of your sewing machine. In the two latter instances, read the instruction book for your machine and practice on a scrap of the fabric so that you will be skillful in applying the braid to the garment or article. Unless you have time and patience, do not undertake an elaborate job of decoration; rather, simplify the design to suit your circumstances. Ends of braids should be carefully pulled through with a tiny crochet hook to the wrong side of fabric and secured in place with whipping-stitches. Never stretch braid in applying it. Military braid must be put on with great care so that each line, each turn, is true.

Braid, like appliqué, often provides a way to cover a tear or break in fabric. When it is applied in a decorative fashion, you have not only repaired the damage, but also added a decorative motif that seems a part of the original design.

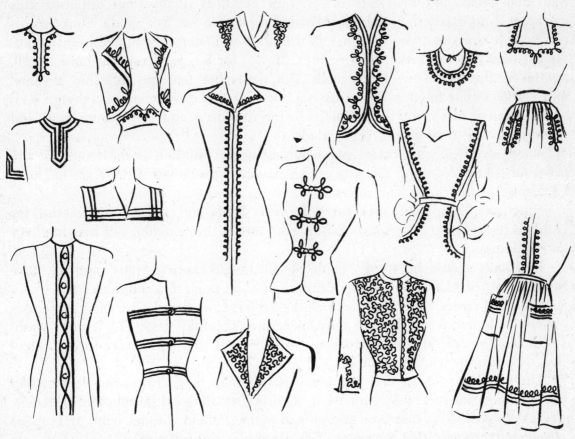

When You Sew For Children

LOOK TO THE LAUNDERING when sewing for children or when buying ready-mades. Fabric manufacturers are giving the best values today that we have ever known, in smart styling of materials, in fastness of color and in insuring against shrinkage.

When planning or buying a child's dress, always think of how it will look after it has been laundered once and then how it will look after being laundered twenty times. Often trimmings are too frail to stand washing, and often they are too tedious or compact to iron.

All mothers of youngsters should insist upon simplicity, good materials, good workmanship, good fit, and becomingness plus practicality.

The first criticism of most ready-made clothes for children is that they are too fussy, which means they cannot be washed and ironed readily. Too often, perhaps, ready-made clothes have better style than "mother-mades," but this need not be true.

One way to be sure of making good-looking clothes for children is first to find a ready-made dress or suit that is exactly right for the child, one that has correct individual style, and then buy material of excellent quality and duplicate this garment. If necessary, buy the ready-made garment to use as a guide. Suppose this ready-made dress cost you $3. You can usually buy material comparable in quality for $1; thus you can make three or four dresses for $3, and you will have, in all, several for the cost of two ready-made. But remember that the style has a value, and you must pay for this. If you have a good eye and can remember a design even to the detail of finish, you will not need to buy the dress and you can make several dresses for the price of one ready-made.

Another critically important point in sewing for children is the length of the skirts, or trouser legs, and the sleeves. All the style can be lost if these are too long. Children's clothes must look smart for their sake and your own.

Ginghams, linen-like fabrics, printed challis, lawns and percales are practical for children. Smocking is ever new and appropriate, as are trimmings of bias bindings and appliqué.

Play suits should be sturdy, made of substantial fabrics. Many mothers make these in lots of half-dozens. They can be cut alike, each in a different color.

Choosing materials for children's clothes differs from the plan of selecting fabrics for adults. Material for children must meet the "Fivefold" test: (1) It must wash. (2) It must wear. (3) It must work up easily. (4) It must give warmth or protection. (5) It must win appreciation.

Use matching thread that you know is fast-color, and always buy first-quality bias binding, rick rack, tape, and, most important of all, good buttons and fasteners. Try to place these so that the children can manage them without help, and, above all, place buttons so that the point of the iron can get in between them.

[158]

Making clothes for children is fun. It really need not be work. Start with an idea for something that will delight the youngster. Choose cheery colors and try to style the dress so it won't be just another garment.

Make a basic muslin that fits perfectly so there won't be too many fittings. Little folks like fittings if the time can be given to admiration, but rippings and tedious pinnings make them fidgety.

Cut all the garments at one time and do all the machine work at another time. Then do the hand finishing at your convenience. Our grandmothers invariably had pick-up work to do when callers came. Now such pick-up work makes good radio sewing. School yourself to have work ready to do, and when favorite programs are on, you will be amazed to find how much you can accomplish. At the same time, you will find you get more out of the radio program because you can concentrate better when your hands are occupied.

When You Cut Out. Tear fabrics when possible. Corded fabrics will not tear, but ginghams, linens, and imitation linens will. Straighten the fabric, use plenty of pins, and cut the seams edges evenly. Cut several garments at once to save time. Cut all the facings, even the pieces for the bound buttonholes. Fold the pieces of each garment together so that there can be no confusion when you are ready to sew.

When You Stitch. Sit down at the machine and regulate the stitch so that it looks right on the fabric. Stitch up shoulder seams. Put on collars before putting in sleeves. Stitch arm bands in place before seaming sleeves. Generally the sleeve can be put in, and the underarm and sleeve stitched at one time. Stitch sleeves in twice, once on the seam line, which is usually ⅜″ from the edge, and once a scant ¼″ outside this. Always stretch the armhole slightly as you stitch so that there is some give in the stitching line. Stitch the top of hems and then slip-stitch the hem in. Use the gathering foot for gathers; the cloth guide for decorative stitching on cuffs, collars, front plaits, and pockets. Make pockets whenever possible because children delight in having them.

You can apply the instructions given in the following pages and at the same time use your favorite make of pattern, the materials, and color you prefer. The order in which the garment is assembled is important to quick and easy sewing; the perfection of detail is based upon an understanding of approved and modern methods.

Bundle Sewing

YOU HAVE already been introduced to the plan of bundle sewing, in this book. It is one of the important steps towards quick and easy sewing, and it is especially important when sewing for children.

Proper Styles. When you plan to do bundle sewing for children, choose patterns with style features that will make them suitable for several suits or dresses for the same child, and still appear different. Jackets will usually achieve this trick. A suit pattern may serve for several outfits from playtime to dress-up time. Shifting the collar, the pockets, the trimming, length of the trousers, and the fabric, will vary the outfits. Cutting all from the same pattern will insure quick and easy construction, for the garments will go together in the same way and practically all finishing details will be the same.

A little girl's jacket dress, too, will provide this same valuable aid for cutting and construction. Several dresses which are entirely different may be cut from the same pattern. There are many such styles offered by pattern companies. Even simple styles, when cut in different materials, and trimmed differently, will provide dresses that are quite unlike each other.

How to Cut Garments for Children. Tots and toddlers require many changes of clothing, so plan all of each season's sewing in advance. When buying fabrics, plan, as far as possible, to select materials of the same width, as this will aid in laying out several layers at one time and cutting from one top mark. Rip apart and clean or wash the fabrics which you are going to make over. Plan all trimming features, and buy what is needed. If white collars are generally used, several of these may be cut out ahead of time, provided a single dress pattern is to be used for several dresses.

There are two plans for quick and easy cutting for children. One is to place two garments, such as a big and little sister outfit, on one piece of fabric and cut at one time. This will prove an economy in fabric as well as time. The other plan is to place patterns for one suit, or dress, on the fabric and then place it all over another layer of fabric, of the same width. More than one thickness may be used, if desired. Cut through all thicknesses at one time.

When all parts are cut out, lay the largest section of one dress, for example, flat on the table, place the other parts in the center, and tie the bundle securely with a piece of string, or selvage. Then mark the bundles so that you can remember the garment when you have time to do the sewing.

To Do Bundle Work. There are several ways to do bundle work. You will find a plan that is satisfactory for your own time. These may aid you: Several bundles may be opened and all small parts, such as collars, cuffs, belts, belt loops, and patch pockets may be made for several garments at one time. Or, open and make the small parts for a single garment, then proceed with the rest of the machine work. Wrap up the bundle again, keeping all hand finishing, such as clipping threads, buttonholes and buttons, hand embroidery or trimming touches, for pick-up work.

"Quickies" for Children's Clothes. In sewing, as in other work, there are prescribed rules for finishing certain details. At times, however, and in children's wash garments particularly, there are quick little turns in finishes that insure speed. Following are a few:

Quick Belt Finish. Instead of making a tube and turning the belt, simply turn in the raw edges, the regular seam allowance, and stitch from the right side, along one edge of the belt, or as a better finish, stitch on both edges. This type of belt is satisfactory for play togs, aprons, housecoats, and pajamas.

Machine Hems and Bindings. An entire dress or suit may be made on the sewing machine. Such sewing will hold up well under repeated launderings, and hard wear. Hems particularly, and also collar bindings, except in fine dresses and suits, may be machine-stitched.

Quick Cuff Effect. A cuff effect may be provided for a wash dress or suit without applying a separate cuff section. For this, cut the sleeve 2" to 3" longer than the regular sleeve. Turn the extra length under and then pinch up a generous tuck, ⅜" to ½", on the right side of the sleeve, catching the raw edge in the tuck. Baste through the tuck, catching only the turned-up edge. See **A.**

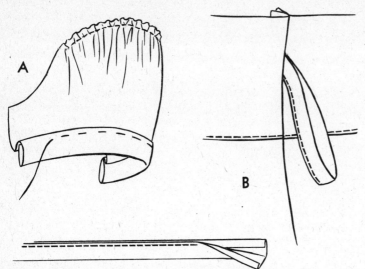

Quick Belt Carriers. Quickly made belt carriers may be folded as directed for the Quick Belt Finish and stitched on the outside instead of making a tube. To attach them to the dress, double the belt loop lengthwise and slip both ends together into the side seam about 1" above the waistline, pin, and catch in the stitching of the side seam. See **B.**

Quick Tie-End Finish. Many children's garments are finished with ties. Belt ties for dresses, sleepers, and aprons are common. A quick finish for the ends of such ties is to fold the end to the right side, diagonally, and stitch the end to the side of the tie as shown in **C.** Then turn this corner inside out, as at **CI.**

Quickly Made Frog Effect. For children's sleepers or house-coats, a frog effect may be quickly made with ready-made bias binding. This is kept folded and put around a regular buttonhole, pinned and then stitched on the machine, in **D.** A number of effects may be worked out in this way. Initials may also be made for such garments from bias binding.

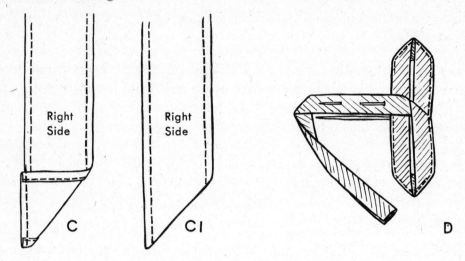

Baby Clothes

MUCH STUDY has gone into the clothing problem for the new baby. The many elaborate garments once made for a layette seem to belong to the past. A baby's first clothing wants are really few, and simplicity and comfort are the keynotes. For his first few months, for example, little one-piece kimonos, worn over shirts and diapers, serve adequately for the baby's waking and sleeping hours. Long nightgowns may be added, if desired.

One or two dresses and slips for his brief "company" periods are important, and perhaps a christening outfit is in order. This, of course, may be as elaborate as time and money permit. White still holds first place for infants' clothes, but pastels are in favor for some of the first dresses; and using soft, light pink for trimming baby girls' clothes and light blue for boys' is, of course, a time-honored custom.

The following chart lists the necessities for the baby's first few months. Many of the items can be made at home, easily and quickly.

The Quick and Easy Layette					
First Clothing Needs	**Necessary**	**Preferable**	**First Bath Needs**	**Necessary**	**Preferable**
Diapers	3 doz.	4 doz.	Towels	3	4
Shirts	4	6	Wash Cloths	3	4
Kimonos	6	8	Mild Soap		
*Bands	3		Sterile Cotton		
			Baby Oil		
			Powder		
First Comfort Needs	**Necessary**	**Preferable**	**First Crib Needs**	**Necessary**	**Preferable**
Cotton wrapping blankets	4	6	Sheets	4	6
			Crib Blankets	2	3
Wool, or part wool, wrapping blankets	1	2	Spread	1	2
			Mattress Protector	1	2
Pads	4	6			
Diaper Covers	2	4			
Safety Pins					
Second Clothing Needs	**Necessary**	**Preferable**	**Out-Door Needs**	**Necessary**	**Preferable**
Dresses	2	4	Hoods	2	3
Slips	2	4	Booties	1	2
Bibs	2	4	Coat, or Bunting	1	
Sweater or sacque	2	4	Carriage Robe		
			Carriage Pillows		

* Used if recommended by doctor: These are required only in the event the baby is born at home as they are generally used for two weeks only.

For Summer or Winter. Whether the baby is a summer or winter baby will naturally alter the items slightly. For example, the weight of the shirts will differ, and a sleeveless shirt, or band, which should not be confused with the navel band, may be worn under the long-sleeved shirt in the winter, and may be worn alone, in the summer. In cold weather, if the house is not very warm, nighties of outing flannel, made quite long and with a drawstring at the bottom, may be added to the garment supply.

Sewing for Infants. The important thing in starting to sew dainty things is to equip the sewing basket with fine cotton sewing thread, fine needles and dainty edging, fine bindings and tapes.

When you have assembled the things with which you wish to sew, and have your patterns at hand, measure the patterns, and decide the length you wish the kimonos, dresses and slips to be. The dresses should be 2″ longer than the slips. If the pattern is too long, fold in tucks to get the right length, and then proceed to cut out several garments at one time.

Cutting Out. Patterns usually allow for ⅜″ seams. If you are using very fine nainsook, lawn or batiste for the dresses, and making French seams, perhaps you will want to trim the seams of your pattern a little, making them ¼″ instead of ⅜″. This is especially desirable in making collar edges and sleeve bands, because the daintier seams are more in keeping with baby garments.

Machine Work. Many of the finest baby dresses that are French-seamed have the first seams stitched on the machine and the second seams done by hand. This is an ideal way because the machine stitching gives strength to the seam and makes it hold better in laundering, and to all appearances the dress is entirely hand-made. A French seam, however, can be done beautifully by machine. Fine tucks can be put in by machine, and then the tucks pulled crosswise gently to give a hemstitched effect. Cotton flannel kimonos should be entirely machine-stitched, because these garments require almost daily laundering and only strong machine stitching will wear well. Slips, pads, bibs and diapers should also be made by machine.

Diapers. The commercial double-gauze diapers are so inexpensive and so easy to launder that it is worth while to buy them. They are light in weight to wash, dry rapidly, have no hems or seams to rub or irritate. In some communities there are diaper services that handle the whole diaper problem of buying and laundering for a fee. This is convenient if it fits into the budget.

The square diaper, 27″×27″, birdseye or cotton flannel, made with a narrow hem, is still a part of many a modern baby's layette, but scientific research has approved the rectangular, approximately 20″×40″, diaper. This permits a change in folding as the baby grows. Such a diaper, made in a light-weight absorbent fabric, is on the market.

In making diapers, pull a thread to cut them, so that they will be straight. Tearing diaper material usually frays the edges, making it necessary to trim them before hemming. Hem diapers by machine, using the foot hemmer. Hem a number at one time, and when all are stitched, remove the hemmer, and with the presser foot in place, reinforce the corners by stitching back and forth on them twice for a distance of 2″ or 3″. Diapers are so frequently washed that only sturdy corners will withstand the wear. For the same reason, number 50 thread is practical in hemming them.

Kimonos. These are usually made from cotton flannel or cotton jersey, open all the way down, and since they must take repeated launderings, they should be made as sturdy as possible, but at the same time, they must be kept soft and dainty. The length of kimonos varies, but make them long enough to protect the baby, yet not so long as to hamper his kicking.

Cut several at one time, and because they must be durable, stitch by machine. Make plain, broad-stitched seams, as these seams will remain smooth and flat. The neck and front may be faced with a fitted facing in a different color, as in **A.** This is effective and substantial, but it cuts into considerable material. The bound neck and hemmed front, as in **B,** are recommended as being easy to make and more practical. For **B,** finish the neck with narrow bias binding of any soft, firm fabric, and use a narrow, firm cotton tape for the ties. Avoid ribbon or silk ties, as they do not wear well and come untied easily. To make these tie-tapes hold to the garment well, stitch them on right side of the material, the width of the hem, before the hem is turned, as at **C.** The hemmed-front kimono may be worn tied in front or back. When the sewing is finished, the little garment may be given some dainty, baby-like touches of embroidery.

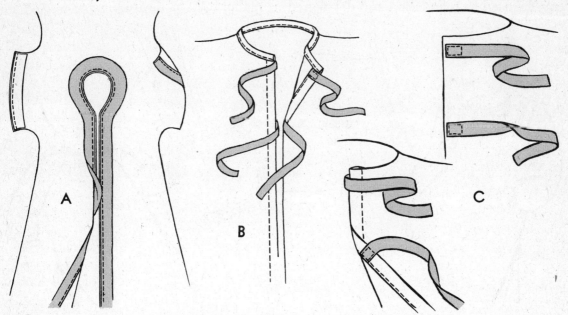

Bands. These are straight pieces of cotton flannel, or similar fabric, approximately 6″ wide by 27″ long. The edges should be pinked, as the bands are drawn snugly around the baby. Hems would be bulky, and would not permit the fabric to give properly.

Shirts. The little knitted shirts that are sold in the stores have so many convenient and practical features that it is best to buy them if you can. However, layette patterns do show several shirt styles, so if you prefer to make the shirts, get a pattern and follow the instructions faithfully. The type of shirt that laps over and ties is better than that which buttons down the front, for it is more comfortable, launders better and is easy to make.

Pads. There are many ways to make pads which may be used under the baby as lap pads or as added protection for the crib. A popular type is one made of two thicknesses of outing flannel or terry cloth, twice as long as it is wide, so that it may be folded and tied to give more protection and it may be opened out for quick drying. It is made approximately 14"×18" and the ends are quilted.

Another pad that is easy to launder may be made from a medium-sized, lightweight Turkish towel. Fold the towel through the center crosswise, and stitch the sides, as for a pillow case. Slip a piece of rubber sheeting or oilcloth in the open end. Sew snap fasteners to the corners so it will hold in position, and close the end of the case with snaps so that the inserted piece may be removed for laundering.

Dresses. Two to four dresses are generally sufficient. The baby may receive some for gifts, and he will grow out of infant styles very quickly. The two styles given here are the foundation dresses from which many variations may be made. If a hand-made christening dress is to be made, for example, the little tucked-yoke dress, as in **D,** may be used as foundation and developed as elaborately as desired.

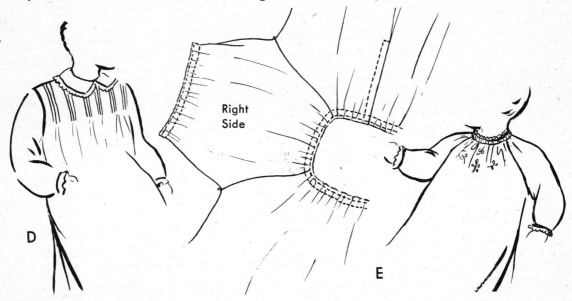

Right
Side

D

E

Bishop Dresses. One of the most practical and popular baby dresses, shown in **E,** is the bishop, or raglan sleeve, dress. This provides a roomy armhole and is slightly easier to make than a dress with a set-in sleeve. French-seam the armholes, hem the neck and sleeve edges, making the hem sufficiently deep for a narrow heading and casing through which a narrow tape may be run. The tape can be drawn up and tied in bows for wearing, yet opened out for ironing.

Another alternative is to gather the edges ¾" in, and stitch the narrow tape directly under the gathering to hold the fulness permanently in place. When this is done, make a loop of the tape on the lapping edge at the back neck so that the loop can serve as a buttonhole. French-seam the underarm seams, stitching from the wrist edge up to the armhole and then down to the bottom of the dress. Gather the sleeves at the bottom and bind them. Put in the hem.

Variations of the Bishop Dress. The neck and sleeve edges may be bound and left plain, or narrow baby lace may be sewed to the bound edges. (The best lace for baby clothes is a fine, washable lace from ¼" to ½" wide and generally called "baby lace.") A ruffle may be added to the lower edge rather than a hem. Rows of tucks and insertion may be used in decorating either a plain edge or a ruffled edge. A dainty embroidery design may ornament either the center of the front yoke portion, the left shoulder of the dress, or each sleeve ¼ of the way up from the wrist, or embroidery decoration may be used at the top of the hem in front or all the way around.

Tucked-Yoke Dresses. Baby dresses should have some fulness provided by means of gathers, tucks, or yoke fulness. Machine-made tucks are very practical and may be put in in groups of two, three, four, or five, as desired. Be sure to make the tucks tiny enough for daintiness.

In making a tucked-yoke dress, decide first on the space the tucks will occupy in width and depth. The front of an infant's dress will measure 8" to 8½" across. The depth of a tucked yoke should not exceed 3½" from the shoulder down.

Measure off the material for the tucks and pin them in, or adjust the machine-tucker so that the markings and spacings will be correct for the space that the tucks will occupy. Put in all the tucks before you shape the yoke and take care in doing this to place the first tuck on a lengthwise thread. In this way, all the tucks will come in a true line with the warp.

The simplest way to cut such a dress is to measure the width of the dress at the lower edge. From 48" to 54" is the usual width, and the finer the material, the wider the skirt.

When the width for the bottom of the skirt has been decided upon, fold your material lengthwise ¼ this distance from the selvage. Use the fold as a center-front and center-back line and tuck on each side of it to make the yoke portion. The tucks are first grouped, the threads pulled through to the wrong side and tied, and then the pattern is put on the tucked yoke, as in **F**.

Many patterns allow an inverted plait at the underarm, as at **G**. The two edges of the plait meet over the seam line, and the plait is made just deep enough to fit the lower part of the armhole. (Illustrations **F** and **G** on next page.)

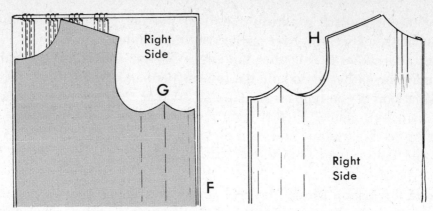

The back of the dress, with tucks at each side of the back opening, is shown in **H.** When the yoke and armhole edges are shaped, French-seam the shoulder and underarm seams and put the hem in. A plain hem 3″ to 5″ deep is usually desirable with a tucked yoke. Embroidery may be used between the tucks and at the lower edge if desired. The sleeves have a ⅜″ to ¼″ finished band at the lower edge with baby lace sewed to the edge.

The tiny collar pieces may be double or have narrow hems. Baste them first, then sew on the lace, making one row of stitching suffice for hem and lace. Those expert in using the hemmer turn the hem and sew the lace on with one operation. A rolled hem may be used, the edge rolled and the lace whipped on at the same time, or the raw edge may be turned once and stitched, then the lace whipped on. The whipping-stitching pulls the raw edge in enough to conceal it.

Stitch the sleeves with French seams and then French-seam them in position in the armholes. Pin the collar pieces in place on the neck and sew them with a very narrow bias facing which conceals all raw edges.

In finishing neck edges for infants' clothes, remember that little necks are short, and that the shirt usually comes up close to the neck, which makes it necessary for collars to be flat and without any bulk in the band or facing. Seams should be very smooth and facings perfectly flat so that they will not rub or irritate. The buttons in the back should be small and flat so that they will not be uncomfortable. Usually one button at the neck and one at the placket opening are sufficient.

Often, when 36″ material is used for baby dresses, a width and a half are used for a dress, the half width coming in the back and the seams being arranged to come at the under-fold of an inverted plait. When you follow this plan, seam the material together first; then put what is left of the skirt fulness in the underarm plaits. A plain dress pattern will serve in cutting the dress in correct proportions.

Slips. The little slip, open on the shoulder, known as a gertrude, is the best type for a baby as it is quickly made and may be put on and taken off easily. To make the slip, use a good quality of nainsook and cut it out according to a pattern. French-seam the underarm seams, and face the neck and armholes and shoulders, using for this a true-bias facing cut a scant ⅝″ wide. Stitch the facing on, on the right side, trim the seam to ⅛″ all the way around, turn the facing back to the wrong side, turn the raw edge in, and stitch it neatly in place. The slip may be trimmed with dainty lace, or simple hand embroidery touches. Make buttonholes and sew buttons on the shoulders. Some prefer the slip that is closed on the shoulder and open all the way down the back.

Flannel Slips. If the climate is very cold, flannel slips may be necessary for a winter baby. These are made the same as the cotton slips except that plain seams rather than French seams are used for joining, and to hold the plain seams flat, the edges may be machine-stitched to make a broad seam or catch-stitched.

Bibs. These may be made small, just to protect the front of the dress, or they may be large apron-like feeding bibs. The little dress-bibs are usually made of fabric, lightly padded, and they may be lace-trimmed or embroidered. The feeding bib should be made of a water repellent fabric, dull-finished oilcloth, or of terry cloth, simply bound with cotton bias binding. Make feeding bibs waist-length or longer, and have tapes to tie them well around the dress. There are many styles from which to choose.

Sweaters and Sacques. These little garments are often hand-knitted or crocheted, but cozy sacques may be made from any soft, warm fabric. Baby should have several, so even with gift sweaters he will need one or two. The sweater that closes up snugly from top to bottom is ideal for wear under a coat or bunting. A slide fastener is excellent for a close-fitting sweater. For the light-weight knitted or crocheted sacques, usually worn indoors for extra warmth, ribbon ties are satisfactory and the edges may be bound, or finished with a blanket-stitch.

Baby sacques may also be made from light-weight wool or silk and these are most practical, as they provide warmth, dress up a plain dress, and are easy to make and launder. The edges are usually bound, or a dainty, blanket-stitched edge is used. If the sacque is to be lined, cut both thicknesses alike; then with the right sides of both together, stitch around the garment, leaving the bottom open across the back. Then turn it right side out and finish by blind-stitching the opening at the back and sew tie-ribbons at the neck.

Hoods. The baby needs at least two hoods, for most of his daytime sleeping in done out-of-doors. Hand-knitted and crocheted hoods are best for his first needs. These may be made to match his sweaters. Make them of the softest yarns, and have them snug, without being tight. He may have fabric hoods for dress-up and these are usually made from silk, rayon, soft flannel, eiderdown, fine-wale corduroy, or fine, crisp cottons for summer. Be sure to line these with soft silk or rayon.

Bonnets. Baby bonnets are not difficult to make, and they make attractive gifts as well as dress-up features for your own baby's wardrobe. Get a simple pattern and vary the fabric and the decoration as the season and your fancy dictate. There are two principal types of bonnet that can be made without a pattern. One has a straight piece that goes all the way from forehead to nape of neck. Two side pieces complete the shape, as in **I**. The other type has a circular piece at the back and a straight piece gathered onto this circle, as in **J**.

I   J   K

Coat, Sweater Suit or Bunting. The winter baby is usually tucked into a sweater suit and a bunting for going out-of-doors. The summer baby may need a coat. Knit the sweater suit, and make the baby's bunting from soft eiderdown or heavy flannel. Cut the lining for the bunting from the same pattern as the bunting, using sateen, or cotton flannel. The outer fabric and the lining are sewed together, right sides facing, and then turned right side out. Bind the edges with bias silk or ribbon, if preferred. Usually a matching hood is made for the bunting, and if this has a collar or a short cape, as in **K**, additional protection is provided.

For a summer coat, select a light-weight wool flannel or good-quality silk or rayon. Fine corduroy or pique may also be used for warm weather. Choose a simple style, and decide whether you want it lined or not. Lining is selected according to coat fabric; silk or rayon for a silk, rayon or wool coat, and sateen for corduroy. If you do not use a lining, bind the seams. If you use a lining, cut it from the coat pattern, omitting the width of the front facing and the hem allowance.

Decorative Machine Smocking

THERE IS AN attractive trimming stitch, decorative, easy to use, and practical but so simple that it is often overlooked. It is made by using #30 crochet cotton on the bobbin of your machine and gathering so that it looks like smocking.

Use a regular mercerized thread on top, the crochet thread on the bobbin; use a long stitch, and work from the wrong side. When doing smocking in this way, test the gathering on a scrap of the fabric to make sure you have the stitch right in length for the amount of fulness desired. The longer the stitch, the more full the gathers. The gathering foot is a real aid when full gathers are desired. Although shown here only on frocks for girls, this method of decoration is just as good for women's dresses, especially summer ones made of medium sheer fabrics, as lawn, dimity and voile.

When smocking by machine, make all rows even and true to a line, draw up bobbin threads, if necessary, and pull threads through to wrong side and tie each row of shirring at each end.

Aside from the practical considerations and the attractiveness of crochet thread for machine smocking, there is another advantage, which is that the shirrings are sturdy and as a rule require no reinforcement from the wrong side.

Two-Fabric Frocks

WHEN MAKING over mother's dress for a tot, be certain that the material is suitable in design. Combine new material with it, if necessary, or use two old dresses that blend well, as new fabric may tend to show up the used material.

In making clothes for children from grown-ups' clothes, it is not enough merely to adjust the size. The whole style must be made appropriate for little figures. Rip and clean the garment and use the fabric as you would brand-new material, recutting on a child's pattern. There is nothing more pathetic than a little girl in a dress obviously cut down from mama's. The sketches here give suggestions for remaking dresses for children. These may be infinitely varied to suit your particular child and to use the fabric at hand.

Often fabric that would not be becoming to a child if the whole dress were made of it can be attractively combined with another color in panels, jumpers, collars and cuffs, etc. The use of appropriate new trimming and the kind of details that little girls love can make a remade dress a favorite instead of a hand-me-down.

Little Coats From Big Coats. Adults' coats, particularly good wool coats, in almost any color, offer an interesting challenge for remaking for children's garments without too much piecing. Rip before choosing a pattern.

Scarves and Handkerchiefs

MANY TIMES SCARVES and handkerchiefs provide color and decoration and help to repair a garment or extend a remnant of fabric into a dress or apron for a child. The sketches on this page are suggestions for using these in sewing for children. You will be able to think of many other ways of working them into your own scheme. All sorts of gay peasant styles can be achieved. Scarves and handkerchiefs vary in size so that each is an individual problem.

Scarves. A scarf may be made into a peasant skirt for wear with a soft white blouse. A 26″ square will make a skirt for a two-year-old. Waistband and straps may be made from plain material. A touch of embroidery on the blouse done in the skirt colors helps in making the dress a unit. Larger scarves may be cut and combined with plain material to make an entire dress.

Handkerchiefs. Handkerchiefs can be very successfully made into aprons, sunsuits, nightgowns, bed jackets, and collars and cuffs. Take your ideas from current fashion and use your imagination to make what you have into what you want. Assemble appropriate colors and harmonizing fabrics and don't forget that all-important point of being sure that what you make will please the little one who wears it.

Bias Binding

OF ALL MEDIUMS of trimming, nothing ever seems to replace bias binding for wash frocks. Possibly this is because binding finishes and decorates at the same time. It provides color and is inexpensive. Once a mother takes the time to master the machine binder and learns that a #5 ready-made binding will slide through and catch perfectly under the needle, she will be forever a binding enthusiast. She will buy piece upon piece of binding whenever she buys fabric for her own or her children's clothes—or for that matter, for kitchen and bathroom curtains, for pot holders, plate covers, clothes cases, shoe holders and all such articles so necessary to housekeeping. Bias bindings have a multitude of uses.

Few women realize that binding comes in a range of widths—white often from width 1, very narrow, to width 17, which is practically 2″ wide. All the narrow and wide widths must be basted on. On the wider ones, some like to stitch one edge on then bring the other edge down and stitch it in place.

When you need a wider piece than you can buy binding for, it is better to make a fold of fabric, this to match the grain of the fabric which it is to join; as a lengthwise fold for lengthwise and crosswise for crosswise.

Here we show examples of what bias binding can do in dressing up wash frocks— row beside row where emphasis or color is desired, single rows only when finish is the requirement. Bias binding goes around curves as conveniently as does a jeep and with almost as much speed. Buttonholes, yokes, and pockets can be bound with bias. Scroll designs can readily be worked out. For this, one needs a tracing to follow so that all the scrolls are uniform. For intricate work such as scrolls and sharp scallops, baste the binding on, then stitch it. Especially is this necessary in doing floral sprays, flower pots and such designs favored for quilts and curtains.

On all straight or long edges or ruffles use the binder, but, please, always practice on a scrap of your fabric with a scrap of binding so that the work is a credit to your time, effort and sewing skill and so that it will look even prettier after it is laundered.

If you have scraps of fabric, as gay prints, especially stripes and checks, you can make your own binding, but do cut it on a true bias of a correct width for your purpose. Press the edges over a piece of cardboard that is exactly the width you want the binding to be. Slide the cardboard along in your binding as you press, so as to keep the width even all the way. Never stretch, tighten, or crowd binding as you sew it in place; let it flow easily under the presser foot, the binder and your fingers guiding gently but never forcefully.

On page 10 we show how to piece bias on the lengthwise grain of the fabric. Neat piecing is important for very nice work. When placing bias bands on a skirt, stitch to within 6″ of the joining. Make the joining, press the joining seam open, then complete the stitching.

[175]

Pajamas, Nighties and Robes

NIGHT CLOTHES AND HOUSE-ROBES made at home will relieve the strain on the clothing budget considerably. There is also the advantage of being able to put better fabrics into them, and they are decidedly easy to make.

Comfort Foremost. A generously cut pajama is important, and a pattern should be tested thoroughly to be sure that it is correct for the child before cutting into the material. The crotch must be long enough, the armholes roomy, and the legs comfortably wide without being baggy, but the shoulders and back neck should fit smoothly to have the garment set properly and be comfortable. The construction principles for nightgowns and house-robes are the same as for dresses. Avoid having them too long. It is better to use a deep hem. Use cotton flannel, broadcloth, percale and seersucker for boys' and girls' pajamas and girls' tailored nightgowns. For light-weight gowns, use nainsook, plissé crepe, batiste and voile.

Styles for Different Ages. For very little children, it is advisable to use pajama pants that button on at the waistline, and make two pairs of pants for each pajama. Little tots may be given greater protection, too, if pajamas are made with feet. Another feature for small children's pajamas is the back belt that slips through side-seam belt-loops and ties in front. This eliminates buttons and permits the child to adjust them easily himself. The one-piece pajama is practical and requires less material than the separate coat and pants, but girls and boys past eight years of age generally prefer the two-piece pajama. If these are made middy-style, there is a saving on mending and laundering, for there are no buttons or buttonholes to pull out, and such garments are very easy to iron.

House-Robes. These are usually made to provide warmth for a child. Any soft wool or cotton flannel fabric that is not too bulky is excellent. Often an old robe, discarded by some grown-up member of the family, will provide enough good material for a child's house-coat. For proper protection, the front must have an ample lap and buttons or a slide fastener to keep the garment in place.

Whimsical Trimmings. Plain, well-tailored night clothes are always correct and no trimming beyond good even stitching is necessary. Such garments, however, permit many types of trimming touches if desired. Binding, piping, braid appliqué, hand-embroidery may be used, and for girls' pajamas and nightgowns, smocking, ruffles, lace, and bows are permissible.

[176]

Clothes for Boys

BOYS' CLOTHING, like clothing for men, falls into types more easily than that for the feminine world.

Sturdy Styles. When material of good quality, good workmanship, and appropriate colorings and fabrics are combined, there is distinct economy in making garments for small boys at home, because these elements are to be found only in the best ready-made garments.

Styling in clothes for boys is just as important as for girls. Fabric and color must be selected correctly and garments must be well cut, thoroughly sewed, and appropriate for their purpose. In choosing fabrics for a little fellow, perhaps two years old, one might use fine poplin or broadcloth, but for a four-year-old one might use percale, while for an eight-year-old a broadcloth or percale shirt and cotton gabardine trousers would be appropriate. Use flat-fell seams in practically all boys' garments and use machine stitching for all work on such clothing.

Fitting. In making clothes for boys, it is a good idea to keep at hand garments similar to the ones you are sewing which fit correctly. Few little fellows relish fittings, so it is best to take measurements and use garments as a guide for measuring sleeve lengths, collar and cuff sizes, pocket positions, and for other details. Check each part, for a collar that is too wide, a cuff that is too heavy, or a yoke that dominates the blouse destroys proportion and detracts from the garment's smartness.

He-Boy Trappings. The fabrics and accessories for boys' clothes are most important. In choosing colors and material for boys' clothes, examine the best garments. Find the colors and types that you know will be appropriate for the child for whom you are planning the clothes, so that you will be sure to have the right style effect. Buy appropriate buttons and buckles, and avoid embroidery stitches except for very little boys' outer garments, and then limit them to initials, nautical designs, or animal appliqué.

Avoid, by all means, all feminine fabrics in boys' attire. The point is to have them just as smartly masculine as possible, even when boys are tiny. The yardage for such garments is small, and one can afford to buy materials that are right for the purpose. A wise mother will see the advantage of making herself proficient enough in sewing so that she can make trousers and shirts look like custom-made garments. The sewing machine and the iron are the two greatest aids to smart, tailored effects.

Boys' Shirts. These are not difficult to make, and when several are cut and made at one time, the work goes very quickly. Make and apply small parts first, such as pocket, plait and sleeve facings. Use flat-fell seams. The collar should not be regarded as difficult, for with an accurate pattern as a guide, the collar-setting is a simple operation. The important thing is to keep the work smooth and tailored at all points.

Boys' Trousers. Boys' trousers and knickers may be satisfactorily made at home, especially in light-weight fabrics. A good pattern is essential. If a commercial pattern seems to require too much adjusting, a pattern may be made from a pair of old trousers. Rip them carefully, press and recut in paper, allowing a generous ½" for seams on all edges beyond the stitching lines. Mark the paper patterns to indicate the sections to be cut from lining fabric, and mark to show the lengthwise thread. If this is not clear, pull a thread in each section about which you may have some doubts. One of the most important points is to have trousers hang properly, and to insure this the pattern must be laid on the fabric correctly. Adjust your machine stitch to the weight of the fabric, and when stitching over three or four thicknesses, try the stitch on scraps of the material to insure uniform stitching throughout.

Make Your Own Fabric Furnishings

Analyze Your Fabric Furnishings. We all desire attractive homes that express the best possible taste. Too often we accept substitutes or make compromises in our plans because of lack of information regarding essential details.

This book aims to help you make, in just the right way, the type of fabric furnishings that please you and that harmonize in every way with your rooms and your furniture. Remember that, in addition to correct construction, fashion, textures, color, line and design are all of almost equal importance. When you successfully bring these elements together, the result is certain to delight and satisfy you.

Know What Is Needed. Styles and fashions in furniture and architecture have a definite influence on fabric furnishings. With Early American furniture, draperies must be simple and frugal. Short ruffled curtains, cretonnes, mohairs and chintzes in the designs of that period, even some modern designs in the simpler fabrics, carry out the spirit of that age. Rooms done in the styles of the luxurious French periods require rich taffetas, brocades, silk voiles, and crisp organdies. On the other hand, ultra-modern rooms need limp fabrics in plain colors, often in two tones, or in conventional designs, made with utter severity, while informal modern rooms speak definitely for unusual cretonnes and limp, neutral curtains, done in the most fashionable manner.

It is not enough to learn to make one kind of drapery or bed or chair cover. Variety in home appointments is an inspiration. Fashion provides change for us, and it behooves us to be alert to desirable new features. Valences may be plain one year, and ruffled, gathered or box-plaited, the next. Tie-backs have a way of moving up and down on the window frame or hiding away entirely. Ruffles come and go. We must be informed about the license Fashion takes with period types and adapt our needs to harmonize with the times.

Furniture should, when possible, be selected a piece at a time, and with deliberation. Yet few homes have been furnished in this way. Our houses generally contain things bought—wisely or unwisely—gifts, bargains and heirlooms, all of which we must try to place together with an aim for harmony and comfort.

Fabric furnishings often constitute the medium of reconciliation. When we realize what paint can do in restoring furniture and then what fabric can do in giving crisp freshness and completeness to a room, we know that it is a matter of intelligent interest and energy to make even dull, inconsequential furniture and rooms new and satisfying.

Who Lives in Your Home? In planning fabric and furnishings, consider the family and adapt your plans so that your results will be appropriate and comfortable for all. Delicate lace rufflings and tiny pillows are out of place for rooms inhabited or frequented by men and grown boys. On the other hand, heavy, dominating furnishings are incongruous in rooms occupied by young girls or petite women.

Whether the room where the family gathers and entertains its friends is called the parlor, sitting room, library or living room is of little consequence. The important thing is that this room should be inviting, cheerful and restful, and suited to the people who occupy it. If it fulfills these requirements, it is in every sense appropriate.

One Room at a Time. Study your home, room by room, and jot down the things you would like to change and the new things you would like to add. Then go over the lists again and alter them to make them suit your budget. Make a game of it. Try shifting things from one room to another—curtains, draperies, chairs, spreads and other furnishings, if they can be made appropriate—so that you can plan most of the new articles for one or two rooms. Then, next season consider making new things for another room, and so on, until you are satisfied with all.

Choosing Fabrics

CHOOSE FABRICS appropriate to rooms, furniture and family. Consider, also, exposures and lighting. Dark rooms require light colors; sunny rooms can take deeper tones.

Plan the room as far as possible before you start out to select materials. Make a little diagram of your room, checking the work you decide to do, such as draperies, slip-covers for sofa and chairs. Know the colors you prefer, and take samples with you of the colors of walls, rugs—those things you cannot change.

Avoid a monotonous effect by combining fabrics different in texture and in design, and by setting off your basic color scheme with accents of another color or two. However, be careful to plan this combination so that it has enough unity not to look "busy." Your room would have a very restless, inharmonious effect, for instance, if you combined stripes, polka dots, checks and floral designs all at once.

Plan for summer and winter. If you can have two sets of fabric furnishings, you will find the seasonal change refreshing and the life of both sets will be prolonged by cleaning and changing. Every season produces new and beautiful fabrics and designs. If you do the work yourself, you will find that you can buy fabric of better quality and enjoy more frequent changes.

Before buying, consider what the cleaning or laundering possibilities of the fabric will be, how well the colors will withstand fading, etc. Don't buy unwashable fabrics if the location of your house (in an industrial city for example) will necessitate frequent cleaning, or if your household budget won't stand frequent cleaning bills.

You will find it well worth while to buy finishes and fixtures for your fabric furnishings that are as good in quality as the fabrics themselves. It is disappointing to have bindings and braids that wear out before the chair covers to which they are applied, or curtain fixtures that do not do justice to your beautifully made draperies.

Tools for Fabric Furnishings

THE THINGS THAT COUNT in the way of tools are those you are quite certain to have. The others you can add as your work requires them. For sewing you need sewing, crewel and milliners' needles. An upholsterers' curved needle is easy to handle for heavy upholstery work, and it slips in and out of heavy fabrics with one motion. There is also a strong, straight needle with a point at each end which permits the needle to be used backwards or forwards, and a sail needle (triangular) for work on leather or leatherette.

Always buy a good quality of thread to match the weight of your fabric. If heavy work requires it, use strong linen thread or carpet or shoemakers' thread. There is also spring twine, which is a heavy thread used to hold furniture springs in place. Darning needles and a firm, steel thimble are best for such threads.

For cutting you will need good 8″ shears, a razor blade set in a handle and a sharp, sturdy Boy Scout type of knife.

For measuring and marking have a tape measure, yardstick, tailors' chalk, tracing wheel, awl, and a pad and pencil. A scrapbook or idea file, as for your dressmaking, is also helpful.

For work on furniture you need a small hammer, a strong screw-driver, a tack-puller and an assortment of tacks. There are the regular carpet tacks in various sizes, upholstery tacks which are similar to carpet tacks, but finer, gimp tacks which are quite thin, with practically no heads, and decorative tacks of various types.

A strong table, covered with a piece of carpet or drill, will serve instead of a professional upholsters' trestle. Such a trestle is usually made 28″ high, 30″ long and 6″ to 9″ wide. A webbing stretcher and a regulator to aid in adjusting stuffing evenly are good additions to your tool kit.

For handling all large pieces of sewing, use a table. Draperies, spreads and other heavy work should be placed so that they will not drag from your machine and break your needles.

Use your machine for practically all of your home sewing. Curtains, draperies, spreads and slip-covers all have long seams and require the strength in their construction that only machine stitching can give. Long stitches are desirable in fabric furnishings. The information given on page 6 will help you to get the most from your sewing-machine work.

Table Linens

DON'T WASTE TIME on over-worn linens, but those that are good enough to make over can, with a little ingenuity and imagination, be made really attractive. If a new hem is needed, use a colored thread and a quick running- or uneven-basting-stitch, or the edges may be bound or finished with rick rack.

Two tablecloths, a colored one and a white one, may be joined lengthwise with a white strip through the center and a colored edge on either side. A well-made flat-fell seam will permit the cloth to be used on both sides.

If there is no border design to interfere, a cloth can be lengthened by sewing a false hem on each end. A piece of checked gingham that just fits your table top may have a wide white border sewed all around. Miter the corners, and join with a flat-fell seam.

Lunch clothes that have small holes, as from cigarette burns, may be given a new lease on life by decorative appliquéd patches. Add a few additional designs for a planned effect. Floral designs are suggested, but if the cloth is for use on the children's table, all types of amusing designs will be appreciated. For more formal cloths; bands, panels or motifs of lace may be used attractively.

Table Cloths and Place Mats. These are an important part of home sewing. Small cotton lunch cloths and breakfast sets can be made in novel designs. Place mats are often used for semiformal dinners. Notice what is being shown in the stores when you plan your linen sewing.

Small lengths of cottons left from other home sewing may be utilized for luncheon and breakfast sets. The design must be appropriate, and the fabric should not be too tightly woven, as this makes it difficult to remove stains. Also, avoid a too-soft fabric; any table linen has to hold its shape well. Gingham, chambray, percale, unbleached muslin, organdie, dimity, and many rayon fabrics that resemble linen weaves are satisfactory. All linen is of course most suitable, and many a well-worn linen table cloth, especially one too full of holes to repair, is worth cutting up into place mats and napkins.

Scraps of seersucker or other sturdy cotton may also be cut into place mats and napkins. Hem by hand or machine. Some even-woven cotton fabrics may be finished by fringing the edges. Ravel the edges about an inch and stay the material from further raveling by machine-stitching.

The important point for table cloths, napkins and place mats, is to cut them on a straight thread of the fabric, to turn true edges and to sew or stitch accurately and well, so that they lie flat and the corners are flat and smooth. The napery hem is used to finish your best linens. In sheer place mats, the seams must be small and very even, as all seam lines show up clearly on a dark table top. A whipping-stitch or running-hem can be used on sheer fabrics.

Slip-Covers for Blankets or Comfortables

PROTECT new or light-colored comfortables or blankets, especially in dusty or sooty localities, with slip-covers of cotton prints, rayon sheers, plain chambrays or any light-weight suitable material. For camps and cottages, some women use fabrics from old curtains or draperies, dyed, if necessary, to give them a fresh appearance.

For comfortables, which usually measure 70"×80", 4⅔ yards of 36" material is required for each side. Join the material lengthwise through the center, taking up no more than necessary in the seam. Fold the ends over, as shown, so that the opening is about 12" from the top at one end. Bind or French-seam the outside edges. Tie the opening with binding or ribbon. Cut tie ends 6" long. If you are using binding for ties, fold the binding in half and stitch, as in **A**. Pin the tie to the cover, as at **B,** with one end under the edge binding. Stitch the edge binding.

Blanket Covers. A blanket cover is made like a sheet, used as decoration and protection for the blankets when the bed is "undressed." Choose a fabric that will not slide or slip off during the night. Washable silk, cotton, challis, crepes, sheers, light-weight pongees, powder muslin—many types of fabric are appropriate. These may be lace or ribbon trimmed, have elaborate monogrammed centers, be truly decorative. Even so, they are never to take the place of a daytime spread.

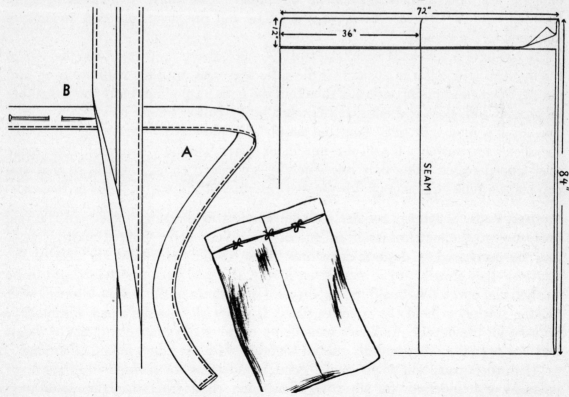

Cuffs for Blankets or Comfortables. Many women make for themselves, and many linen shops sell, removable cuffs or bands 12″ to 24″ wide that fit over the end of a blanket or comfortable to protect the binding. These cuffs are attractive when made of rayon sheers, especially delicately flowered prints on light backgrounds, or of dimity, handkerchief linen, lawn or voile. These originally were often embroidered or monogrammed to match the sheets and pillow-cases.

When a blanket binding is badly worn, a cuff will conceal it. Sometimes it is best to remove the binding from both ends, blanket-stitch the bottom end with yarn of matching color and cuff the top. Sometimes such cuffs can be made of marquisette to match the glass curtains. In any case, cuffs should be easy to put on and take off for laundering.

Mattress Covers and Pads

Mattress Covers. Many women make protective covers for their mattresses. A sturdy fabric is necessary, because the cover gets hard wear and frequent laundering, and is often put on and taken off the mattress. Unless you have used material that is strong enough, use new unbleached muslin or Indian Head fabric. Unbleached muslin sheeting is ideal, because you have few seams and the sheets are easy to remove and send to the laundry.

If you have a full-sized bed, take two 72″×90″ sheets, put one over the top of the mattress, pinning it in position at the sides and ends, turn the mattress over, and put the other sheet on this side and then fold the ends in; pin and baste them together all around both sides and ends. If you use a heavy cotton thread (say, No. 8 or 16), you can use stitches 6″ or 8″ long and simply clip these when you want to remove the sheets for washing. If you use muslin or other fabric by the yard, then make over-lapped seams, using only one stitching, and have enough widths so that you can make a tube large enough for the mattress to slide in easily. Fold in the ends.

Mattress Pads. Mattresses require pads for comfort in sleeping, and a pad is a real protection to the mattress itself, so buy or make your pads. Quilted mattress pads may be purchased in department stores. They should be almost the size of the mattress—they usually are 2″ smaller each way. If a pad becomes stained, it can be washed and covered with old tender sheets. Catch these to the pad at intervals with tacking-stitches to hold the cover in place. If you wish to make a pad, muslin may be used for the outside, the inner pads being made of old blankets, quilts or sheets laid one over the other and all quilted together, with the edges bound all around.

Discarded pads, cut to fit, make good foundations for padded headboards or valances or foundations for slip-covered wooden chairs that have no upholstery.

BECAUSE THE INITIAL cost of bedspreads is usually high, your object is to make them last as long as possible. To prolong their life, mend bedspreads at the first sign of wear. Handle them carefully at all times and, after laundering or cleaning, examine them for wear before putting them away.

An old spread may be rejuvenated by using the best parts for the top, piecing it, as in **A,** and covering the seams with binding, ribbon or other trimming, as shown. Attach a ruffle of contrasting fabric, or set on a plain fitted side piece, using godets for fulness, as shown. **B** shows how to cut a number of godets for this purpose. **C** shows a corner of the bed as it will look with godets in place.

If the whole top of the spread is faded, set in a new top, joining it with plain or welted seams, cording or binding. When using 36″ fabric for the top, use the full width in the center and narrow strips on each side. Always allow ½″ for seams.

When spreads have lost their usefulness because your color scheme has changed, dye them if you can, or convert them to draperies. Cut them lengthwise and hem them, or use contrasting borders, hems, or bands.

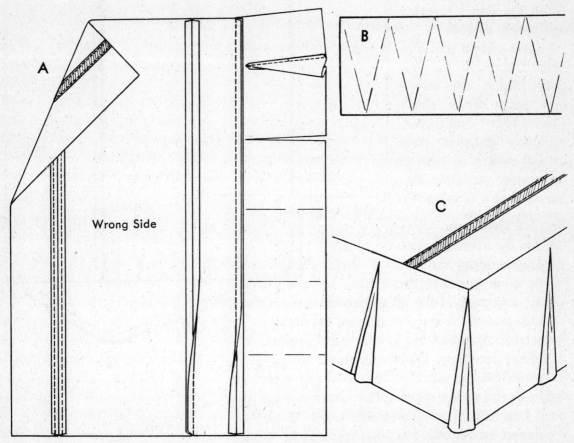

Wrong Side

Sometimes a plain oblong spread used on a daybed will drag on the floor at the corners. To overcome this, round off the corners and finish the edge with a narrow hem.

An ordinary spread can be made into a tailored cover for a day bed, as in **D.** Lay the spread over the bed, wrong side up. Center it accurately. Then pin the corners together in a boxed effect. Make this easy, rather than tight, for convenience in using. Cut away the extra fabric, as at **E.** Bring the edges together and stitch, as at **F.**

Save scraps and discarded spreads, for drapery fabrics are strong and may serve again, even if faded and frayed, to make garment bags or slip-covers to protect household articles that are used only occasionally.

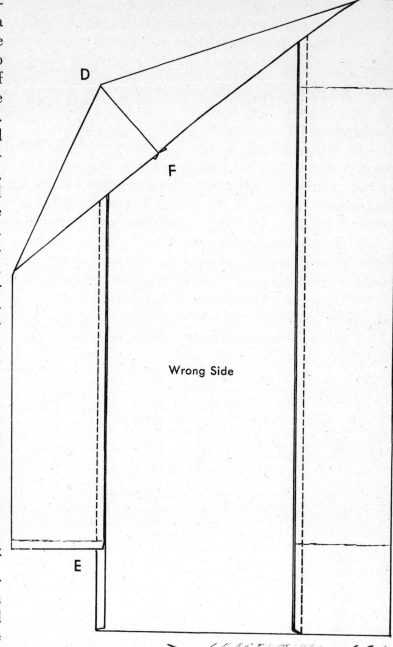

Banded Overhang. Measure for the overhang with all the bedding on, and cut it 2″ longer than the mattress is deep. Take all measurements on the bed, so that the length, width and overhang will be correct. A spread can have a band applied to make the overhang. Widths of fabric 10″ or 12″ deep are stitched together and sewn to two sides and one end of the spread. The lower corners of such a spread are usually rounded, as in **G.** Often a covered cord is used between spread and band.

Box Corner Overhang. If a ready-made spread is used, or if the fabric is wide enough to make an applied overhang unnecessary, put the spread on the bed, wrong side out. Adjust it carefully so that lengthwise threads are true with the bed, and the overhang the same depth on each side. Then pin it in place. Turn the corners back, as in **H.** Make sure that the corner line, **I**, is true. Pin this. Remove spread, stitch this seam, and cut away the surplus fabric. Press the seam open. The finished cover should appear as in **J.** If you prefer not to cut corners away, whip the line from **H** to **I** together, as shown. These overhangs can be used over any type of flounce.

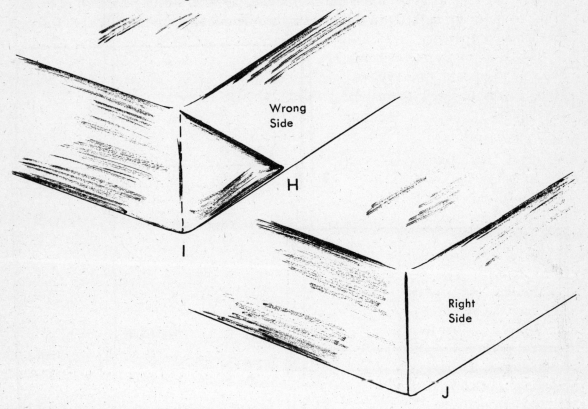

To Line a Bedspread. Place the spread on the bed, wrong side up. Seam the lining so that its seams correspond in position to those in the spread. Press the seams open. Pin the lining in place. Tack the seams together at intervals. Turn the bottom edges in and slip-stitch them. Make the lining ½″ shorter than the outside so that it cannot sag and show.

For a machine-made spread: Place the spread on the bed, right side up. Place the lining over this, wrong side up. Pin edges together. Seam the two sides and lower edge. Turn the spread right side out. Turn the open ends in and stitch or bind them to finish.

Slip-Covers for Pillows

Flat Cover. Cut the fabric long enough to cover both sides of the pillow plus allowance for two 1″ hems. Hem both of the short sides with these 1″ hems, as at **A.** Overlap these hems, as at **B,** to make a tube of the fabric. Stitch both ends of the hems together, as in **C.** Turn to the wrong side and fold the tube so that the hems are near one end, as at **D.** Stitch the side seams, as at **E,** turning back at each end of the seam for strength. Turn the cover right side out and slip the pillow in through the hemmed opening.

This is a simple but decorative way to protect your pillows. Make covers of fabric to match your spread.

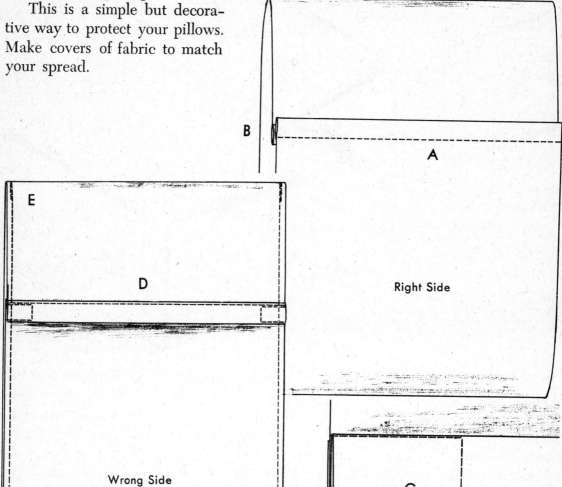

Box Cover. Cut two pieces large enough to cover the sides and half the depth of the edge, plus seam allowance. Stitch the two pieces together, leaving an opening, as in **F,** so that the cover may be turned right side out. Fold each corner diagonally and stitch across, as at **G, H,** and **I** to make box corners. Turn the cover right side out and insert the pillow. Then stitch or slip-stitch the edges of the opening together. The covered pillow will then appear as in **J.** This is a practical cover, because it can be used for a pillow or cushion of any thickness. You can make two or more sets of these covers to give variety to your color scheme.

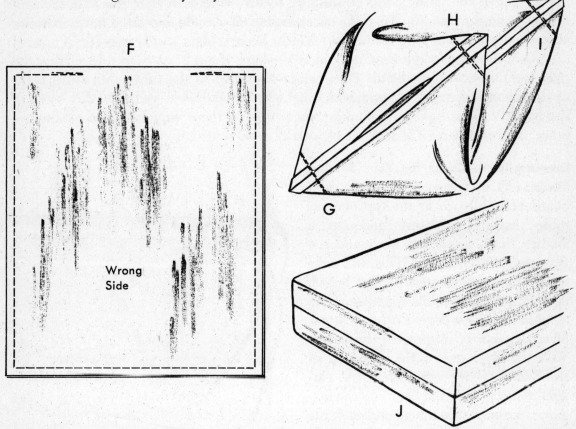

Sofa Cushions. Sofa and chair cushions are a happy solution for leftover materials. Backs and fronts may be of different fabrics, or scraps may be pieced together for innumerable interesting effects.

Narrow strips of fabric may be joined in many interesting ways. Plain seams covered with braid or embroidery stitches are effective, or cording or binding may be used for seams.

Cover extra bed pillows as day-bed or sofa cushions. Make removable covers or lap the corners or ends of the pillow tick over and baste them down to make the shapes square. Then cover the pillows as regular sofa cushions.

In doing all of this work, watch style trends for current finishes and styles of cushions.

Dressing-Table Skirts

MAKE THESE FROM used curtains, bleached or tinted, gay draperies, or old sheer dresses. Use them to cover shabby tables or drape over home-made dressing tables.

On kidney-shaped tables the skirt usually opens in the front. To provide sufficient fulness, use one-and-one-half or twice the distance around the top, depending on the weight of the fabric. Add at least 4″ to this length so that the material will extend around to the back a little on each side. If a ruffle is desired at the bottom, make a strip twice as long as the skirt width. Make a plain sturdy band to fit around the top of the table and extend around to the back about 2″ on each side. Gather the skirt and fasten it to the band. Then fasten the band to the table with small tacks or use a snap tape, one strip of which is tacked to the table and the other sewn to the band. Various types of trimming are usable on these very feminine creations— bows, flowers or lace. The latter is especially good with taffeta or organdie.

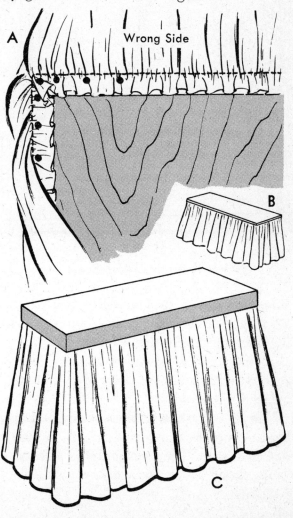

Dressing-Table Cover for Your Sewing Machine. Cut a board (even a craft board is usable) to fit the top of your table machine. Measure and cut a flounce to go across the front and the two ends of the board. This will take twice the measurement of the board. Seam the fabric widths together. Hem or bind the lower edge. Gather the top. Strech a piece of fabric over the board. Take the edges over to the underside of the board, taking care to fold the corners in nicely. Lay the board on the machine, covered side down, and tack the gathered top to this, as in **A**. Place tacks 2″ apart and nearer at the corners. When the top is turned over and laid in position on the machine, it should appear as in **B**. Ribbon, lace, braid or flowers may be added as trimming if desired.

Glorified Kitchen Tables. Many women like to buy a wooden kitchen table and dress it up as a dressing table, as in **C**. To do this, first pad the top with very old bath towels, sheets or drapery fabric. Cover the padding with a plain fabric or with fabric to match the skirt. Tack this cover on, stretching it taut on all sides and ends. Make a flounce. Hem the bottom. Turn raw edge to wrong side and make two rows of shirring at the top. Tack this in place at the two ends and across the front. Make 2¼″ bias fold from a strip of fabric 5″ wide, folding the strip through the center and turning the edges in, as in **D.** Stitch the edges together. Place the band around the top of the table, stretching it in place. Tack it as in **E.** Drop the band down over the tacks; then you will have a very nice finish.

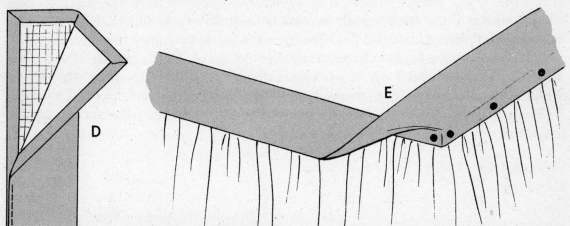

Dressing Tables from Shelves. Decide how long and how wide you want your dressing table to be. Have a board cut to this size—a board 10″ or 12″ wide is usually very satisfactory. Secure this to the wall with brackets, as in **F.** (These can be purchased at any variety chain store.) Hang a plaited or gathered flounce to the board, tacking it in place on the top of the shelf. Take a strip of fabric ½″ longer all the way around than the board. Turn the raw edges in ½″, press, and lay this over the board. Catch it with stitches or cover with plate glass that has been cut to fit the top. Or bring the raw edge down over the skirt, tack it, then place a ribbon band all the way around the edge to conceal the raw edges and to give a finish. Ribbon may be finished off with a bow at the center-front, or with small tailored bows at each end of the shelf. Rayon, satin or taffeta is ideal for such a table. Seam widths together, put hem in, then plait the flounce or have it done by a professional plaiter.

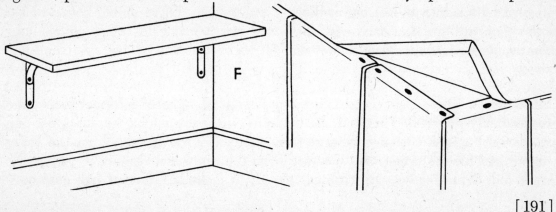

Curtains and Draperies

Measuring for Curtains and Draperies. Use a tape measure for fabrics, and a yardstick or steel rule for measuring windows. Measure from top of woodwork to the bottom, then from center of the rod to the sill, allowing, of course, for hems, headings and casings. Make your curtains the length you want.

Glass Curtains. These are generally measured from the center of the rod to the sill. To this measurement is added the allowance for the bottom hem, top heading, and casing. An allowance for shrinkage should also be made. This is usually about 1″ to the yard for rayons, and 2″ to the yard for cottons. If double hems are desired, as they are for some very sheer fabrics, twice the regular hem allowance is required.

For a window that measures 74″ from rod to sill, the extra allowances may be as follows:

Window Measurement	74″
Bottom Hem (2″) plus ¼″ turn	4¼″
Top Heading (1½″) and Casing (1″) plus ¼″ turn	5¼″
Shrinkage (Approximately 2″ per yard)	4″
	———
Total	87½″

Glass curtains usually hang straight and close to the glass, but they may be on the frame, tied back, especially in bedrooms where ruffled glass curtains are favorites. An additional allowance of 12″ to 18″ may be required for this draped effect.

If over-draperies are not used, glass curtains that hang entirely on the outside of the window casing and below the sill, are preferred. Floor-length glass curtains are used for a formal atmosphere, or to aid in giving the windows or the room an appearance of height. Such curtains are not draped on the floor, but just clear it.

For casement windows that open in, and also for French doors, make glass curtains with a heading and casing at the top and bottom. These should be held close to the glass with a rod at each end. After washing such curtains, many people hang them in place on the rods when wet and let them dry, thus saving stretching and ironing.

Sash Curtains. These glass curtains are popular for all types of informal rooms and are decidedly practical. They may be made in two sections to cover the upper and lower sash. For sash curtains, measure from the center rod to the sill for the lower section; and for the upper one, measure from the top rod to 1½″ or 2″ below the center rod. Often ready-made curtains are cut to make this type of half curtain.

Cottage Curtains. A variation of the sash curtain is the cottage curtain, in which the upper section is looped back and is often made of a different color and material. An additional length of 10″ to 12″ is necessary for the upper section to provide for the tie-back feature.

Draperies. Measure these from the rod to the desired length, usually to the floor. If they are to be looped up or draped on the floor, an additional allowance is necessary. In formal draperies, 4″ to 6″ are provided to lie on the floor. Then, as for glass curtains, the allowance for hems, hem-turns, and heading must be added, and if the fabric is very heavy, ½″ to 1″ is required for "take-up." For washable draperies, a shrinkage allowance is always necessary. The type of drapery determines the depth of the heading, the hem, or both, but in general, the plan for measuring for draperies is the same as for glass curtains.

Fixtures. After draperies and glass curtains have been planned, examine your windows and decide what type of fixture you will need.

The fixture must be of the correct length, and sturdy enough to hold the draperies properly. All large department stores have a department, usually near the drapery and curtain sections, with all types of rods and fixtures on display. Study these and discuss your problems with the sales girl, who can help you decide the best type of fixture for your needs. If possible, take her a sketch of your window with all measurements indicated.

Making Glass Curtains. These curtains, which hang close to the glass and give privacy and a uniform appearance to a house, are generally made in neutral colors, as ecru, peach, eggshell, champagne, cream, white and similar tints.

Straighten one end by tearing or pulling a thread. Measure from this end and, if necessary, straighten the fabric. If fabric has design, watch this so that it will come in the proper position. If selvages draw too tightly, consider cutting them off and using a hem on all lengthwise edges. The selvages do usually shrink slightly more than the rest of the fabric.

Hems, Heading and Casing. If selvage has been removed, make a hem on the outside edge ¼″ wide. Then turn and stitch the hems of the edges that come in the center, making them 1″ to 2″ as desired. Put hems in the bottoms ¼″ deeper than the front edges. Make square or mitered corners at the bottom. The hems may be finished in a number of ways, if plain stitching is not desired. Hemstitching is always a good choice if the fabric lends itself to such work. Insertion, rickrack, colored binding are effective, and darning stitches in harmonizing colors make a quick and pleasing finish.

Finally, stitch a hem at the top, wide enough for the casing and a heading, if one is planned. The heading may vary in depth from ½″ to 1½″. The casing depends on the rod; it may require from 1″ to 1½″.

Tuck for Shrinkage. When an allowance has been made for shrinkage, a tuck may be run across the curtain on the inside below the casing. This may be made on the machine, with a long stitch, or it may be basted in position.

When Making Draperies. Never stretch drapery fabric except to straighten it. Pull a thread and cut on the pulled thread line. Measure all the lengths of the drapery material before you start to cut, making sure that if there is a design, it runs correctly in each length. Flowers, you know, should always run up. Measure and match the designs throughout all the lengths, if necessary. If this makes you short of material, face the draperies at top and bottom, but, naturally, it is better if your material allows to make hems. These should be at least 2″ wide. Draperies tend to shorten in making, so allow ¼″ per foot for this.

Baste the interlining to the lining, using long stitches in matching thread on the lining side. Lay the drapery right side up on the table, floor or bed. Turn the side edges in 1″ to 2″. Make the lining narrow in keeping with these turns. Place the lining right side down on this, and pin it on on both sides; clip or cut away the selvage edges so that they cannot draw or tighten. Baste generously, using plenty of pins.

When you stitch the drapery, do the top first and then the sides, stitching from the top down. Support the weight of the drapery on chairs and tables so that it cannot pull under the needle and thus distort your stitch or break your needle. Use a long machine stitch and remove pins as you stitch. If crinoline is to be used to support plaits, stitch this to the lining before applying the lining to the drapery. Also, slip-stitch the hems in the drapery fabric and stitch them in the lining. Turn the drapery right side out and press the hems and edges.

Decide what type of plait you will use. Measure for these. Mark the spacings with pins, and make sure all spaces are even. If cartridge or pipe organ plaits are used, baste; then stitch, pull thread ends through to the wrong side, and tie. For cluster plaits draw each group together and secure with catch-stitches. If the fabric is loosely-woven, it is sometimes necessary to cover weights and sew them to the lower corners to hold the edges straight.

In making what are called in the trade "table-made draperies," you turn the edges of the drapery in from 1″ to 2″ and then make the lining this much narrower. You baste the interlining to the lining, turning an edge of lining over on the interlining, as illustrated, and then slip-stitch this lining to the drapery edge. This makes a very soft edge and helps to overcome any tendency to tightness.

Valances for Style or Necessity

WINDOWS IN SOME ROOMS require valances to give the correct finish to the tops of the draperies. Oftentimes a valance is a veritable "curtain stretcher," as it helps you to extend short curtains by using another material at the top and covering this with a valance of a harmonizing fabric—velvet with brocade curtains, or brocade with velvet, or plain chintz with figured, etc. Valances also help you to redesign windows—to make two windows seem as one—to make a room harmonize with furniture. Valances may be made of building board or of ½″ lumber; these are padded and have fabric tightly stretched over them. Paper or buckram or crinoline may be used as stiffening and covered with fabric. Think of a valance as the finish for the top of the drapery. If your ceilings are low, begin the valance flush with the ceiling. Shape the lower edge of the valance as best suits the width of your draperies and the decorative effect desired.

Details for making and lining a buckram valance are shown in **A** and **B**. Center the motif of the fabric as you desire it to appear, and measure from the center to the ends. Cut the fabric 1″ wider than the finished dimensions. Line this piece with muslin or flannelette, then buckram. Fold raw edges back over buckram, clip any curves for ease, and baste together, as in **A**. Cut the lining the size of the finished valance and turn ½″ under all around. Pin this as in **B**; then whip or baste it down.

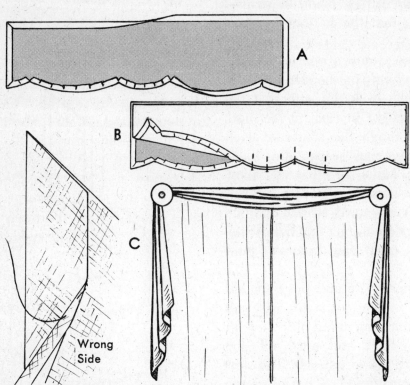

For attaching this to the valance frame, whip twilled tape across the top and put tacks through this tape.

C shows a draped valance. This is simply a width of fabric with the ends cut diagonally and slip-stitched. Draped over two important-looking tie-back pins, this is an ideal finish for glass curtains.

Slip-Covers Are as Easy To Make as Pie

IF YOU ARE VERY NEW at making slip-covers, choose a plain fabric that does not have a motif to match or an up-and-down design to give you concern.

To determine the amount of fabric, measure the height of your chair and its size around. You need twice as much in width as your chair measures, plus ⅓ extra in height, plus enough to go around each cushion. When you measure and figure it out, you will find that a slipper chair takes 3 yards of 50″ fabric; an overstuffed, 4½; a huge armchair with reversible cushions, 6. A love seat also takes 6 yards; small couch, 7; very large couch with reversible cushions, 9. Decide how much your chair or couch requires. Add ¼ yard extra for each yard where there is a design to be matched. If you are using a remnant or very expensive fabric, then cut a pattern from newspaper or a worn-out sheet. This way you can place the pattern pieces on more economically and can make sure of having enough. Bottoms of cushions can be made of other fabric, or can be made of strips— these nicely paneled so that the bottom looks as nice as the top.

Fit a chair just as you would a box or a body. Allow for seams. Pin the fabric on the chair, usually wrong side out, as shown in **A.** Be sure that the grain of the fabric is straight in each piece; mark the straight of goods through the center of each piece, as at **B**; allow generous seams. Pin, baste and stitch; press and fit. Make sure that you allow enough ease to insure a good fit and ease the fulness in around curves. Don't crowd, stretch or stitch a crooked line. Use a medium-long machine stitch and remember to press each seam before it joins another.

If you want a slipper chair and have an old chair that needs to be put out of sight, why not make something new from something old? Saw off the top of the old chair, as in **C**, and saw 3″ off each leg. Cover the chair with fabric, as in **D**. The skirt can be plain, plaited or gathered. A bat of cotton

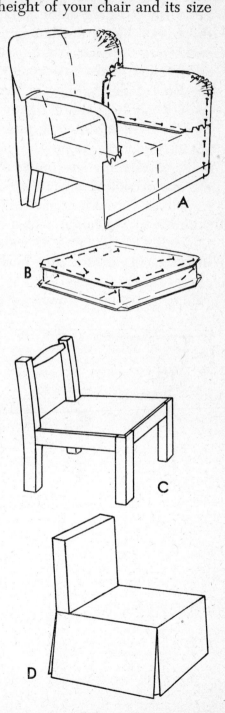

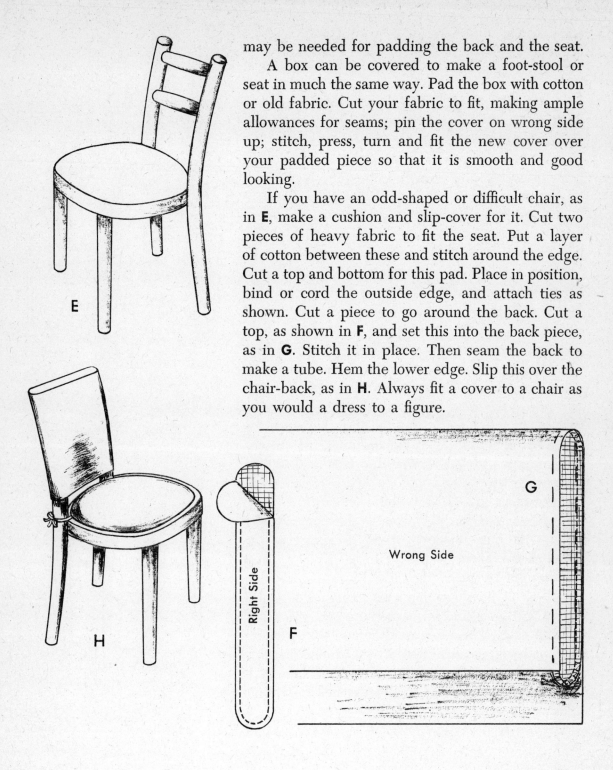

may be needed for padding the back and the seat.

A box can be covered to make a foot-stool or seat in much the same way. Pad the box with cotton or old fabric. Cut your fabric to fit, making ample allowances for seams; pin the cover on wrong side up; stitch, press, turn and fit the new cover over your padded piece so that it is smooth and good looking.

If you have an odd-shaped or difficult chair, as in **E**, make a cushion and slip-cover for it. Cut two pieces of heavy fabric to fit the seat. Put a layer of cotton between these and stitch around the edge. Cut a top and bottom for this pad. Place in position, bind or cord the outside edge, and attach ties as shown. Cut a piece to go around the back. Cut a top, as shown in **F**, and set this into the back piece, as in **G**. Stitch it in place. Then seam the back to make a tube. Hem the lower edge. Slip this over the chair-back, as in **H**. Always fit a cover to a chair as you would a dress to a figure.

E

H

Right Side

F

Wrong Side

G

Index